PASTORAL CARE

A Practical Guide

Bill Merrington

Augsburg Books
MINNEAPOLIS

PASTORAL CARE
A Practical Guide

Original edition published in English under the title PASTORAL CARE by Kevin Mayhew Ltd, Buxhall, England.

This edition published in 2020 by Fortress Press, an imprint of 1517 Media.

Cover image: © iStock 2020: Small White Church with Green Steeple stock photo by dbvirago
Cover design: Emily Drake

Print ISBN: 978-1-5064-6011-6

To my wife,
for her patience in all the time I have given to writing and caring for others, as well as her willingness to offer wise advice.

And to all the laity in my previous churches,
who allowed me to learn pastoral care on the job.

Contents

Appendix

About the author

Bill Merrington has been an Anglican priest for over 29 years. Originally an analytical chemist, after a serious illness he retrained in ministry and has since led churches in city, town and countryside in the West Midlands. Bill has a PhD in Psychology, specialising in the understanding of the long-term impact on parents when a child dies. He has carried out research in Britain, Lebanon, Africa and Japan, looking at the cross-cultural impact of death. He has spoken at a number of national and international conferences, and lectures regularly at universities. Bill is a qualified supervisor of counsellors and teaches regularly in counselling topics. Bill has written a number of books for both adults and children. He is currently the Lead Chaplain at Bournemouth University. Bill is married with three grown-up children.

Other books by Bill Merrington published by Kevin Mayhew:
Grief, Loss and Pain in Churches (1501273)
Death, Funerals and Heaven (1501189)
Coping When Your Parents Separate (1501017)
When Someone Dies, 101 Ways for Children to Grieve (1501144)
101 Ways to Cope with Grief and Loss (1501016)
The Hideaway (1500192)
Alice's Dad (1500274)

Introduction

Christian pastoral care is the Church's holistic action of unconditional love where individuals (and communities) are encouraged to become all that they were created to be in Christ.

Grace to you and peace from God our Father and the Lord Jesus Christ. I give thanks to my God always for you because of the grace of God that has been given you in Christ Jesus.
(1 Corinthians 1:3, 4)

The moment a baby leaves the safety of the womb, it requires considerable care. The child requires air, milk, warmth, protection and affection, and these mainly come from the chief caregiver. These are, hopefully, things that are given to us throughout our early childhood. Unfortunately, in the turmoil of life, we all get battered about. Our experience of relationships both in the family and in the community can at times seem inadequate.

Along comes the Christian faith and the local church, where we aim to bring healing and harmony. 'Pastoral care' is the term we use to cover how we engage with this ministry. It is a place where people experience acceptance and forgiveness, where their gifts can blossom and hopefully develop. Those who have been cared for will soon develop their own ministry of caring for others, and so the Jesus 'model of care' progresses.

It is a great privilege to care for others, be it in the church, at work, at home or in the community. Pastoral care often develops naturally as we copy others or follow our own instincts. However, all Christian ministry can be enhanced with wisdom and reflection, and by learning from the mistakes of those who have gone before us. This book is for the laity and the ordained; it attempts to provide a basic guide, a kind of highway code to enable Christians to pause, reflect and then practise a Christ-filled ministry. This involves a resolve to never make a situation worse, and to seek the best for another while also being aware of our own parameters, strengths and weaknesses, hence keeping us appropriately safe. The term 'pastor' is used to encompass all who are engaged in pastoral care and does not just refer to ordained clergy.

The book begins in Part one with a biblical definition of care and looks at the basic elements of ministry. This includes an understanding of a human being's basic needs, how to visit and get alongside another, and how to listen, suffer with and pray for another. Part two looks at developing particular skills that come out of the world of counselling, healing and deliverance ministries. Part three looks at how we can keep ourselves safe within a professional approach. Part four looks at the individual issues that we face in church life, ranging across all ages including singleness, marriage, old age and bereavement. Part five looks at health issues, from basic anxiety and stress to the more serious matters of eating disorders and dementia. Part six looks at how we need to care for our families and ourselves and how we can engage in pastoral ministry for the long haul.

We all come into pastoral work with our own experiences and context of ministry. No one model will therefore fit all. However, whether your ministry is in a large, thriving city church or in a small rural context, I hope that you will find the chapters encouraging, and that you will be able to apply certain aspects to your church and community so that your ministry proves to be a blessing both to others and to yourself.

Part one

The basics

Chapter 1

A biblical view of pastoral care

Jesus Christ meeting you at your point of need.
(Morris Maddocks)[1]

Pastoral care in the Old Testament

At the beginning of the Bible we are told that God wanted to have a relationship with his creation and especially with humankind.

> They heard the sound of the Lord God walking in the garden at the time of the evening breeze, and the man and his wife hid themselves from the presence of the Lord God among the trees of the garden. But the Lord God called to the man, and said to him, 'Where are you?'
>
> *Genesis 3:8, 9*

'Where are you?' is a fundamental question at the heart of pastoral care ministry. We are engaging with people who often need to be drawn out from their hiding place. This is not usually a location but the emotional and spiritual condition of a person's well-being. For Adam and Eve, it was their guilt and shame that caused them to hide away. Many people we encounter are so busy that they are unaware of their personal condition. Without realising it, they live their lives hidden among the trees just outside the garden. They find themselves disconnected from themselves and those around them. At the heart of our Christian message is the belief that people are special. They have the right to have their own 'needs' met. However, if a person fails to recognise their own needs, they remain disconnected with themselves and those around them. As we discover our own connectedness with God, others, and ourselves, we are called to speak out on God's behalf.

The question *'Where are you?'* is the beginning of our pastoral care message. What was God asking in this question? I think it incorporates three aspects. Firstly, 'Where are you in relation to yourself?' Adam was ill at ease with himself as he came to the realisation that all was not well. 'Adam, where are you? Are you at peace with yourself? Do you know who you are, do you know what you have done and do you know where you are going?'

---

1. M. Maddocks (1981), *The Christian Healing Ministry*, SPCK.

Secondly, God is asking, 'Where are you in your relationships with others?' We quickly discover that Adam and Eve are not at ease with one another. Adam blames the woman and Eve blames the snake. This becomes a common theme in 'community', where relationships break down and we fail to take individual responsibility. The outcome is that we seek to find a scapegoat to appease our conscience. This disharmony then quickly spills over into everything around us. It creates isolation in the community and environment. 'Adam, where are you in relation to Eve and those around you?'

Thirdly, God is enquiring whether we know where we are in our relationship with him. Adam hides because he is not just guilty but ashamed of himself. This shame comes about only because he has something much higher with which to compare himself. Here, right and wrong, moral standards and the consequences of his actions manifest themselves. 'Adam, where are you in relation to me? What have you done to our relationship?'

Outside the garden, Adam now knows that he is not what he could have been and that he must live with the consequences of his actions. He is on a journey to find himself again, to restore his relationship with those around him and to bring harmony to his friendship with his creator. It is into this complex story that the pastor engages and journeys with an individual or a community.

The theme of 'the pastor' progresses throughout the Old Testament as God relates to individuals and communities. We see how Abram's obedience to God comes totally out of God's total commitment to him. Here, the care is not short term; it is so long term it becomes generational.

We then have the account of God's care for his family as he guided Moses to lead the Israelites out of bondage to a better land. God also showed his 'delicate touch' when he recognised Moses' weaknesses and provided Aaron for support.

We then come to David, who through the Psalms provided us with wonderful imagery of our God as a shepherd to his sheep.

God provides direction but not directions.

This image straddles both the Old and the New Testament. The pastor is called to shepherd his or her sheep, whilst also reaching out to the lost sheep.

Psalm 23 is the main text in the Old Testament that enables us to focus upon the image of a shepherd. Here the shepherd has an active role to fulfil: he restores my soul, he leads me in right paths, he comforts me with rod and staff, he reduces the fear within me, and he journeys with me through the valley of death. The shepherd therefore offers both a presence and a guidance that leads to the restoration of a person's soul.

Many of the psalms echo the inner turmoil that is a human's experience of a fallen world.

> For my iniquities have gone over my head; they weigh like a burden too heavy for me. I am utterly spent and crushed; I groan because of the tumult of my heart.
>
> *Psalm 38:4, 8*

Here, personal sin has led to physical pain. The psalms reveal a deep need within humans to express their thoughts and emotions, be it in praise, confession or supplication. In other situations we need someone to listen to us when turmoil overwhelms us and we can't see the way forward.

Ezekiel 34 develops the role of a shepherd who is willing to work through our complexities. In the first 11 verses God uses the prophet to chastise the leaders of the nation for failing to lead the people rightly in their walk with God. They are told that they should have been shepherds, caring for God's flock, but instead they have been feeding on them for their own selfish gain.

Ultimately, God shares that he would be a shepherd to his people:

> For thus says the Lord God: I myself will search for my sheep, and will seek them out. As shepherds seek out their flocks when they are among their scattered sheep, so I will seek out my sheep. I will rescue them from all the places to which they have been scattered on a day of clouds and thick darkness. I will bring them out from the peoples and gather them from the countries, and will bring them into their own land; and I will feed them on the mountains of Israel, by the watercourses, and in all the inhabited parts of the land. I will feed them with good pasture, and the mountain heights of Israel shall be their pasture; there they shall lie down in good grazing land, and they shall feed on rich pasture on the mountains of Israel. I myself will be the shepherd of my sheep, and I will make them lie down, declares the Lord God.
>
> *Ezekiel 34:11-15*

In this case God was speaking directly to his chosen people, the Jews. But he cares for all his people in the same way today. Listen to this explanation of how he cares for individuals:

> I will seek the lost, and I will bring back the strayed, and I will bind up the injured, and I will strengthen the weak, but the fat and the strong I will destroy. I will feed them with justice.
>
> *Ezekiel 34:16*

We can see that God speaks to the whole Church of his love and care. However, he would not have us miss the fact that he is a God of justice, and he will also execute judgement.

Perhaps the account of Jacob going to meet his brother Esau gets to the core of what happens when we seek to care for another. Jacob wrestled all night, wounding himself before he was able to move forward. What was he wrestling with? It is only when we are willing to look into the mirror and see ourselves as we truly are that we are released into caring as we should. It is here that we see ourselves warts and all. We are not ministering to another who is different from ourselves but we are reaching out to ourselves, to a different facet of who we represent. 'To live is to wrestle with despair, yet never to allow despair to have the last word.'[2]

Since a great deal of pastoral care focuses on supporting people through their trials and tribulations, the book of Job has much to commend itself to a pastor. It is not just a discourse about suffering but it also reflects something of God's concern for an individual. Problems came one at a time for Job until they piled up against him. With his back against the wall, he found himself with nowhere to turn.

There is no shortage of people today who arrive at church with a quiver full of enormous personal issues. The fact that they survive is a miracle in itself. Job's friends collectively agreed to support him (Job 2:11) and sat with him in silence for seven days as they attempted to feel his pain and understand his situation (2:13). For Job, it was not enough, and he began to see, think and say things that he would never have said weeks previously. Eliphaz reminded Job that he had been a carer himself; surely he realised his problem was one of sin? We don't have Eliphaz's limited awareness, as we are told in the narrative that Job's plight had nothing to do with personal failure. This is a pastoral warning to us all to not jump in with quick assumptions.

> I am not at ease, nor am I quiet; I have no rest; but trouble comes.
>
> *Job 3:26*

2. C. West (1997), in K. Sealey, *Restoring Hope*, Boston, MA: Beacon Press.

In Job's suffering he observed how others reacted around him. He observed how others saw his suffering and how it filled them with fear for themselves (6:21). It is certainly not uncommon for people to avoid those who have extreme problems in life; I guess we all have a self-preservation button that makes us veer away from situations that are just too hot to handle. It is often when we are feeling most uncomfortable that we dive in and make inappropriate comments.

Bildad the Shuhite felt he had to defend God with his comments. Zophar the Naamathite implored Job to turn more to God, but Job was still an equal to his friends and he reminded them so (12:3). Here is a sharp lesson to everyone in ministry who finds themselves talking down to others. Job had much to say, if only someone would listen to him. Unfortunately he felt that he was surrounded by 'miserable comforters' (16:2). Perhaps this warns us that there are times when people are inconsolable, or at least that there are times when we need to be very careful what we say to a sufferer.

Elihu, son of Barakel the Buzite, at least showed humility in his ministry as he waited for the right time to speak. Yet he, too, got caught up with the situation, feeling frustrated and angry both with Job's so-called friends and with Job himself. Elihu felt he was convicted by the spirit to speak (32:18). He confessed that he too was vulnerable like a piece of clay (33:6), yet he believed in a God who speaks into situations. Christian ministry is founded on this premise, yet Job shows us that despite all our well-intended words of wisdom, we don't always have the answers. God finally spoke to Job 'out of the whirlwind' (38:1).

It is not an objective, cold approach; rather, God appears to be intensely present with his holistic listening ear. He doesn't appear to prevent Job from expressing his feelings, nor does he reject his strong outbursts. In fact, God twice affirms Job for speaking rightly about character. However, God doesn't leave Job as he is, to wallow in self-pity. God rebukes Job more with regard to the truth than from a knee-jerk defensive position.

God mirrors to us the practice of being involved yet not consumed. God is not surprised by what he hears from Job. He doesn't overreact but offers a way forward to redeem the situation by finding meaning amidst the suffering. Here the Lord uses metaphor, images and pictures to help Job see a broader canvas of creation, which involves humility, mystery and contemplation.

There are no quick-fix answers here; these might have satisfied Job initially but later would have led to frustration and disappointment. There is no manipulating or condescending speech as God conveys a commitment to Job that actually says he is pleased with him but not yet satisfied. There seems to be a process going on, not just a one-off encounter. All of this shows us that pastoral care is not simple or formulaic but more of an art form, requiring knowledge, wisdom, patience, experience and humility. It also reveals how ministry is never straightforward or neatly resolved. There are still many questions left unanswered in Job's experience of life. There is also no dialogue as to what Job's wife or family felt; they were simply pawns in what appeared to be a cosmic game. We can't make a full theology from the Job account. It is simply a snapshot account of one aspect of suffering and pastoral care.

Part of the pastor's role is to be able to live with unanswered questions and to carry this tension, yet still to be able to minister effectively. There may well be times when the person being cared for finds answers that they find acceptable but that the pastor is far from satisfied with for himself. To engage in pastoral ministry means we will always be on a journey of an evolving yet turbulent faith.

Jesus and pastoral care

On the one hand, it is natural to assume that pastoral care would be a call to behave like Jesus. On the other hand, however, it is not that simple. Andrew Pratt rightly points out that Jesus' life was rather unusual, to say the least.[3] He didn't marry, he didn't seem to baptise anyone, he moved from place to place, he delayed when a friend was ill or when called to comfort the bereaved, he raised people from the dead and when he was finally attacked by others, he put up no resistance. Follow that!

Yet Jesus was still the supreme pastor, the shepherd of the sheep. What can we learn from his ministry?

Jesus formed what appeared to be ordinary relationships and friendships: his family; the disciples; three special disciples; Mary, Martha and Lazarus, along with others. Here he reminds us of the importance of friendships. In one sense, this is the heart of pastoral care – one friend helping, supporting and enjoying the company of another.

However, some of Jesus' friendships might not have been welcome in church! He did hang out with zealots, extremists, rebels, prostitutes and the misfits of society. If our pastoral care only reached those we liked, it would not be very Christlike.

Jesus' care of the leper, the Samaritan woman, the demonic Legion, the Roman soldier and Gentiles communicates something about caring for those who are different to ourselves. This was at the

3. A. Pratt (2010), *Practical Skills for Ministry*, London: SCM Press, p. 24.

heart of what the Pharisees didn't like about Jesus. He pushed the concept of loving one's neighbour too far in their eyes. If we look in detail at the various encounters that Jesus had with individuals, we will learn some interesting lessons about how to handle people.

In John 1:43-51 we see Jesus confronting Nathanael's prejudiced and assumptive views: 'Can anything good come out of Nazareth?' Jesus opened Nathanael's eyes to the truth. Nathanael has an 'Ah ha' moment of self-realisation. It is as we engage with people that we get to know them, and in so doing we discover their biases, be they racism, ageism, gender, sexual orientation, etc. Like Nathanael, we are called to enable people to gain a heavenly perspective that changes the earthly view.

With the woman at the well in John 4:1-29, Jesus engaged with a woman whom many would have ignored. She was impressed by his acceptance of her but then rather defensive. He then drew out from her a deeper perspective of life. However, she was still bound by her history. Jesus encouraged her to see the potential before her very eyes, and this led to an honest exchange about her past. The woman began to see things more clearly, which resulted in her changing her actions.

In another situation Jesus challenged a person's negative, trapped perspective of life (the man at the pool of Bethesda, John 5:2-16). Here, not only physical healing took place but an inner change of attitude also occurred. Jesus challenged the man as to whether he really wanted to be healed. The man seemed to have all sorts of excuses as to why things couldn't change. Jesus gave the man a new power to believe in himself again, which resulted in the man following Jesus' advice. The man met Jesus later and was encouraged to live life in a new way. Whether the man did or didn't we are not told, but he was clearly left with the choice of his own actions.

Elsewhere, Jesus challenged individuals to not hide but to bring out their inferiorities, imperfections and shame in order that God's light might bring healing and restoration to those around them (e.g. Luke 6:6-11).

Throughout Jesus' ministry, he was constantly relating to the Father and the Holy Spirit. The Trinity captures something of the wonder of mutual care. However, this was not some narcissistic inward-focusing obsession but rather an outward concern both for each other and for the world they had created. Each of the 'persons' in the Trinity is distinct and fulfils their own role and desires, yet they are also entwined closely together in a way that does not hinder their individuality and encourages the full, free expression of their individual persona.

There seems to be a confidence within the Trinity of knowing who 'the other' is, and assurance that they will always be there for each other. We see the terrible pain when this finally breaks down on the cross and Jesus sees that the Father is not there; there is only silence and an echoing call, 'My God, my God, why have you forsaken me?' (Matthew 27:46). It is impossible to fully grasp what this separation must have been like. The nearest anyone can get to this is when we experience the loss of a long-standing partner. Imagine a husband who has been getting up every morning for 40 years and making a cup of tea for his wife, and now she is no longer there.

As Jesus cried out, 'My God, my God, why . . . ?' we find ourselves also crying alongside others who are suffering. There is a silence here we must not become content with, although we must at least be comfortable enough with it to endure. Most of Jesus' ministry was forward looking, not backward. Often in pastoral contexts we find ourselves surrounded by people asking 'Why?' It seems that Jesus preferred to focus less on the 'why' and more on how to transform a situation. We see this when Jesus met a man who had been blind from birth. When asked why was he blind, Jesus replied that it was neither the man's fault nor the fault of his parents, but that this was an opportunity to look forward and be creative (John 9). People need to claim responsibility for their errors of life; confession is healthy, but they need also to change their behaviour for the future.

When a person embarks on such a forward task, it is always easier if others are alongside to support and enable them to move forward.

There was another side of Jesus that we can often ignore – his strength of character and firm resolve. We see this with the Phoenician woman who begged for her child to be healed (Matthew 15:21-8). Jesus was firm in his response that he had not come for this. Knowing the end of the story, it is easy for us to soften the account and feel that he was leading the woman forward, but perhaps he was just being firm and definitive. Without clarity of what he was doing and where he was heading, Jesus would never have left Galilee. We, too, need to have some clear perspective on our ministry.

Jesus seemed to reflect upon what the woman said and was amazed at her faith. Was this a developmental moment for Jesus himself, that his message was indeed for the entire world? It is inevitable that any ministry involving people will cause the pastor's beliefs and attitudes to be challenged, shaped and deepened.

In all of these situations, we see Jesus functioning with an acceptance of individuals, recognising their uniqueness, offering forgiveness, not domineering; empowering and bringing freedom, yet all set within a framework of boundaries of what he himself would and would not accept. Ultimately it was all at great cost to himself.

We must now consider how we put this theology together so that it has a cutting edge in today's society.

Reflections

- God sought out Adam. How have you experienced God seeking you out?
- How does the concept of 'the shepherd' speak to you of your ministry?
- What would be a modern interpretation of the shepherd's role?
- Can you see how Jesus' encounter with individuals is similar to your ministry?
- Does your church mirror the breadth of pastoral care in the Bible?

Chapter 2

Pastoral care today

We do not experience things as they are: we experience things as we are.
(Talmud)

At the very heart of the life of a church are its relationships. When they are healthy, they create a healthy, dynamic community.

Throughout our lives we need relationships. For some people, their human relationships have been so damaged that they look to different types of relationships that are less threatening, such as animals or even plants. All types of relationships help us express who we are, provide a basis for giving and taking and allow us to be able to see who we are through others.

Alas, all of this is not simply worked out in a person's life. There are many twists and turns before we are able to get a clear grasp of the landscape before us. Hence people get hurt and lost along the way.

> They are darkened in their understanding, alienated from the life of God because of their ignorance and hardness of heart. They have lost all sensitivity and have abandoned themselves to licentiousness, greedy to practise every kind of impurity.
>
> *Ephesians 4:18, 19*

This is where the Church offers a new beginning in relationships. It is here that Jesus builds his family afresh. It is a place that should allow wounds to be healed, friendships to be formed and relationships to be deepened in a safe environment. This is where pastoral care comes into its own.

Our aim is to produce a healthy Church where people enjoy holistic relationships. However, this is the end point and not the starting line. People often enter a church with hurt, distorted relationships that they need to work through. Some need to be delivered from abusive or oppressive relationships that have squashed and distorted their view of themselves and others. This type of domineering relationship might be all an individual has ever experienced in his or her life. It would clearly take time for this individual to build trust and security so that they can begin to find out what a healthy relationship is all about. Jesus is the beginning of this discovery, which is worked out in the church.

It is not what happens to us that matters; it's what we make of it.

This requires a careful balance between the amount of attention given to an individual and space for them to work things out alone at their own pace. If we shepherd in a heavy, controlling way, the church just becomes another problem for the person and confirms to them that all relationships are abusive and to be avoided. On the other hand, if we just leave people alone, they can feel deserted, lost at sea with no one offering a life raft. Frank Wright suggests that people need to find three components for healthy relationships:[4]

- Firstly, a sense of identity where we can discover who we are
- Secondly, the ability to give to ourselves openly, recognising that there may be hurt and joy along the way
- Thirdly, a rhythm of aloneness and togetherness.

The pastoral worker is just one part of the church that can bring about this balanced perspective. Clearly the preaching, teaching and belonging to a home group will all contribute to each of these three points. But the pastoral worker is often the oil in the engine that brings these components together.

It is the pastoral worker who gets to know a person well enough to observe whether their identity is healthily formed without being tied to things or people in the past. It is this pastoral presence that gets to know people well enough to be able to identify gifts and abilities and match them up with the needs of the church.

It is often the gentle touch of a carer's presence that gives an individual the courage to agree to read, pray or simply help to hand out books, etc. The other side of the coin is helping an individual stay in church not only to give but also to receive healing ministry. Having someone pray for you or lay hands on your head requires both courage and trust.

It is only with a supporting carer that people find the strength to begin to allow the church to bless them. Here a person finds themselves on a journey of relationships. They move from relationships where people have exerted power over them to a relationship which, though cautious and controlled, is at least safe, and finally enables them to enjoy a loving relationship where both parties are blessed.

In such a situation, people are given the freedom to come and go as they feel able within a church community. This requires trust from both sides. Churches can easily fall into the trap of either being

4. F. Wright (1996), *Pastoral Care Revisited*, Norwich: SCM Press.

authoritarian (checking up on you if you miss a service), or not being aware (e.g. that you have not been to church for the past three months). There has to be something that is a healthier 'in-between'. A church that gets this right demonstrates maturity and being at ease with itself. This is the very heart of pastoral care.

A church that can't let go is very insecure, while a church that doesn't notice your absence is uncaring and selfish. We need to see that in any healthy relationship there is the need for togetherness and for times of separation. Paul wrote about this in the Epistles where he recognised that a time of absence can awaken the heart to all that it has been taking for granted.

> The rhythm of aloneness and togetherness ensures both the preservation of identity and the joy which relationship brings, and deepens its creativity.[5]

A church that is concerned about pastoral care cannot purely see it as an individual's problem. It is easy for a church to appoint a pastoral worker to care for the elderly and the sick and then claim to be a pastoral church. We have to look at the subject from a corporate perspective.

> When I give food to the poor, they call me a saint.
>
> When I ask why the poor have no food, they call me a communist.[6]

The message is clear: you cannot help people fully unless you also do something about their situation, as it is their situation which makes them what they are. It is all too easy for churches to duck political issues only to then complain about the local counsellors or politicians who are elected. We can too easily adopt an ancient Greek idealistic view and make our Christianity private and spiritually self-centred, rather than embracing the idea that our faith should be about action and community.

This takes our pastoral care outside the church and into the community. It is here that we do what is called, 'open cast theology',[7] following Jesus' example of relating our faith to the local community situation. If this can be done across the denominational divide, then all the better. After all, what good is a church if it can only love its own?

---

5. F. Wright, *Pastoral Care Revisited*, p. 60.
6. H. Camara (2009), *Essential Writings*, Maryknoll: Orbis Books.
7. F. Wright, *Pastoral Care Revisited*.

In a university chaplaincy context, we are constantly working in situations where the university is not meeting the needs of an individual or a group. It is here that we work, often until the university takes up the mantle and makes our work redundant. This is not seen as a threat but as a positive thing, and it enables us to seek the kingdom in other aspects of the community's life. This should be just as true in a church community context: healthy pastoral care involves starting initiatives and then being willing to close them down when the need moves elsewhere (something we often struggle with).

To do this we need to begin to listen to people's stories well before we contemplate any new development. Otherwise we end up ministering to people rather than ministering with and alongside them.

A healthy pastoral care policy will straddle the structure of the whole church.

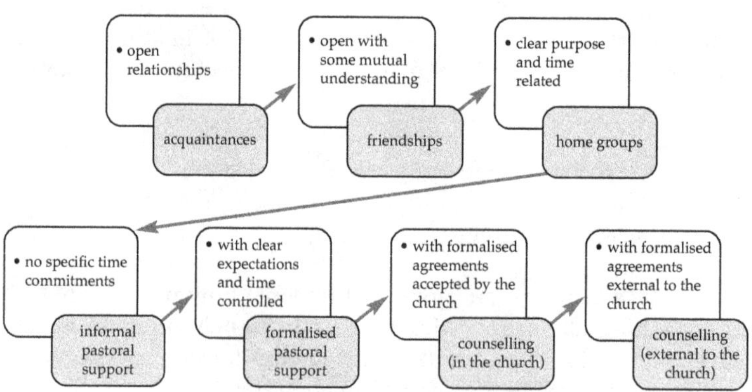

Figure 1: A Typical Church Pastoral Care Policy

Figure 1 helps us to see what expectations the church member and the carer are creating. It is when one or both parties confuse these boundaries that problems so often arise. This equally applies to our relationships with those outside the church. The underlying aim of this book is to seek to reduce some of these misunderstandings.

Reflections

- How would you describe the relationships within your church community?
- How does your church balance the need to care and yet provide space for people to be themselves?
- Does your church have a pastoral care policy? Who would develop it?
- Is your pastoral care inward- or community-focused?

Chapter 3
Human needs

Pastoral care is all about quality relationships.
(Teresa Onion)[8]

Life experiences (often out of our control) mould us and shape us more than we can ever appreciate. It's like a potter with his clay. It takes two hands to mould the clay into the desired shape, just like it takes two inexperienced parents to shape a child through the early stages of life.

A little too much force from one finger, or turning the wheel too fast or too slowly, will affect the final shape of the pot. How much more so with a child?

Erikson's life cycle identified eight stages of life with degrees of conflict in each stage.[9] For healthy development, the understanding between these conflicts needs to be balanced.

Erikson crisis stages	**Life stage/issues**	**Basic virtues**	**Maladaption/ malignancy**
Trust v mistrust	Infant/feeding/comfort from mother	Hope and drive	Sensory distortion/ withdrawal
Autonomy v shame and doubt	Toddler/adventure and play	Willpower and self-control	Impulsivity/compulsion
Initiative v guilt	Preschool/exploration/ adventure	Purpose and direction	Ruthlessness/inhibition
Industry v inferiority	School child/achievement and accomplishment	Competence and method	Narrow virtuosity/inertia
Identity v role confusion	Adolescent/resolving identity/becoming grown up	Fidelity and devotion	Fanaticism/repudiation
Intimacy v isolation	Young adult/intimate relationships, work and social life	Love and affiliation	Promiscuity/exclusivity
Generality v stagnation	Mid life/children/ community/contributing	Care and production	Overextension/rejection
Integrity v despair	Late adult/meaning and purpose/ life achievements	Wisdom and renunciation	Presumption/disdain

Figure 2: Erikson's Life Cycle

8. Pastoral coordinator, Association of Christian Counsellors.
9. E. Erikson (1994), *Identity and the Life Cycle*, London: Norton.

Pastoral care is about engaging at each of these stages. In fact, we may be dealing with more than one stage at a time. We also need to recognise right from the beginning that there will be things we are simply unaware of. Effects in the womb will be unknown to the parent and to the child.

How much do we know about:

- Union / violation?
- Fusion / invasion and consumption?
- Wanted / unwanted?
- Accepted / rejected?
- Secure / insecure?
- Growing / stunted?
- Engaged / non-engaged?
- Emergence / expulsion extraction?

Abraham Maslow's hierarchy of human needs is a good starting point to see the various aspects of how pastoral care can help an individual.[10] It is a humanist approach but it can also be seen through a Christian perspective.

- **Physiological needs.** We all need to know where our next loaf of bread will come from. God didn't place us in a vacuum but in a rich garden where there was no shortage of physical resources.
- **Security needs.** We all need to feel safe. God explained to Adam how to be safe in the garden, what to do and what not to touch. I recall a curate who lived in a very tough part of a city. Every time he went out in the evenings to work, he needed a minder to look after his wife and children. We can imagine the anxiety of living in such a situation. When either or both food and security are removed, people can become extremely aggressive and violent until both are obtained and some kind of order is restored.
- **Belonging needs.** We need to have a home, a place where our emotional needs can be met. We are told in Genesis 2:18 that it is not good to be alone; we need relationships. Relationships are where we can relax with friends and let our hair down. In an increasingly individualistic society, this is an aspect that more and more people are having difficulty with. To belong means dealing with the requirements of others. This is so much more

10. A. Maslow (1968), *Towards a Psychology of Being*, New York: John Wiley.

than just joining a group, whether it be in church or on an internet group such as Facebook. Joining is not the same as belonging. We live in a complex world where we have better communication than ever before, and yet people are experiencing increased alienation and loneliness. To belong is to be accepted, warts and all; it is taking the mask off and knowing that you are still loved and wanted.

- **Esteem needs.** We all need places where our self-respect is developed and strengthened, both for ourselves and for others in our lives. When we feel valued, it allows us to begin to work through issues that concern us. But if we feel that we are not of value to anyone, it is much harder to choose to begin to work out our personal issues.
- **Self-actualising.** This is the need to become everything that we are capable of becoming. Here we are helping an individual to become genuinely themselves (all that God has made them to be and wants them to become). This is not about making people as we want them but helping them to discover their own unique specialness that makes them who they are. There is no manipulation here to try to make people Christians. It may be a happy by-product but it is not our primary aim as we engage with people.

I feel that my whole ministry has been one of leading people one step further towards Christ, which is not the same as leading them to where I am.

In my spare time I enjoy woodcarving and creating portrait heads. As I carve, it is as if I am releasing the form that is already there. I have my desires and hopes but the wood itself determines the end product. I might want the carving to have no knots or burrs or colour changes, but that is not in my will to choose. In the same way, we might believe that everyone cannot reach their full potential without becoming a Christian. But if that is the only reason we are caring we will miss out on the true needs of the individual at that particular moment. As I carve, it feels as though I am peeling back an onion, layer by layer. At each stage I am producing a portrait of the same person. It is not just the final form that I'm interested in, but each stage also gives satisfaction, interest and challenge. The journey itself is worthwhile even if I never produce a carving that I am fully satisfied with.

The next chapter will take us further into the needs of individuals.

Reflections

- How aware are you of your development in the womb and during your early childhood years?
- Where do you see yourself within the Erikson's life cycle?
- Can you identify with Maslow's concepts?
- Do these concepts help you to reflect upon where a person might be with their personal needs?

Appendix 1 is a description of what a mature Christian human being might look like.

Chapter 4

The need for forgiveness

To forgive is to set the prisoner free and discover that the prisoner was you.
(Lewis B. Smedes)[11]

All humans need to be able to forgive if they are to travel with little baggage in life. Unfortunately, most people are not taught how to forgive or what it means to truly forgive. The Church, of course, should be an expert on the subject. Pastors will come across the issue of forgiveness time and time again. We need to know clearly what is and what is not forgiveness in God's eyes. John Patton suggests:[12]

- Forgiveness is not forgetting. We cannot forget because these experiences have much to teach us.
- Forgiveness is not condoning. It is not saying that what happened was acceptable or not really serious.
- Forgiveness is not absolving those who have hurt us of all responsibility for their actions. People are still responsible for what they did and must deal with it themselves.
- Forgiveness is not a form of self-sacrifice or swallowing our pride and being a martyr.
- Forgiveness is seldom a quick one-off decision. It usually takes time to confront the pain that has been caused and to allow healing to take place.

Forgiveness is a discovery and a by-product of an ongoing healing process. The failure to forgive is often because wounds have not yet healed. We need to recognise that we no longer need to hold on to our hate and resentments. We no longer desire to punish the people who have hurt us, wanting them to suffer as much as we did. We realise that punishing another does not bring healing to us. What forgiveness does is to release our energy that was consumed with rage and resentment and focus it towards moving positively forward in life. Forgiveness can take place when we have a positive self-esteem, when we no longer build our identity around something that has happened to us. The injuries that we have are just a part of who we are and are not all of us.

11. L. B. Smedes (1997), *The Art of Forgiving*, New York: Ballantine.
12. J. Patton (2005), *Pastoral Care: An Essential Guide*. Nashville: Abingdon Press.

It is here that a pastor who fully understands the depth of forgiveness can bring Christ's ministry to bear upon people in a healing and holistic way. Unfortunately, some people are so damaged that they are ill-equipped to forgive. They need a pastor's hand to help them first experience forgiveness, be it divine or human, before they are able to learn how to forgive themselves. It is in the light of God's forgiveness that we are able to see clearly enough to forgive others. This is not a DIY, self-help task that individuals can achieve alone; rather it requires others alongside to support, accept and encourage. When Carl Rogers, a key founder of modern counselling techniques, was talking about counselling being a place where a person receives positive regard and empathic understanding in a genuine and sincere way, he was talking about what the Church should be.[13] Each Sunday we remind ourselves of our failures and seek to get back in the flow with God and others through repentance, acceptance and love.

It is important to accept that forgiveness can be a long process. The pastor needs to understand that a superficial approach might only deepen a person's resentment and entrapment in an unforgiving state. There are at least four stages to forgiveness.

The first is the uncovering stage, where the person recognises the impact of their hurt and anger. The person may need to accept that the event may have challenged their understanding of life and faith. They need to be given the opportunity to safely express the emotions that have built up. Too often people are encouraged to forgive without first fully articulating and releasing their story. The person may say that they forgive but they find that they are still not released in peace. The hurt and anger remain hidden under the surface.

Secondly, the person needs to accept that their current approach of denial or anger is not releasing them to move on healthily. A commitment is needed to begin to forgive the perpetrator, and perhaps God and themselves. Part of this is the acknowledgement that we all need God's forgiveness.

Thirdly, viewing the offender in a broader framework can help the person. This means trying to see the situation from the viewpoint of other people, including God understanding the other person's past and weaknesses can help to ease the pain.

Finally, if the person can find some meaning in the event and journey, they are more likely to be able to move on in a positive and creative way.

---

13. C. Rogers (1967), *On Becoming a Person*, London: Constable & Robinson.

Alongside forgiveness is the need to begin to accept and love oneself. We are commanded to love others as we love ourselves, yet many people seem to find this difficult. No one is born hating themselves, but early experiences of hurt, guilt and fear can produce people who have extremely low self-esteem. Fear is very easily passed on to our children. We can quickly internalise our experiences and think that we are always bad and never good enough. We take in what is said to us and adopt attitudes from our parents' lives. This can produce a vicious circle of negative thinking and thought processing that is hard to break free from. This is tragic when we think that the Christian message is one of forgiveness, of affirming that we are made in God's image and that God wants us to reach our full potential. We could all do with learning how to love ourselves a little better. Pastors can find themselves regularly helping people deal with low self-esteem and yet not recognise their own issues of self-image.

Reflections

- How do people know that you are available to talk about emotional issues?
- What have you learned from others ministering to you?
- How can you and the church be realistic with regard to your expectations of handling people's emotional problems?
- How important is it to build links with other supporting agencies?
- How can your own journey of forgiveness be helpful in ministering to others?
- Can you see yourself using the stages of forgiveness in your ministry?
- Who helps you meet your own personal needs?

Chapter 5

Suffering with others

Out of suffering have emerged the strongest souls; the most massive characters are seared with scars.
(Edwin Hubbell Chapin)[14]

Although the world is full of suffering, it is also full of the overcoming of it.
(Helen Keller)[15]

The word Almighty means that there is no suffering that God cannot bring good out of.
(Sister Frances Dominica)[16]

My wife worked at a university with students who had additional learning needs. One particular student had severe MS. They had an arrangement whereby the student would be ready for work by 10am when my wife would arrive to scribe his academic work. However, if the carer were late arriving, the student would still be in bed. He couldn't get up, wash himself, get dressed or have breakfast without considerable help. It was only as my wife began to grasp what it was really like for this man each day that she was in a position to help him academically.

If we have eyes to see, there will be someone each Sunday in some kind of wheelchair who has to grapple with several hurdles just to get to church on time. Unless we choose to see more deeply, such challenges can pass right over our heads. It takes discipline and knowledge to be truly empathetic with another person's difficulties. It is often not until we ourselves have had some kind of major issue or struggle in our lives that we become fully aware of other people's situations. Often other people's pains go unnoticed because they are either invisible to us or it is just too painful for us to take them on board.

We need to be able to develop our own understanding of 'suffering theology' if we are going to engage with people in a

14. E. H. Chapin (2012), *Lessons on Faith and Life (Classic Reprint)*, Hong Kong: Forgotten Books.
15. Letter to Dr James Kerr Love (1910), published in J. K. Love (Ed) (1933), *Helen Keller in Scotland: A Personal Record Written by Herself*, Methuen.
16. Quoted by Helen House Hospice, Oxford, speaking on Radio 4 about suffering, March 2009.

pastoral way. Our own experience of life may have been fortunate and we may not have had to encounter significant 'suffering issues'. Hence we can easily feel inadequate and overwhelmed. Yet if we pause and reflect upon our own lives, we will see that we all have had times that have challenged and stressed us. If we are able to tap into our own past experiences and reflect upon how we felt and reacted, we will be more equipped to at least understand other people's stories.

We have a wonderful biblical resource available to us in the books of Job, Lamentations and the Psalms. In addition, a good selection of autobiographical and other works is available of Christians who tell tales of suffering and difficulties.[17]

The next step is to listen to people within your church community who have testimonies to tell of past difficulties and present trials. Often we listen to the stories of famous people but ignore those under our noses who also have remarkable stories to tell. We must also remember the unsung heroes who are busy caring for relatives on a daily basis. These are people who don't have the luxury of choice or of choosing to care. Many feel trapped with the responsibility of supporting a relative. If we can begin to understand with true empathy what this must be like, it will open up to us a huge window of insight and awareness. Indeed, if a church can offer support to the carers, what better place to begin a care ministry?

In order to care for others, we need to use all the resources that God has given us. These days we have considerable knowledge about what makes marriages work, how to cope with bereavement and depression, how to build a healthy self-esteem, and so on. We would be negligent if we failed to equip ourselves with the appropriate knowledge when it comes to our Christian role of carer.

More will be said through the book about how suffering plays a role in pastoral care; for now we need to accept and be prepared for the reality that any pastoral ministry will be costly. I have seen a good number of ministers with whom I trained fall aside, partly because of the cost of ministry. I have also witnessed too many lay workers finding themselves overwhelmed by other people's problems that have affected them both spiritually and physically. This, however, may be no reason not to engage in a caring ministry; after all, we do follow one who was rejected and suffered.

We cannot predict where ministry will take us nor how it will affect us. We are people of faith on a journey. What we do know is

---

17. Examples include *The Shack* by W. P. Young, *When Bad Things Happen to Good People* by H. Kushner, *The Problem of Pain* by C. S. Lewis, *Lament for a Son* by N. Wolterstorff.

that any Christian ministry will involve a cost, both to ourselves and sometimes to our families. Yet we must bear in mind that Jesus does not expect Christians to go looking for suffering. Hopefully some of the guidance in these chapters might steer pastors away from that temptation.

Reflections

- Can you tap into your past experience to enable you to understand others?
- What stories inspire you in your ministry?
- How aware is your church of those who are carrying long-term burdens?
- How do you know when something is your cross to carry?
- How do you decide when to put down the cross and move on?
- How can you prevent the pain of caring from leaving you worn out and resentful?
- What do you see as the cost of your ministry?
- Can you minister in Jesus' name without suffering crucifixion?

Chapter 6

The core elements

In a moment I will be looking at the different elements and contexts that pastoral carers find themselves in. But first let us just think of some of the key tools that a carer has at their fingertips that makes their Christian ministry unique. At some point in our ministry we will encounter the need for:

- listening
- empathising
- repenting
- bringing hope
- praying
- touching
- being present
- silence
- learning
- rescuing
- encouraging
- confronting
- suffering alongside
- reflecting
- celebrating.

These experiences will manifest themselves in different ways. We will have one-off encounters with people whom we will never meet again. Others we will accompany on a long journey and have the privilege of seeing change over months and years.

A slight *change of heart* often brings people to us as they seek help and support. Today people feel more sinned against in life as they experience injustices and make complaints; they feel victimised. Today's society has a willingness to sue anyone and any organisation. Yet when it comes to thinking about our own sin, it is a term seldom used. Part of a pastoral ministry inevitably involves helping a person think about their context and enabling them to be open to having a *change of heart,* which can lead to reconciliation and healing. These days, it might not be appropriate to use a word like 'sin' if it simply doesn't relate to the person's ideology. But there are many other words and conversations that can help a person to see that they are perhaps on the wrong road and heading in an unhealthy direction. For example:

- offended
- had a lapse in judgement
- gone wrong
- strayed
- made an error
- misled
- succumbed
- erred
- gone amiss
- disgraced
- shamed
- feeling guilty
- low
- blameworthy.

Acceptance is the first thing that a person is looking for when they arrive at the pastor's door. They are wondering whether their unique story will be accepted, whether they can tell the whole story and not just a part. They are concerned whether this religious person will judge and condemn them. This is a very vulnerable place to be in. But we as carers are also putting ourselves in a vulnerable place. We are being willing to open ourselves up to a story that will affect us, a story that might draw upon painful feelings of the past.

If we are able to convey genuine emotional acceptance of another's story, we have set the foundation for a good beginning for ministry to take place. As a companion for what follows, we are recognising that their story could be ours. This is at the heart of what empathy conveys. Yet, at the same time, their story is different from ours. We don't actually know what it is to be them with their experiences. This draws us into the encounter with openness, inquisitiveness and willingness to recognise that the 'other' is the expert here; they are the author of their own story. When true acceptance has taken place, you will hear people say to you that they feel so much better by simply having their story accepted and not rejected.

Hope is at the heart of the Christian faith. But we need to bring the right kind of hope into people's lives. The hope of a cure when a person is terminally ill is a false hope. So how can we bring meaningful hope to someone when they are in despair? It begins at least with ourselves and our awareness of our own hope and what we put our trust in.

This reminds us that any pastoral ministry begins and ends with *prayer*, be it corporate prayer or our own private prayer life that sustains us. Prayer, of course, is never static; it helps us move forward into a living learning arena. It is hard to imagine being in the caring profession without finding ourselves constantly learning new things, whether it be about other people, ourselves or lessons about life generally. Hunter puts it this way when talking about hospitals:

> The primary task of a hospital in society is to enable patients, their families and staff, to learn from the experience of illness and death how to build a healthy society.[18]

In the context we find ourselves in, we need to be open to the *learning possibility* and seek to enable a person to become wiser and stronger despite the pain and heartache.

We are in the healing business, and that at times requires *rescuing people* when appropriate. Jesus was constantly rescuing people from the traps they found themselves in. For us, it might mean providing an opportunity for a person to escape an abusive and violent situation, opening up possibilities for a person to move on, or directing them to other support agencies with appropriate knowledge and care.

I will say more about rescuing later (Chapter 32, Dangers in pastoral care) as we have to be careful that we are not in fact helping a person to remain a victim because we like playing the role of the rescuer. Churches can attract people who need to be needed, so we need to be careful that we do not cause more harm than good. This shouldn't stop us, though, like many other agencies that have become so afraid to help people for fear of bad press and the risk of getting it wrong. Social workers find themselves in a terribly difficult situation today where they are damned if they do and damned if they don't intervene. Often Christian voluntary workers venture into situations like innocent lambs going to wolves. There is no doubt that we need to be as wise as possible in new situations and ensure that we operate good practice (see Chapter 27, Ground rules and boundaries). But we mustn't avoid the cost to Christian ministry that requires us to go the second mile and to seek to help a person, particularly where other agencies have given up. We have to acknowledge that at times we can get caught up with a short-term rescue, only to discover that what is required is a much deeper rescuing by society and God's 'kingdom plan'. Having this balanced perspective can help to prevent us from failing to see the wood from the trees.

Confrontation might not be what is commonly expected from a pastoral worker, but we all find ourselves at times in situations that

18. T. Hunter (1967), 'Self-run hospitals', *New Society*, 14, pp. 356ff.

make us angry. Pastoral carers are not to be 'doormats' to be trampled on by all who pass by. Neither is it an excuse for us to pass it off as an act of 'taking up our cross'. This is just bad theology. Jesus spent most of his ministry confronting those who were mistreating the poor and vulnerable; we should do likewise. This requires Christian maturity and the prayerful advice of others. Our confrontation may be to an individual if we feel we have a strong enough relationship to cope with it. In other instances it might be to speak out on behalf of another to the church, an agency or the local council. It is hard to imagine being a care worker and not having to speak out forcefully at some point in one's ministry.

There will equally be times when one chooses to suffer alongside another. W. H. Vanstone puts it this way:

> The dignity of being human is expressed not only in our activities but also in passivity when things just happen to us and we endure them.[19]

We will meet people in families where one person, whether unknowingly or willingly, plays the role of a 'pain bearer'. It can be an important role, providing they themselves don't become crushed under the weight of responsibility. For pastoral care workers, we are actively putting ourselves into situations where pain exists. It is impossible not to be affected by it. Suffering with God's children to bear the unbearable is a high calling. At times it is impossible to fulfil our calling without experiencing pain. To sit alongside another with them on their painful bench is in fact the only way of understanding and getting alongside another in their grief, earning you the right to speak. We, too, have to make sure that this endurance is not making us bitter and hardened and having a negative effect upon our first calling – our families.

Repentance is part and parcel of the Christian ministry and message. Calling people to a new way of thinking and being will inevitably involve a call to repent. Here there is the desire to be right with God, with our neighbours and with ourselves. Repentance involves turning from one's present way and finding a new way of life. This involves understanding what is wrong about the old way and current attitude of life, acknowledging this to another (the divine and the human) and seeking to walk in a new way, a 'new kingdom' way. This includes:

---

19. W. H. Vanstone (1982), *The Stature of Waiting*, DLT.

- leaving behind old ways of thinking
- dealing with negative thought patterns that might be compulsive and habitual
- altering fixed understandings of the past
- changing attitudes that focused purely on the self.

This is not just a one-off event. Conversion is a life-transforming event but it is also the start of a journey. Here we begin to live in the new kingdom yet surrounded by the old kingdom. No wonder there is tension.

The Christian life is a desire to remain within the flow of the river of the 'living water' and not to be pushed into the stagnant pools that are always nearby. A pastoral carer is always working on the edge of the two, drawing others from the static waters into the living stream while ensuring that they do not become trapped themselves.

Finally, we mustn't forget the role of *thanksgiving and celebration* within our ministry. Releasing joy, thanksgiving, remembering and celebrating goes hand in hand with our caring role. In a university context, I deal mostly with tragic and difficult situations, but I also love to hear stories from students and staff of their successes. Sometimes there is no one else to share such good news with. And when you are aware of the struggles some have undergone to get this far, the joy is even greater. Having an opportunity to share good news allows the giver of the news to deepen their satisfaction and pleasure. As carers, we in turn can find that it makes all the long hours and heartache worthwhile.

I was stopped on a staircase one day by a student I didn't recognise. He shared that he had been looking for me to say thank you. Four years previously, when he had just arrived at university and was extremely unhappy, I had suggested that it was OK to go home, that there is an option other than going away to a university. He told me that when he went home he had been given a hard time by his family, but in the end it was the best thing for him. Now he had graduated from home and was doing an MA at his first university.

But what makes these attributes Christian? First of all, we are supporting and encouraging someone who is wanting to get in touch with his or her inner self. In Christ we are bringing a basic degree of courtesy, respect and compassion. We are presenting one 'Christ-created being' to another 'Christ-created being'. This is a movement that involves confronting pain and finding faith in a God that asks for all. The pastor uses skills of focusing on the content of the conversation. We listen to what is being said, not what we assume is being said. This also includes observing non-verbal clues in the way the person speaks and gives off body language – posture, facial expression, tone of voice, blushing, etc. This listening skill is not special to the Christian environment but is fundamental in our belief in a God who hears our prayers.

We are helping a person to express their anxieties and fears by expressing them both to us and to God himself – i.e., we are helping to make what is known to them and to God known openly to another. Here we are making it safe for a person to express their feelings in a safe, non-judging, accepting environment.

We work on people's landmarks and stepping stones as they journey in life. This maintains a Christian direction that leads to forgiveness and holiness. It is where we are different from a social worker or secular counsellor as we recognise the spirituality of a person's life and seek to engage with it.

We also allow the 'God' question to be asked. Many care workers, counsellors and bereavement workers shy away from the God issue. They feel less competent to deal with God issues. But here is where the Christian pastoral carer should be confident and well able to handle it. I'm far from suggesting we dive in with answers and give people our theology. This might be a backward step. But we must allow questions relating to God to be discussed in a safe environment without judgement and condemnation. What questions might arise?

- Where is God in this situation?
- Is God punishing me?
- Why is God not healing?
- I thought God had a plan for my life.
- Why did God allow this?

Allowing someone to express their thoughts will always be more positive than ignoring them, suppressing them or turning them inwards to negative despair. Just allowing someone to release these questions allows a process of healing to begin. The danger for the carer is that we want to dive in with the sticking plaster and get rid of all doubt and pain. This might make us feel better, but is this helping the person? We need to embark on a journey of companionship in which we resist diving in with our directions and quick answers; rather we must journey with the person till they find satisfactory answers that are appropriate for them.

Finally, we point to and use appropriate Christian symbols, images and stories that allow a person to see their horizon more clearly. Pastoral visiting is far more than just having a cup of tea with someone and talking about the weather and everything under the sun in a trivial way. However, the skills need to be taught in the context of the church where they can be recognised, encouraged and developed.

Of course, the foundation of any caring ministry begins with the skill of listening, and it is this developed skill we now address.

Reflections

- Can you analyse a pastoral visit you have made and see the different components that made up your encounter?
- Can you think of different ways of talking about 'sin'?
- How can you know when to confront an individual?
- How easy do you find it to bring in the Christian gospel to a conversation?
- Do you find it easy or hard to sit with difficult and challenging questions about God and faith issues?
- With whom do you rejoice and give thanks?

Chapter 7

Listening

I know that you believe you understand what you think I said, but I am not sure you realise that what you heard is not what I meant.
(Robert McCloskey)[20]

It is strange that at school level we are taught how to speak English but are rarely given lessons on how to listen effectively. It is something we all take for granted, and we assume that we are good at it. However, effective listening is not as easy as we might think. It's rather like passing the driving test and never looking at the Highway Code again until you get a speeding ticket and head off to a driving awareness course. If we are about to go on a car journey, hopefully we will reflect upon what we will need:

- Is it a new route?
- Is the car roadworthy?
- What will the weather be like?
- Do we need a map and directions?

Just as driving depends upon the situation, listening also requires different approaches and skills. So much of pastoral care involves listening, yet there are many distractions that prevent it:

- Are you easily distracted?
- Do you fake attention when thinking about other things?
- Do you react to emotional words?
- Do you often interrupt the speaker?
- Do you try and get your point across at the sacrifice of hearing what's being said?
- Do you tune out of uninteresting topics?
- Do you daydream if the speaker speaks slowly?
- Do you jump to conclusions?
- Are you busy thinking about what you need to say?

All of these things are common and can become roadblocks to a person feeling that they have been heard.

---

20. R. McCloskey (1920), *Make Way for Ducklings*, New York, Viking Press.

Before we can begin to listen to another person, we need to learn how to listen to ourselves. If on encountering another we emit a signal of anxiety, it will impact on the other person, who in turn will not feel that they are being heard. We need to identify the source of our own anxiety to decide whether it is useful or just interfering. Useful anxiety is generated when we feel that we are in danger. But more often than not the anxiety we create in ourselves comes from a fear that we will not succeed in the relationship. Anxiety comes from a thought process that often has a root that says, 'I'm not good enough.' If, however, we can be at peace with our own persona and accept that we are 'good enough', we will regain our ability to truly concentrate on another and listen. A very simple deep breathing technique can relax us enough to enable us to re-engage with the present situation. By focusing on our breathing we can become more aware of what our thought patterns are and will be able to address them. When you are about to go and meet a person, there is nothing worse than suddenly remembering that you have forgotten to phone someone else. In such a state of mind we are certainly not ready to listen to another person.

Next, we need to come with the right attitude. We need to reflect how we like to be treated when someone listens to us. We must come with a gentle approach in which our beliefs, values and priorities take second seat to the one we are caring for. Otherwise we are tempted to see ourselves as an expert and come to the situation not as equals but with a superior attitude.

It can be helpful before beginning a pastoral work session to be quiet in prayer, listening to one's own breathing and asking the question, 'Is there anything that is keeping me from being present with others and myself?' This needs a few minutes to allow things to surface. We need to acknowledge our anxiety and agree to deal with any issues that arise. In this way we can feel more prepared to face whatever ministry throws at us. In this way, our breathing will be less tense, our hands will warm up and our stomach muscles will relax. As we make our first encounter for the day, we will find that we are more available for the person and are less distracted.

- Focus upon understanding the other person rather than first being understood yourself.
- Pay attention to the other's differences and appreciate their uniqueness.
- Do not be judgemental.

When we communicate with a person in ministry, several things occur. We have the sender, the message, the channel of communication and the receiver. Much of our time is spent trying to decode what someone is trying to tell us. We have to achieve four things if we want to achieve good communication:

1. Sense – this is becoming aware of the message, picking up the sounds that seem relevant.
2. Interpret – this is trying to understand the meaning and purpose of the message. What is the person trying to convey?
3. Evaluate – Is it urgent? Serious? Does it require action?
4. Respond – this might range from simply recognising that the message and the messenger have been heard to taking immediate action.

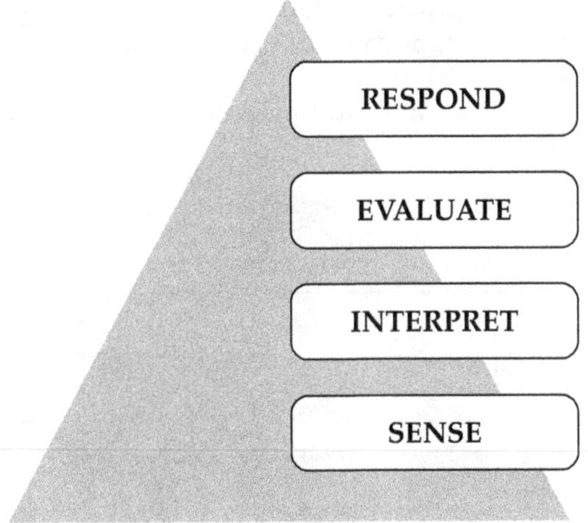

Figure 3: Signs of Good Communication

Listening empathetically requires practice. We first have to learn how to manage our own feelings, especially when we struggle to understand another person's story. Whether we like it or not, we are always communicating something, be it through our voice, our gestures, our expressions or our behaviour.

Secondly, we need to listen by learning how the person is talking to us so that we can use appropriate language to engage with them. We all bring with us our own history, culture, personality and belief perspective, which influence how we communicate.

Thirdly, we need to check what we are hearing so that we can correct any distortions or misconceptions that we have assumed. We do this by paraphrasing and repeating back what we have heard. This does not mean repeating what has been said verbatim but expressing it in our own words. Examples might include:

- As I understand it . . .
- You seem to mean . . .
- What I hear you say is . . .
- Correct me if I'm wrong but . . .
- In other words . . .

By doing this we are focusing in on the essence of the conversation, the content and on feeling involved. More will be said about this when we talk about counselling skills, but a helpful approach is to try and visualise the experience that is being described. In this way, we can tap into any past experiences we have had that create similar feelings. This will attune us to their situation. We need to be aware of silences and reflect upon their meaning. What we are doing here is not collecting statistical data but getting to 'know' the situation being described.

What often frustrates our listening skills is the noise around and within that distracts us.

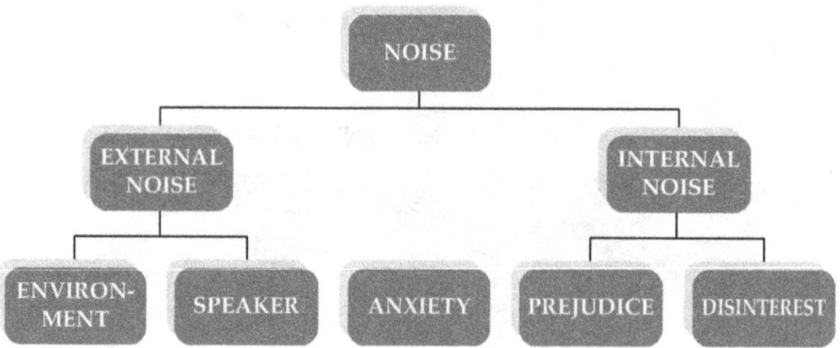

Figure 4: Noises that Distract

External noise might be the telephone, mobile phone, TV or other people around us. But there are also internal noises such as anxiety, prejudice, a fixed religious belief system, or focusing on style rather than substance. We need to grow in awareness of our own triggers that get in the way of our ministry. For example,:

- How do we react if the person shares with excessive emotion?
- Do we quickly judge the situation and person before they have finished speaking?
- Are we busy thinking about what to say next?
- Are we easily distracted?

Many of us who enter into pastoral ministry have been carers in our own families. We are used to engaging with people's problems and playing a role in fixing things. In ministry, people will often come with the expectation that we will be able to fix whatever the problem might be. However, we need to learn to pause and not slip into that 'fix it' mentality. This is so important for several reasons.

Firstly, the reality is that we can't fix other people's problems.

Secondly, we need to recognise that it is the person themselves who needs to deal with the issue, not us.

Thirdly, we need to be aware that often the first issue that a person brings to us might not necessarily be the main issue of concern that needs tackling. So when someone says that they need help, we need to remain in listening mode until we can work out exactly what the main issues are. It may be that all they need is someone to listen to their story. Some will have already made up their minds about what to do but need someone to act as a sounding board. Others need support as they work through their issues, while others will need help to be directed to the right support agency.

If we can develop an ability to take a deep breath when someone is asking for help and resist thinking in a 'problem-solution mode', we will create space and time to allow a person to develop their thoughts, reflect on the issues and have a fuller picture of the circumstances.

Reflections

- Think of someone you know personally that you like and highly respect. Are they good at listening? What does this tell you?
- Spend a day observing people's encounters. Are they listening?
- Over one working day, reflect upon the types of listening you practised (social, entertainment, information, persuasion, catharsis).

Chapter 8
Visiting

The meeting of two personalities is like the contact of two chemical substances: if there is any reaction, both are transformed.
(Carl Jung)[21]

When I was a maternity hospital chaplain, I asked for help from a couple of lay readers. Unfortunately, not having had any training, one went around the wards waving a Bible at the door and shouting, 'Anyone want the Bible?' I soon received complaints.

This was very different from my first ever experience of a pastoral visit. I was four years old when my grandmother became bedridden in our lounge. She was dying of cancer, having had both breasts removed. I have vivid memories of various events at that time, but one in particular stands out. It was when the local curate came to visit. He knelt down by the bedside to pray. As he did so, we noticed he had big holes in the soles of his shoes. In those days, being a curate meant that one lived little above the poverty line. My family seemed to be really uplifted by his visit. It was clearly done with sensitivity, respect and care.

Visiting might seem to be something you naturally do, without thought. Some people are indeed able to do it naturally, putting people at ease, and they are always invited back. But if you analyse it, there are certain elements that are required in order to make it successful.

There are two types of visitors: those that you want and those that you definitely don't want. It is so easy to generate a bedside manner that never engages with the person you are visiting. You probably know the kind I mean: the person who comes to see you when you are in hospital, eats your grapes and never once listens to what you are actually saying to them. Their aim is to cheer you up at all costs while at the same time keeping their emotional health safe and untouched by another.

In this case, the visitor can use God as a way of hitting you over the head with compassion while communicating that you should be grateful to be alive. It can feel almost as if God has inflicted you with an illness so that this obnoxious person can visit you and be fulfilled in 'their' ministry.

---

21. C. Jung (1933), *Modern Man in Search of a Soul*, London: Kegan Paul Trench Trubner.

This is a detached visitor who may feel that they have helped by their visit, but actually leaves the client annoyed and frustrated. What is needed at a visit is a commitment to long-term support rather than emotional, over-involved indulgence. It takes time, experience and maturity to be able to fully care for another, to engage with them while not being so attached that you can't walk away.

We can all wear masks of one form or another to help us cope with a situation. We can wear the mask of the religious dog collar, the Bible, a particular way of praying, quoting verses of cheerfulness, citing positive examples of healing and happy endings, and so on. All of these can prevent us from personal, costly involvement in a situation. Sometimes we have to be willing to engage in a helpless situation that we ourselves would crumble under, and all we can do is simply sit with the person and try and grasp what it must be like. And once we understand, we remain sitting there without platitudes. This is honesty at work and produces the kind of visitor that many long for.

One thing that should characterise good pastoral presence is how we approach visiting. We must have the ability to accept and love people regardless of their beliefs, doubts, intense anger or prolonged sadness. If the person thinks you are just visiting to sell them Christianity or to give your advice, we may be better off not calling in. Our task is to be more about journeying with a person, to listen to them in such a way that enables them to resolve their issues. We are there to help an individual negotiate their spiritual crisis knowing that they are not alone.

Prayer is what marks out the Christian worker from a social worker. There is a spectrum of approaches to take with regard to prayer. At one end there is always the need to simply inform the person that you will pray and go on praying for them. We can then offer them the choice of whether they would like the church to pray. This is very much their choice. Not everyone wants their situation, however tactfully done, to be aired in church. We can do great damage to a relationship if we put someone's name in a news sheet or pray for them by name in church without their permission. It really is their choice, and we must have the humility to let them decide what they would prefer. The other side of the spectrum is where we pray with a person on each visit, and perhaps they join in with us in this prayer ministry. A wise pastoral care worker is mature enough not to have a blanket approach but adjusts their ministry depending upon the situation and what is appropriate at the time.

There is no standard way to pray, although churches often develop their own particular style. Some of us are more at ease using prayers that have been thought over and written down and have stood the test of time. Others prefer a more extemporary approach. What is important is that we function within our own comfort zone. When we begin to feel uncomfortable, the other person will soon pick up our vibes.

Unless we are ministering to someone who is at ease with long prayer ministry, we are better advised always to keep our prayers on the shorter side. After all, it is the heartfelt prayer that God listens to, not the long-winded meaningless prayer (Matthew 6:7). We would do well to take a fresh look at Jesus and how he prayed. On the whole, his prayers tended to be short and to the point (see Chapter 11, Prayer).

When people ask for a pastoral visit, they usually say why they want to talk to us. However, we mustn't assume that this is the main reason. A person might say after a church service that they want to speak to us because the sermon spoke to them. However, this might be just a safe way for someone to ask to see us. Often the main reason is not disclosed at the time the appointment is made. This means that when we do visit we mustn't jump to a conclusion of what the meeting is about. We need to create space in the conversation and allow silences in order to provide an opportunity for the person to pluck up the courage to address what is really on their mind.

Endings

We arrange a meeting with someone and we agree the time and the place. We have developed a very natural way of initiating a conversation and trying to put someone at ease. But how much time do we give to thinking about the ending of the meeting? Endings are as important as beginnings. There are at least four issues to be clear about with endings.

Firstly, there is the time constraint. People will visit a doctor and know that they will be given 10 to 15 minutes at the most. But when they see a pastor, they seem to think we have all the time in the world. I find this in my university student ministry where students will often arrive late for meetings. They will then want to chat as if this is the only reason they are at university. Right at the beginning, as I close the door, I need to be clear just how much time I have available and explain this to the student. It focuses their attention remarkably, as well as my own. By saying we only have 30 minutes does not mean we are not taking their issue as important. In fact, what we are saying is that we have their undivided attention for that period, and if more is required then it can be arranged for another time. People understand this if it is stated at the beginning. However, if you don't mention any time constraint at the beginning you find yourself trying to end a conversation and making an excuse to leave. The ending becomes confused and unsatisfactory for all concerned.

Secondly, it is important to recognise that everything can't be discussed in one meeting. It is common in a counselling room for a person, just as they are about to leave, to raise another subject. The professional counsellor, with their clear boundaries and time control, will suggest that they discuss the topic at the next meeting. Sometimes a pastor's time is not so tightly controlled, but it doesn't mean we have the attention span to handle another issue with clarity.

Thirdly, we need to develop the ability to not open up an issue when closure would be more appropriate. It is easy to suggest that someone should come and see us to talk about an issue that the person has already put to bed. In this way, we can inadvertently make a situation worse. Alternatively, it can be tempting to suggest that a person requires additional support well before they are ready to receive it. Our problem can be twofold: we can be too inquisitive and begin an extra conversation that is just not necessary, or we can see the bigger picture of a person's life and want to bring about change at a rate the person is just not ready for. People only change when they are ready, not when we think it is necessary.

People do not change when we try to change them.

We need to develop the patience to allow people to choose when they want to face and work through their issues.

Fourthly, we need to be clear with the person and ourselves whether we will be visiting them again. Although it might be nice, for example, to keep visiting a person post the funeral service, the reality is that there are just too many deaths in the community to continue to visit people endlessly. We need to be clear about this, otherwise people raise their expectations and are then upset when we fail to visit (more is said about this in Chapter 46, Bereavement).

Finally, there is the issue of general visiting in the church. It is not uncommon for a church worker to hear someone mutter that they have never had a visit from the church leadership team, or specifically the vicar. There are two things worth mentioning when we do visit people in their homes. When visiting, we represent the church leadership, which includes the vicar/leader. Otherwise you will be constantly going back to the vicar/leader and saying that such and such wants them to visit. You will be just stirring up more work for the leader.

It is important to remind people that we can't pop in all the time but we will see them every Sunday in church. People seem to forget easily that we are available on Sundays and that they have spoken to us recently in church. However, we need to be clear about how we make ourselves available on a Sunday so that people know they can arrange a meeting with us. Some church workers turn up to church on a Sunday deliberately without their diaries as a way of controlling their week. This approach pushes the emphasis on the members of the congregation to phone during the week, usually via a secretary, to make an appointment. We have to consider what message we are giving here. When people see that Sunday is one of our main days of work, it can seem odd that we are not willing to bring our diaries. I wonder how many times a worship occasion touches someone's life such that they want to follow it up with a one-to-one, but they are then put off by the approach of the leadership team and find that the desire wanes during the week?

A person might think that their issue is simply not important to the pastor, while the pastor might equally be closing the door to the work of the Holy Spirit and an opportunity to minister when someone is open and responsive. A caring, professional approach perhaps could be to have the secretary available on a Sunday morning with the diary with set times available. It is important that the diary is clearly planned before Sunday so that we retain control of what times are available. In this way we are showing that we are professional and take people's needs, post Sunday, seriously. The more organised we are with regard to our contact with people, the better equipped we are to handle how we engage and end our meetings.

Reflections

- What experience have you had of people visiting you?
- What makes you feel at ease when visiting?
- How do you prepare yourself before a visit?
- How can you make the length of stay more controlled?
- Do you feel comfortable about introducing prayer?
- What ways can you initiate the ending of a meeting?
- Do you ever feel frustrated and struggle to end a meeting? How can you prevent this from happening?

Chapter 9

Hospital visiting

Time doesn't seem to pass in the same way in hospitals as it does in other places.
(P. Almodovar)[22]

I recall many years ago, as a 22-year-old graduate, attending an outpatients' clinic in a large hospital. Six hours and a handshake from a consultant later, I was told 'best of luck' as a nurse took me in a wheelchair to a ward where I was given pyjamas. Over the course of the next few hours I saw six doctors, and at 9pm that evening I was finally told I was seriously ill. The gravity of my illness didn't dawn on me until I woke in the middle of the night to urgent medical care being given to the man in the next bed. Suddenly I realised that, if the man next to me was that critically ill, I must be in an unhealthy state too. In the midst of a sea of strangers I was very relieved when my local vicar came to see me. Here was someone with whom I could share my fear and worries. I needed that reassurance several times over the following weeks. I was moved to a neurological ward in another hospital that was full of men with brain tumours of one kind or another. The other patients' stresses and worries spilled over constantly and had a negative effect on me. Fortunately, my story had a happy ending.

Sooner or later, every pastoral worker will be expected to do some hospital visiting. For those who consider hospitals to be alien and frightening places, visiting can be a tall order. Here, a person who works in a faith context enters a very scientific domain. Yet at the heart of hospitals are vulnerable people, and that is the primary ministry of a pastor. We mustn't allow the environment to intimidate us. After all, we are all working towards the same aim – to bring comfort and healing to a person, be it physical, mental or spiritual.

Most hospitals have a chapel, which can help you to begin or end your visit with prayer and calm. Sometimes a patient will be well enough to come with you and will appreciate a change of environment. Pastors are usually allowed to visit out of hours, provided we don't interfere with any medical procedure or prevent a patient from resting. However, on arrival we need to seek permission from

22. P. Almodovar, Spanish Film Director.

the ward sister or senior nurse and assure them that we will only stay for a brief visit.

Hospitals consist of only people, yet we attribute names to the different roles people play. Doctors, nurses and physiotherapists all have recognised roles. But what is the role of the sick person? They suddenly become a patient in pyjamas, confined to a hospital bed in a ward shared with strangers. The world shrinks to a bed, a locker, a chair and perhaps a television that might work if you have remembered to bring some money. All of this focuses the attention of the patient on the fact that they must be ill in one way or another.

It is into this small world that the pastor enters, often but not always to visit someone they know. It is a little more awkward if you don't know the person because you instantly become aware of a sea of faces staring at you as you enter the ward. I always check with a nurse as to the exact position of the patient, so that I can go with confidence to the right bed. Even if you know the person, it is best to check; very often people look different under hospital conditions.

The initial encounter will inevitably involve a bland conversation, often about the weather, parking the car, television, sport and the quality of the food. This is a very natural and healthy conversation. After all, just because a person is now being called 'a patient', it doesn't mean that they are not still interested in everyday things. This is an important time during which the visitor is building a rapport with the person and putting them at ease. We are bringing the normality of the world into the hospital environment.

This is also an important time for the person being visited as they decide whether they want to trust us with deeper personal issues. The one thing we have to remember in this work is that the patient must retain control of the conversation. We can ask open, general questions, but they must decide whether they want to take the bait and share personal spiritual concerns.

It is easy to feel rather bereft of skill when you visit a person in hospital. We need to remember that the role is far more about 'being' than 'doing' or 'achieving'. If we can grasp this then we will be more relaxed in the context. When Dame Cicely Saunders, the founder of the hospice movement, became terminally ill and was asked what she wanted from a chaplain, she said she wanted 'someone who has been battered by life'.[23]

This is wise advice. It's less about what you say and more about what you are. Some people will choose to be polite and want to leave it at that without desiring prayer or further conversation; just the fact that people in the church are thinking and praying for the

23. C. Saunders (1990), *Beyond the Horizon: A Search for Meaning in Suffering*, London: Darton, Longman & Todd.

person can be enough to bring comfort and reflection. However, it is surprising how quickly some patients get into a deep conversation.

As a young maternity hospital chaplain I would visit the wards before women gave birth. Many were in bed for long periods of time in order to keep their blood pressure down. It was difficult to know what to say, but I was often touched by how quickly women would share with me their stories of previous miscarriages and losses in life. These were the issues that dwelt on their minds. Having someone who was willing to listen and offer a prayer seemed to be an important part of comfort and hope to the expectant mother.

Being seriously ill in a hospital or a hospice can create an atmosphere in which faithful people suddenly lose their faith and their trust in rituals and rites; they can find that everything they have relied upon for years now seems meaningless. It is inevitable that we will meet people who feel lost and frightened. It is also a time when people reflect upon what they have done in life as well as things they have neglected. All of this focuses the mind. It is here that our gentle ministry of listening, asking open questions and allowing a person to share is so important. It is into this context that we can bring our prayer ministry, be it an audible prayer or a silent one.

You and the patient might feel more at ease with the curtain drawn for a few minutes' solace. Sometimes an appropriate, gentle touch of someone's arm can be very uplifting. If you are unsure or feeling uncomfortable about this, be discerning to your own spirit and don't reach out, or simply ask the person if they are happy for you to hold their arm as you pray. Short prayers are best; the last thing we want to do is to tax a patient's patience when they are unwell. It is not always the illness that is the main thing a patient wants you to pray about. This is why it is important that we ask them what they would want us to pray about. Often a patient's concern is their relatives. Offering to visit and support those at home can be very reassuring to someone who feels trapped in hospital.

I generally keep my visits to about ten minutes. In this way neither the patient nor the nurses will mind us returning.

After a visit to a particular person, it is common for other patients in the room to look on. They often appreciate a friendly 'hello' and might well desire a pastor's presence and prayer as well. Sensitivity is required to assess how far to go when talking to others. If in doubt it is better to just be friendly. You could remind the patients that a chaplain exists who would be more than willing to visit if they inform the nurse.

All in all, hospital and hospice visiting can be extremely rewarding, but there is no doubt that some in pastoral roles and church leadership feel very uncomfortable with this type of work. We have to recognise that not everyone is suited to it, and there should be no shame or guilt in acknowledging this. Visiting in a mental health hospital might be one such example. In one sense it is just like any other hospital, with staff and patients. On the other hand, you may find that the doors are locked; it may be more difficult to gain access and you may feel very unsure as to how to care for a parishioner with mental health issues. In such a situation, it is important that we recognise the feeling of discomfort and hold on to that feeling. This is a valuable insight as to how the patient might be feeling in the hospital. We have just to think about the story of Legion who was isolated, rejected and feeling out of control to begin to understand what it can be like to be mentally ill (Luke 8:26-39).

We don't have to understand a person's illness to care for them. What we can do is to be human and share our common humanity with the patient. This simply means hearing a person's story. We can't assume that this has fully taken place in a hospital; patients tend to get asked questions rather than be given the freedom to just talk about what is on their mind. Jesus began with Legion by finding out his name. Our visit brings a touch of normality and continuity with the community, and that is so important to a person when they find themselves in a strange place. When they are feeling more recovered they often report how valuable they found a simple visit from a pastor.

When we visit someone in hospital it is to be expected that we find ourselves reflecting upon our own health and how we would cope in such a situation. We need to allow ourselves the time and space to digest our thoughts and feelings from such experiences and allow them to shape our ministry and maturity. Otherwise one day we may find ourselves in a hospital bed and be unprepared for how it will impact upon us.

We mustn't forget that hospitals have their own hospital chaplains. If we are uncomfortable with medical environments or are unable to visit, especially if we live in the countryside miles away, then the chaplain will willingly carry out ministry on our behalf.

Reflections

- How do you feel as you walk into a hospital?
- If you have been a patient previously, what kind of visitor did you want?
- Would you feel more comfortable talking with the curtain drawn or open?
- Could you visit the local hospital chaplain and build a working relationship for the future?
- What resources do you have that you could leave with a patient?

Chapter 10

The ten temptations of a pastoral carer

Good habits result from resisting temptations.
(Ancient proverb)

As a teenager in a fairly unreligious home, I started to go to church. I didn't find it easy; the members of the church seemed more interested in my family members than in me. But the curate took an interest in me and one day invited me to his home. I have never forgotten the conversation. I was exploring my faith and reading the Gospels. I wanted to know why my life was flat and boring whilst life in the Gospels was dynamic, with God clearly at work. The curate's wife was listening while she was busy ironing. She interjected with a rebuff to me, 'Who do you think you are? You're not a disciple. God isn't going to work in your life like that.' I left the house deflated and disillusioned.

Sometimes we can understand a subject better by seeing it from a negative aspect. What does poor pastoral care look like?

1. The carer forces or misinterprets the message and the need of the person. This can lead to embarrassment for the person who may well feel trapped and intimidated.
2. The pastor simply doesn't listen, which may delay any healing process and indeed become a blockage for the person to develop their walk with God.
3. The pastor projects their own beliefs and struggles on to the person. We can easily do this when we feel we are struggling with a situation. We can be tempted to simply give superficial answers and platitudes rather than grappling and going deeper with the issue. The cost to us might seem too great to cope with and so we hide behind platitudes saying things like, 'It's God's will,' or 'God knows best'. Such statements may be correct but they can leave the person feeling more trapped. In any case, how do we know it is God's will? And yes, God does know best, but it may still leave us sitting in a hole.
4. The pastor fails to keep a reasonable emotional distance such that they become overwhelmed with the pain of the situation

and lose their objectivity and direction. This is common when a pastor gets too emotionally wrapped up with a person.

5. The pastor may be like Eliphaz and his friends in the book of Job, who assume that everything is down to one problem – sin! Here is a theological model that cannot cope with mystery and the unknown. Yet there are many situations to which we simply do not have the answers. Not all situations are black and white. Life is complex enough to provide us with a whole range of grey tones, and these can be difficult to differentiate. This is not to say that Eliphaz and his friends might not have been right in a different context. But here they failed to show any compassion, sensitivity or humility. In fact, their behaviour may well have led to Job seeing God in a negative light. Jesus, on the other hand, speaks about serving others through simple tasks of offering a drink or providing food, visiting, and binding up wounds as well as comforting. These are basic, tangible actions of love.
6. When a person is enduring a difficult experience, it is not the time to speak with confidence about God when we have never been in their situation. The Bible reveals how often even Moses, Elijah and Peter were brought to their knees. We cannot presume how we would act in such situations. We need a heart response rather than a head reaction.
7. Pastors can easily develop the habit of filling every silent pause with their presence, words and wisdom. Alas, there are times when we need to be comfortable with silence, to sit alongside another and to remain there. This enables us to both get in touch with our own feelings and allow the Holy Spirit to speak into the situation. So often when we echo back what feelings we are experiencing, we find that the sufferer is also encountering the same feelings. This allows for affirmation and attuning with one another and provides a basis to move forward. In the story of Job, his friends come and sit in silence with him for a week, as was the custom in times of grief. This silence allowed Job to gather his thoughts, conscious and subconscious, and to clarify the issues that he wanted to tackle.
8. It is easy for a pastor to feel ill at ease when someone begins to express their feelings and thus close down the conversation because of their own discomfort. Yet the Bible is full of lament. The psalmists often freely expressed their feelings to God. Job also let rip with how he saw his situation. Lament allows several things to take place. It allows anguish to be expressed and frustrations to be acknowledged. This prevents alienation from developing between the carer and the sufferer. The

release of controlled anger prevents this emotion from turning inward and becoming depression. Once the lament is expressed, it has the potential to be a catalyst for either growth or for inward bitterness. However, a skilled pastor can help a person be constructive in resolving their feelings and formulating an adequate theology that they can live with.

9. Pulling out moral judgements may give us a feeling of power, but it belittles the person, increases their guilt and fails to enable them. Words like, 'should', 'must' and 'ought' are a no-go area in pastoral or counselling work. The key role of a pastoral carer is more of a friend than a teacher. That friendship breaks down when we start to tell people what to do.
10. Finally, when a pastor works alone with no supervision or regular spiritual direction, they will quickly find themselves overwhelmed with people's personal issues and may find themselves burning out very quickly.

Reflections

- Can you recall any negative experiences from a pastor visiting you? What can you learn from this?
- Do you recognise any habits you have developed that might be inhibiting your ministry?
- Could you invite another to come with you on a pastoral visit and be an observer, who could then give helpful comments afterwards?
- How do you recognise when you are feeling uncomfortable in a situation, and how do you handle it?
- How can the Christian gospel be heard in such a pastoral context?

Chapter 11

Prayer

And now I commend you to God and to the message of his grace, a message that is able to build you up and to give you the inheritance among all who are sanctified.
(Acts 20:32)

Prayers can be very powerful when they are heartfelt. I was taught a very simple prayer that I echoed for several years as a young person. 'Lord, wash me out like a car petrol tank. Wash out the old petrol that has dirt in it and makes me splutter and stall. Fill me afresh with your Holy Spirit that I might become all you want me to be. Amen.'

Prayer in ministry is a book in itself. Karl Barth described the activity of theology as rooted in prayer.[24] This challenges us to see our entire caring ministry as being one of prayer in all contexts. Here, prayer is more than calling upon God to act; it is also seeing and believing what God is already doing in a community's midst.

Firstly, there is the prayer that acknowledges that God is already at work well before we get involved.

Secondly, we need to pray that God might open up our eyes of listening and learning.

Thirdly, we need to find out what others might want us to pray rather than be presumptuous that we already know best. Not everyone will want prayer for healing; they may have greater concerns on their minds. Often when people ask us to pray with them they have deeper questions attached to their request. Some of the considerations we need to bear in mind are:

- What are they expecting from the prayer?
- What kind of God do they think you are praying to?
- Do they think they won't get better if you don't pray?
- Do they think their own prayers are ineffective?

A seemingly simple request for prayer can be complex. We at least need to be aware that the request may not be as straightforward as it first seems.

24. G. Bromley (1979), *Introduction to the Theology of Karl Barth*. Eerdmans, p. 148.

Fourthly, prayer is far more than getting God to 'do a miracle'. When a person recognises that someone is much bigger than the present issue, it brings a whole new perspective into a situation. Just creating this space allows room for God to bring something of his kingdom into the person's life.

Fifthly, prayer reminds us that we are not in control. The conclusion and outcome are greater than ourselves. This brings a degree of humility into our ministry.

Finally, prayer will inevitably lead to change in our own perspective and understanding and therefore will influence and bring change to our faith. For this reason spiritual supervision is essential when pastoral carers are grappling with issues which may challenge their faith altogether (see Chapter 33, Supervision).

Prayer in a pastoral situation can be seen as the internal task without which the external activity of pastoral care cannot function correctly. It is very easy in ministry to get caught up with the here and now, to rush around being important as carers as if the world and the church couldn't function without us. Alas, this just produces hollow ministries which, with close scrutiny, people see through. It also leads to a spiritual dryness that then produces exhaustion.

Should one always pray in a pastoral situation? The answer has to be yes. However, that doesn't mean it has to be an open prayer that another person hears or participates in. We shouldn't carry out any ministry in God's name without soaking it in prayer before, during and after the encounter. Otherwise we are simply doing social work (good though that might be).

Our prayers should be offered to God well before we venture out into a working day of pastoral ministry. By starting the day with prayer, we are making sure right from the beginning that we do not get in the way of God's work and prove to be a stumbling block to others. Hence we begin praying in an adorational and confessional way. This enables us to put ourselves right with God before we even think about relating to another person. Through our prayer, as well as offering praise and thanksgiving, we seek wisdom, help, fresh direction and blessing in our work. We invoke the Holy Spirit to be at work well before we engage with others and to continue his ministry well after we have moved on. Prayer therefore reminds us of our place in this godly ministry: that it is his ministry and we are simply an instrument under (hopefully) his guidance.

I always include a prayer of protection for myself at the start of any ministry. As we gain experience we realise how often we can find ourselves in dangerous encounters with others. This might be because of the possibility of violence, sexual attraction or finding oneself in an occult situation (see Chapter 22, Deliverance ministry).

As you pray this prayer, it is also a subtle reminder to yourself to consider whether you should be working alone in this situation or whether you should call on another to be with you.

I have always found prayer an important part of my travelling time in ministry. Often as a pastor one visits people without a set appointment. There are, of course, many times when appointments are arranged and kept in a professional manner. But having time and space to choose whom to visit allows room for discernment. I can think of many situations over the years where I have changed direction and visited someone unexpectedly, only to hear them say at the front door, 'How did you know?' Such situations have included the unexpected news that a wedding was cancelled because of a relationship breakdown, news of a sudden death or discovery of a serious illness. Being open to prayer allows the Holy Spirit to bring a new dimension to our ministry.

Prayer plays an important role in every pastoral situation. This will mostly be silent prayer seeking God's help and discernment. But there will be times when it is important to pray out loud with another. If the person is a Christian it should be automatic. I always ask for permission to pray with someone, as it is important that people feel comfortable in their own homes. We can't assume that even a Christian will feel comfortable to join in, but it is rare that they would object to you praying. In situations where I have little knowledge of the person's religious belief system, I rarely find that they say no to me. Indeed, they usually feel comforted and blessed at the end of the prayer. This is not just some internal meditative exercise that makes a person feel comforted and more at peace, although this might be a by-product. Any prayer is reaching out to the living God to be present, God who is omnipotent and all-powerful.

When people are willing to pray aloud themselves, it can be like turning a light on in a dark room. Sometimes this is when we discover what is right at the heart of the issue for the person as they open their soul to God. It is also an opportunity for a person to confess, to offer thanksgiving and gratitude for a particular situation. Alternatively, it may be a turning point when a person makes a prayer of commitment concerning a major decision in life, or indeed to become a Christian. It is such a joy and privilege to lead another to Christ in prayer. It is something you never forget.

Prayer, however, is never just the answer to any situation. A healthy prayer will always request God's guidance concerning what to think and do in the situation. We must also follow sound biblical direction, advice from those we respect and follow our conscience.

What about handling unanswered prayer? Is that a contradiction in terms? Does God not hear all of our prayers? Jay Adams suggests several reasons why we may not see a conclusion we were expecting:[25]

- Hypocritical prayer (Psalm 66:18)
- Unbelieving prayer (James 1:5-7)
- Resentful prayer (Mark 11:23, 24)
- Pharisaical prayer (Matthew 6:5, 6)
- Self-centred prayer (James 4:3)
- Unbiblical prayer (John 15:7)
- Self-addressed prayer (John 14:13, 16:24-6)

We need to see prayer as part of our journey with God and not the whole answer. It is the developing of a relationship, which ultimately concludes with trust and faith.

An additional benefit of praying with another is that you are providing a template for them to develop their own prayers. It can give them the confidence to pray by themselves. We can easily forget that we are guides and models to others. Just as a mature Christian will look back and see how their prayer life has developed and changed over the years, the pastor can also be key in enabling a person to blossom in prayer.

Reflections

- How has your prayer life changed over the years?
- What is your more natural style in prayer?
- Could you produce your own written prayers to take with you in ministry?
- How do you rationalise what can appear to be unanswered prayers?
- What has encouraged you in your prayer ministry?
- Keep a prayer diary, which you can reflect upon months and years later.
- What have you learned from other people's prayers?

25. J. E. Adams (1979), *Prayers for Troubled Times*, Grand Rapids: Baker Books.

Chapter 12

Gossip, small-talk and neighbours

Live in such a way that you would not be ashamed of lending your pet parrot to the local gossip.
(Will Rogers)[26]

For years I would preach against gossip. I would use the Epistle of James as a starting point and convey the message that gossip was divisive and damaging to the local church. I still agree with this hypothesis and have seen much damage where negative backbiting has been allowed to work its way through a church.

One day I moved to the countryside to manage six rural churches. I was told that the local community survived on gossip. Every Saturday morning I would walk about 800 metres down a small country lane to the local shop to buy a newspaper. A five-minute walk could take anything from 30 minutes to one hour. People in the rural context just wanted to stop and chat.

I discovered that without such conversations I was totally ignorant of what was happening in the community. If I had chosen not to participate I would have ostracised myself. It was in this context that I learned who was ill, where marriages were struggling, what the local council was up to, where people had practical needs, who was new to the village and what people really thought about the church. I also had to develop an ability to recognise the difference between talking that was destructive and damaging to others and conversations that were opportunities to bring the gospel.

Some of us are good at small talk; we could do it all day. Others find it boring, annoying and unproductive. Whatever personality types Christians have, we are made for small talk. It enables us to begin to formulate relationships. Everyday conversations for a pastor take place across the spectrum of the church and the community. In church we are involved in welcoming newcomers and regulars to our corporate worship. We hover around after the service to detect those who want to talk or need prayer or want to book an appointment to talk. As lay pastors we might think we are

26. W. Rogers (1879-1935).

off duty some Sundays and are ordinary members of the congregation. However, every conversation we have over a cup of coffee is part of our caring ministry. It does mean that a pastor – paid or voluntary – may feel as if they are never off work. Yet this is all part of the role of a Christian using their gifts and skills.

This role of having a 'pastoral presence' at all times applies equally when we are out and about in the community. It is not just the vicar or leader of the church who is being 'read' by the community. As we chat in the local shops or have a drink in the local pub, the role of pastor is ever before us. These small encounters are so important as a godly presence in the community. I have found that seemingly trivial conversations with individuals often bear fruit later. This has applied as much in town churches where I would meet people shopping as it did in the countryside as people would stop and talk as they walked their dogs. Jesus himself seemed to be very flexible in his ministry to handle whatever came his way as he travelled the countryside of Galilee.

> Truly I tell you, just as you did it to one of the least of these who are members of my family, you did it to me.
>
> *Matthew 25:40*

It is inevitable that the work of a pastoral carer will not stop at the door of the church. Christian caring is an attitude, not just a role or job. Carers are usually people who have their antennae up and quickly detect needs in the community. This can bring about evangelistic opportunities and new friendships as well as burdens of responsibility. Often we can find that individuals in the community latch onto us and we can become rather trapped in our care. It is important to recognise that a process needs to take place that we are aware of and attuned to. This involves building a relationship of trust and respect. Hopefully it will also include helping an individual develop their faith. But the encounter must not stop with us. We need to introduce the individual to others in the church both individually and in groups so that we can be released to move on to other work.

Philip's encounter with the Ethiopian eunuch (Acts 8:26-40) is a good example of this. Sometimes a person might be reluctant to get closer to the church and wants to keep us just to himself. It requires strength of character to recognise that this is second best. There has to be a time limit on our work if we are to have a developing ministry, and we need to draw others into the pastoral care role to help us. This doesn't mean that the person in question cannot become a friend outside our church role. We just have to be realistic about what we can achieve and how much time is available for work, family, friends and for oneself.

A vital skill for anyone in pastoral ministry is to detect when a conversation is becoming unchristian and learning how to stop it. It is easy to get sucked into a negative conversation that results in putting another person down. We need to be determined not to allow this to happen. Hopefully our discernment and conscience can be a good alarm for us, and we have to practise becoming aware of when this siren goes off. Bravery is then required in order to acknowledge that we do not want to be a part of a negative conversation against another. This might not please the person we are talking with, but we are not called to be people pleasers; rather to stand by our convictions. This means that eventually some people will not appreciate us and may well work against us. This is the cost of ministry and a desire to maintain a Christian stance. Hence we need fellow pastors around us to support and encourage us in times of conflict. During the hardest times of my ministry I have learned that it wasn't the time to withdraw and hide but to get out and visit more, endeavouring to live out what I preach.

Reflections

- How do you view your ministry on a Sunday?
- What pressures does it put upon you to think that you are always on duty?
- How does your ministry spill over from the church to the community?
- How can you engage in gossip without it turning negative and unhealthy?
- Who is there to support you when a conversation turns nasty?

Chapter 13

Home groups

The most important work we will ever do will be within the walls of our own home.
(Harold B. Lee)[27]

In my current diocese I help to facilitate what we call work-based learning groups, where about five or six ministers meet each month for about two hours. We commit to meet for a period of two years and to make it a first priority in our diaries, apart from holidays. We have very clear ground rules of confidentiality, of listening to each other, and of not giving advice but offering support and understanding. Gradually trust is developed which allows the members to share in a deep and personal way. It amazes me how each person's story develops with ups and downs and twists and turns in ministry. It is very easy to be in ministry surrounded by the church fellowship and yet be very lonely. The reason these groups work is because of the ground rules that make the sharing safe and confidential. What we are doing is practising group pastoral care.

It is commonly thought that pastoral care is really about one-to-one relationships. We need to remind ourselves that our aim is to help a person with their spiritual formation. This begins within the family, well before we are involved. It is in the full experience of the 'koinonia' (a Greek word meaning 'fellowship') that we are able to grow in our Christian transformation.

Our childhood experiences of relationships and the family grouping travel with us into adulthood. We find ourselves playing roles of a leader, joker, carer or pain-bearer, often without making the connection with the past. These roles might not be always helpful or healthy. Since these influences are harder to identify in one-to-one work, individual pastoral care will never be enough for a person to develop holistically. This is where groups within churches play an important role. They can be safe places where people develop a sense of well-being and where they can experience different views in a non-judgemental and supportive environment.

There are a number of books that can guide us in understanding group dynamics as they go through the stages of forming, storming, norming and performing.[28]

---

27. H. B. Lee (1973), *Strengthening the Home* (Latter Day Saints pamphlet).
28. J. Heron (1989), *The Facilitators' Handbook*, London: Kogan Page.

Any new group will go through an initial time of getting to know each other and formally or informally working out what the group is for and where it is heading. During this *forming* period, each individual will work out how they fit in. This is usually a time where group members avoid confrontation, which means serious issues are avoided.

These more serious issues must eventually be faced. They might relate to how the group functions, what the group is doing or who leads it and what the group believes. This *storming* period can be unsettling for some.

Gradually the group begins to move in the same direction and focuses on its aims and targets. Now the group members are able to listen to each other and actively support each other. This *norming* is a comfortable time for the group. Some groups go on to *performing*, where they all trust each other and are able to achieve new things. Loyalty has been developed and the group has a high morale.

The final stage of a group is *adjourning*, where it begins to break up with thanksgiving for what it has achieved. This might also produce *mourning* at the sadness that the group is ending.

Whatever role we play as a pastor, we will inevitably have to deal with different groups. If we can come with some knowledge of group work, it will equip us to understand our role. A few pointers can help us steer a steady course.

Begin by having ground rules of what is expected. This might mean you will spend the first session clarifying what people's expectations are for the group. This will include timing issues such as the starting time, duration, ending time and number of sessions. Joining a group shouldn't be a life sentence where people feel let down when someone leaves the group. Other ground rules might include confidentiality, respecting each other's views, allowing differences to exist, only one person speaking at a time, telephoning if unable to attend, etc.

Boundaries need to be set concerning what is acceptable and what is not allowed in the group. Someone needs to be responsible for protecting vulnerable individuals, and to prevent scapegoating or accusative attitudes to those who have different biblical understandings.

There needs to be time for personal reflection and sharing. This means we have to be comfortable with moments of silence. Some will want to jump in and fill the gap every time, but they must be gently encouraged to remain silent at these times. 'Rumination time' can lead to significant comment and reflection.

Pilot sessions can be helpful. These allow a degree of playfulness and prevent people from becoming rigid. There should also be regular reviews to give people the opportunity to express how they would like the group to develop. Consideration needs to be given to the size of the group, which ought to reflect the size of the room and the expectations for the group. There clearly needs to be a leader/facilitator whose role it will be to help the group to stay focused. This person needs to have their own support and mentoring system. The leader will guide the discussions on issues such as praying styles and whether silence will be allowed. They also need to control the 'overkiller' who would be happy to talk all day and, if care isn't taken, will monopolise the group.

Care needs to be taken to prevent church groups from being a place of coercion, preventing any creative thought or development. If people are not allowed to express their own thoughts then they are likely to simply remain silent and may eventually become part of the many who have drifted away from the church.

Any church group needs to consist of people listening, empathising, being alongside, offering spiritual encouragement, practical help and prayer. It is the pastoral carer in the church who is called to be the prophet and the banner waver to make sure these aspects are present in all the church groups.

Reflections

- How positive has your experience of church groups been in the past?
- Have you experienced groups that had no clear ground rules?
- In what ways could you handle someone who dominates a group discussion?
- How can you make sure individuals are comfortable in the group?
- What is a safe way of allowing disagreements in a group?
- Why is it important to keep to the times agreed?

Chapter 14

Ministering to friends

Adversity teaches you who your real friends are.
(Lois McMaster Bujold)[29]

I will never forget being called to visit a family that was very involved in the church – a middle-aged couple with three children. It was clear that there was tension in the room. The mother explained that she was pregnant and, although she didn't believe in abortion, she didn't believe she could cope with another child. It was a difficult dilemma. Here was a friend with clear Christian beliefs but terrified of the consequences either way. What can one say as a vicar and as a friend? Together we began to explore all the options and possible outcomes. This also included whether to share anything with other people in the church. People don't always see things in the full context and can quickly make judgements. We concluded that we would keep the whole process confidential. The final decision was never going to be mine; my role was to support, pray and journey with the couple through their decisions. There was no win–win outcome here for anyone. We are still close, many years later, perhaps because of this experience.

Pastoral ministry in the church is very different from external professional care or counselling. In the church we are ministering to friends, fellow members of the Christian community and the body of Christ. On top of this we can easily find ourselves in a situation where we have too much knowledge about a person.

In my role as a counsellor, people come to me whom I have never met before. They agree to a certain number of sessions and at the end I will probably never see them again. This is very different if you meet every Sunday the people you are caring for. Because you probably know a person's family and friends, you may well have heard other versions of events that cloud your judgement.

This therefore requires a unique skill that many counsellors struggle with – the ability to move from role to role with an individual. The good news is that the task is not yours alone. If the person is a part of the Christian community then there are others in the church to support you and the individual. It is within the

29. L. M. Bujold (1999), *A Civil Campaign*, New York, Baen Books.

community that a person can find their healing and wholeness and not through the help of one pastor alone. If we can enable a person to become a part of the Christian community, then we provide access to good soil that can support a plant in need. Here the roots of the individual can draw strength from others in the church as well, and not from you alone. So although it is difficult to minister to those you know, the benefits outweigh the drawbacks. This doesn't make it easy, however. We therefore need very clear understanding of how we are to care for those who are our friends.

We need to acknowledge that there may well be times when we will need to direct a person outside the church community for assistance. Not all Christian communities are healthy. Some have 'illnesses' of their own, be it unhealthy gossip, prejudice, pressure and even an inability to forgive. There will be times when we feel uncomfortable and will need to encourage a person to seek help at a deeper level outside the community. Our role in that case will be to continue to support on a simpler level. In the meantime we need to work hard at creating a church community that is safe, inclusive, just and loving regardless of the cost. Good grace is needed in a church community if people are to feel safe to share their needs and be supported. This is a grace that is above gender, race, sexual orientation, age, class, culture and language. If we can create a church that has ground rules of seeking to understand each other without judgement, it will be a safer, more relaxed environment to minister into.

A pastor's role is complex. We can find ourselves caring for friends who are ill or caring for strangers who are ill. At times they may take up our time and prevent us from caring for our friends. All of this adds strain and stress to our ministry. Later in the book we will consider how to look after ourselves. The key is to recognise the tension and not deny the strain.

Reflections

- How do you find your ministry differs between caring for friends and caring for strangers?
- How do you balance workload commitments when caring for a friend?
- How comfortable do you feel in allowing another person to minister to a friend?
- How do you handle the tension of individuals you have ministered to wanting to become friends afterwards?
- How do you maintain personal friendships while in a position of ministry?

Chapter 15
Teaching

Teachers open the door, you enter by yourself.
(Chinese proverb)

As Christians, we have all been blessed by teaching in the church. It has perhaps led us to Christ, built us up in the faith, encouraged us when we've felt down and planted seeds of hope when all has seemed lost. Having led churches for many years, I now spend as much time sitting in the pews as I do preaching. I appreciate the good in preaching and teaching but also experience the negative. Sometimes I wonder why people keep coming to church. We have welcome strategies to embrace newcomers when there is no one new in church; we preach evangelistically when everyone in the congregation has been sitting in the church for years. We expound the text of Scripture but fail to make it relate to the everyday problems that those in the pews are facing. It only takes a brief chat to people in the congregation to hear about the issues that they are grappling with. For example,

- Struggling to live with an autistic teenager
- Grown-up children who have rejected Christianity
- Adult children who want to sleep with their partner in their parents' home
- Caring for parents with dementia
- Struggling with the threat of redundancy while the church is asking for more sacrificial giving
- Frustrated sitting in the pews when they feel they have gifts to offer the church
- Struggling in a boring job with no career prospects
- Living with mental illness in the family
- Being a part of a patchwork family
- Reaching midlife with a marriage that seems stuck and dry
- Coping with retirement yet feeling fit and well

Somehow the church needs to find ways of bringing pastoral care into its teaching and preaching. Training in pastoral care begins with our preaching and continues through teaching in small groups. If the church has a preaching rota, it is essential to ensure that it is not always organised by an evangelist. Otherwise each week the preaching will have a clear message but will miss out on many of the needs of the congregation.

One aspect of church life is to draw people into the church and the kingdom of God, build them up in their faith and then liberate them to put this into practice in the community. This means that scriptural teaching needs to be applicable to modern-day life with clear, real applications. The teaching should incorporate Christian lifestyle issues and cover character, attitudes, values and moral behaviour. Scriptural knowledge that incorporates Church history should be taught. Teaching needs to be educational in the sense that it analyses modern-day thought and focuses on relationships with all their complexities. It is all too easy for preachers to give priority to doctrine and Scripture at the expense of the personal qualities of the Christian life that grow through suffering and love.

We need a balance between:

- Individual and membership
- Casualty care and growing community
- Holy place and everyday place
- Professional and laity
- Objective (arm's length) and subjective (mutual sharing)
- Service and friendship
- Therapy (disease and sin) and growth (suffering)
- The fall (look back) and the fulfilment (purpose)
- Love (private faith) and justice (public issues)
- Mind (vision) and matter (practice)
- Left brain (verbal) and right brain (artistic)

It helps if the pastoral worker is a full member of the church leadership and has clear input to the planning of the preaching and teaching so that a balance is obtained to develop a healthy congregation. The pastor has an important role within the church leadership team to bring an awareness of the issues that the congregation is grappling with. This might be done objectively rather than subjectively, and keeping confidential information. This kind of information can guide the leaders of a church to prayerfully produce appropriate preaching topics. If the lectionary is used, at least the preachers are able to look at the passages from the viewpoint of their congregation and offer appropriate application. This enables the pastor to be attuned into what the preaching topics will be about and therefore be more aware of ways in which the congregation might react. 'Knowing a congregation' means that the pastor can look out for individuals who might be particularly spiritually and emotionally affected by the preaching. In this way we are keeping the congregation safe and well cared for to a high degree of professionalism.

Reflections

- How pastoral is the preaching in your church?
- Do you have input into the preaching topics/home group teaching material?
- What kinds of topics would be a help to your congregation?
- How does the church receive feedback from its teaching?
- What mechanism does the church have for pastors to care for individuals after a service?

Part two

Specific skills

Chapter 16

Crisis ministry

Crises refine life. In them you discover what you are.
(Alan K. Chalmers)[30]

One day in the university chaplaincy while my door was open, a new first-year student walked in. As I offered her a chair, she immediately told me that she was very stressed, had accommodation and boyfriend problems, was addicted to heroin and had a tendency to be violent. I closed the door and said, 'Hi,' while mentally reminding myself where the alarm button was placed.

Much of pastoral care is dealing with the fragility of people's lives. This is seen most of the time in the day-to-day problems of Christian living. Sooner or later we all encounter a blow to our routine that causes a crisis in the foundation of our beliefs.

Every pastoral worker will find themselves with people who seem to be in a moment of crisis. What might be a panic situation for one person may of course seem trivial to another. However we view a situation, we need to see it from where the person involved is standing. There seem to me to be two clear temptations for carers to fall into.

The first temptation is to think that the problem is well within our grasp and we therefore try and take over and sort out the problem. This can seem to be a quick and easy solution, but in reality it simply undermines the person. The problem is not ours but theirs, and we need to be able to help them grow by enabling them to deal with the issue with our support.

The other common temptation for Christian carers is to say we will pray with them and leave it to God. As much as prayer is important, it can also be a great cop-out. If we have the appropriate knowledge, skills, know-how and connections, surely we are called to do more than pray? It can be like bumping into someone at a railway station who asks for 30p to gain access to the toilet. Offering to pray while you have change in your pocket is greedy, thoughtlessness and just abusing the gift of prayer. Sometimes we need to be honest with ourselves. We can use prayer when we simply don't want to go the extra mile with someone.

---

30. A. K. Chalmers (2009) in *Quote Me*, Uplifting Publications.

Crisis comes when someone feels overwhelmed and out of control. So what can we do? First of all we need to bring calm to the situation and in a sense put a sticking plaster on the problem. Here we are simply trying to stop the bleeding. This means reassuring the person that we are going to listen and stick with them as they work through to find a satisfactory answer to their problem. This might include having a cup of tea, beginning with prayer and finding a safe quiet place where you will not be interrupted.

Sometimes it is just not convenient to deal with an issue there and then – for example, when we have been caught at the end of a Sunday service with another event to go to or have family waiting at our heels. It is important that we say clearly at the time how long we have to listen to them, and that a further time and place can be arranged when the issue can be discussed more fully. We cannot promise that we will sort out the crisis, as some problems are beyond us. What we can do is to reassure them that they are not alone in their situation.

We need to be aware that over time, some people can become very adept at helping people in crisis; it can almost seem like their bread and butter. But we must never ignore the fact that each 'crisis' is unique and upsets a person's stability, perhaps producing panic and disorder.

Crisis problems often come from common issues and emotions. The issues can range from violence, rape, abuse of alcohol and/or drugs, loss of a home or property, illness and mental health to legal problems. Often in these situations the best thing to do is to use our knowledge and connections to link the person up with other support agencies that are more skilled than ourselves. It is helpful to have a range of telephone numbers at hand. If we have links with a safe house for the abused or know charities that provide shelter and food, then our task is so much easier.

We then need to be clear about what we are attempting to do. After all, if we are unsure, it will only increase the panic in the person. A simple way of managing crisis is to think about the ABC of crisis management:

- **A** Achieve good contact with the person. This means settling them down and getting them to steady their breathing. You might do a breathing exercise with them or just offer them a glass of water and some tissues. Do this before diving into the issue.
- **B** Boil down the problem. Get the person to explain what has occurred. This may take some time if the person is still in shock and a state of trauma. Reassurance and encouragement

will result in the story being told. Then ask:

- What is the most pressing problem right now?
- Have you been here before? If so, how did you handle it then?
- Give the problem a number from 1 (worst situation) to 10 (best situation).
- What would make you feel better in the short term?
- Feed back what you have heard to make sure you are both talking on the same wavelength. Remember a person in shock will not easily take in what you are saying. You may need to repeat yourself.

C Cope with the problem. What could you do to move the problem one number up the scale? Help the person to work out the solution to their problem. This might be to examine together a range of options and let the person decide which one feels the most appropriate. Find out what the person is willing to do themselves to meet their needs and then think together what extra support may be needed and where it may be sought.

Finally, recap what has been said, and perhaps write it down for the person. Provide contact details of sources of additional help and arrange a follow-up meeting. If it's likely that you won't be available when you are needed, offer other sources of help; it is important that the person doesn't feel trapped.

In all crisis situations, emotions come to the surface. We need to beware of these emotions and acknowledge them, although it might be more appropriate to address them at another time.

Reflections

- Reflect upon a time when you experienced a crisis moment in your life. What did you want from a friend?
- What has been the greatest crisis situation you have ever had to deal with?
- Who would you call upon to support you with a crisis situation?
- Do you have to hand the local telephone numbers of agencies that might be able to help?
- How do you know when the crisis is resolved?

Chapter 17
Conflict

The greatest conflict is not between two people but between one person and himself.
(Garth Brooks)[31]

As a young curate and youth leader I was in charge of a large youth group. We had a new influx of 14-year-olds and it was evident that it was going to be difficult to find balance between the 18-year-olds and the younger teenagers. It was decided we would initiate an 18–20s group. However, it would mean that some of the 18-year-olds would have to take on some leadership responsibility. I became aware of the tension I had created when a mature Christian member of the church took me to one side after a Sunday service and pinned me to the wall. He accused me of damaging his daughter's chances of getting good A level results as she would have to give more time to the new youth group. It wasn't what I was expecting on a Sunday morning.

Conflict can be a major source of anxiety for a pastor. However, if we are aware of the process of handling conflict it can give us confidence and reduce our feelings of fear and anxiety. If we can't handle conflict, we can become a 'people pleaser' and always say yes. However, in the end this only generates frustration, anger and resentment in ourselves, and everyone is a loser.

Rather than discussing in a calm, respectful manner, some people just don't say anything until they're ready to explode, and then blurt it out in an angry, hurtful way. This might initially appear to be a less stressful route – avoiding an argument altogether – but it usually causes more stress to both parties in the end, as tensions rise, resentments fester and a much bigger argument eventually results. It's much healthier to address and resolve conflict by dealing with the issue as soon as possible.

First, we need to ensure that the person's aggressive response does not prevent us from attempting to bring negotiation and resolution. This requires determination not to be caught up with side issues. Along with this we need to keep ourselves safe. It is a good idea to meet in a public place and to let others know where we are. It is also good practice to take an additional person along to

31. Garth Brooks, American Country singer.

the meeting who can keep a clear and objective record of what took place.

We need to endeavour to separate the person from the problem, otherwise we will find it hard to support the person after the issue is resolved. We need to seek to understand the person's viewpoint and what is motivating them. It is important not to assume that we know what the other person's motives are, especially if we think they're negative. When in a discussion, don't forget to listen and ask questions and try to understand the other person's point of view. In a conflict situation, most of us primarily want to feel heard and understood. We talk a lot about our point of view to get the other person to see things our way. Ironically, if we all do this all the time, there's little focus on the other person's point of view, and nobody feels understood. Try to really see the other side, and then you can better explain yours. (If you don't 'get it', ask more questions until you do.) Others will more likely be willing to listen if they feel heard. We may need to paraphrase back what they are saying to prevent misinterpretations.

Be aware that some people respond best face to face while others function better using the written word. The better we know a person, the more likely we are to choose an appropriate form of communication with them. There is clearly less scope for misinterpretation with face to face meetings, however, provided both participants are comfortable with the arrangement.

Next, we need to generate possible options to allow further understanding between the two parties, to seek a win–win situation. That means being neither aggressive nor apathetic, rather being assertive. 'Winning' the argument can mean you lose the relationship. The goal of effective communication should be mutual understanding and finding a solution that pleases both parties, not 'winning' the argument or 'being right'. Make sure your body reflects confidence: stand up straight, look people in the eye and relax. Use a firm but pleasant tone.

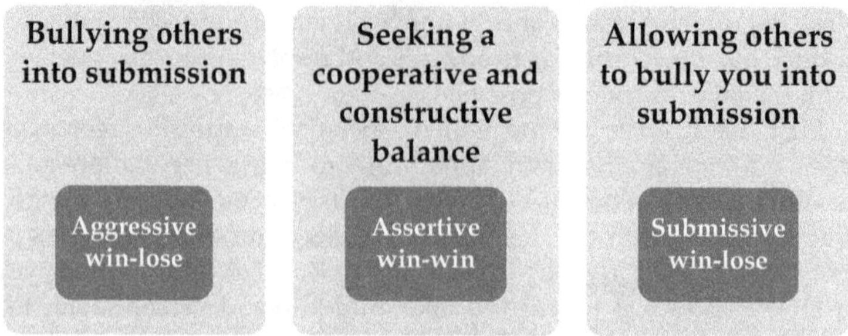

Figure 5: Types of Relationships

Choose to respond to criticism with empathy When someone comes at you with criticism, it's easy to feel that they're wrong and to be defensive. While criticism is hard to hear and is often exaggerated or coloured by the other person's emotions, it's important to listen to the other person's pain and respond with empathy for their feelings. Also, look for what's true in what they're saying; this can be valuable information for us as it allows us room to agree with the other person and provides a platform to build upon.

It is damaging to decide that there's a 'right' and a 'wrong' way to look at things and that your way of seeing things is right. Don't demand that the person see things the same way, and don't take it as a personal attack if they have a different opinion. Look for a compromise or agree to disagree, and remember that there isn't always a 'right' and a 'wrong'. Two points of view can both be valid.

When something happens that a person doesn't like, it is easy to blow it out of proportion by making sweeping generalisations. Avoid starting sentences with, 'You always . . .' and 'You never . . .' – for example, 'You always come home late!' or 'You never do what I want to do!' Stop and think about whether or not this is really true. Also, don't bring up past conflicts; these will throw the discussion off topic and stir up more negativity. Such an approach will stand in the way of true conflict resolution and increase the level of conflict.

Stick to factual descriptions of what the person has done that's upset you, rather than using labels or judgements such as, 'You're so rude!' or 'You're always late.' It is better to use assertive communication like, 'We were supposed to meet at 11:30am, but now it's 11:50am.'

Use 'I messages'. Simply put, if you start a sentence off with 'You', it comes over as more judgemental or attacking and puts people on the defensive. If you start with 'I', the focus is more on how you are feeling and how you are affected by their behaviour. It also demonstrates more ownership of your reactions and less blame. For example, don't say, 'You need to stop that,' but 'I'd like it if you'd stop that.'

Try and use the formula 'When you [their behaviour], I feel [your feelings].' When used with factual statements rather than judgements or labels, this formula provides a direct, non-attacking, more responsible way of letting people know how their behaviour affects you. For example, 'When you yell at me, I feel attacked.'

LADDER describes a six-stage process for handling problems in an assertive way. These are:

L Look at your rights and what you want, and understand your own feelings about the situation.

A Arrange a meeting with the other person to discuss the situation.
D Define the problem specifically.
D Describe your feelings so that the other person fully understands how you feel about the situation.
E Express what you want clearly and concisely.
R Reinforce the other person by explaining the mutual benefits of adopting the route of action you are suggesting.

Reflections

- Who triggers your emotional buttons? Do you avoid those people?
- How have you coped with conflict in the past?
- Can you recognise when you are getting hot under the collar?
- What is your coping mechanism in conflict situations?
- How does your church acknowledge and handle conflict?
- How can the pastoral carer bring healing when divisions arise in the church?
- Is there ever a time to bring in an outside mediator?

Chapter 18
Counselling skills

The most important thing is this: at any moment to sacrifice what we are for what we could become.
(Charles Dubois)[32]

As a young, keen Christian, I worked voluntarily in what was called a Christian home of healing. We attracted individuals who had considerable needs. They would stay in the home for several weeks as we prayed for and supported them. The love and care provided certainly had a big impact upon the individuals. However, it didn't take long before we realised we were totally out of our depth. We simply had not developed enough self-awareness, let alone psychological skills, to fully handle the issues we encountered.

The concept of counselling is rooted in Christian tradition, although many churches seem sceptical about its usage. Paul talks about how Christians should grow in maturity and become rounded individuals filled with Christ's Spirit as they discover their gifts. God-given natural talents should culminate in a sense of purpose and direction in life (Ephesians 4:11-16). At the heart of this is the belief that a person can change from a distorted image to one that reflects Christ.

The world of science has revealed conflict between nature and nurture: the influences of genes, family background, what happens in the womb as well as early childhood. However, as Christians we hold on to the belief that Christ can transform all, although we recognise that this change will not be complete this side of the kingdom. This is a process, and a slow one at that, according to Paul (2 Corinthians 3:18).

Counsellors may also be pastoral carers in the church. Pastoral carers are not necessarily counsellors, although they may use counselling skills. A pastoral carer links an individual to the faith community. The pastoral carer brings a clear Christian presence whereas a counsellor may not be a Christian at all. Counsellors should be qualified to a certain standard, preferably accredited, and on a government regulatory body's list. They may work individually although they must always have supervision.

32. C. Dubois (1804–1867).

'Pastoral carer' is a much looser term. A person in this role may be paid or work voluntarily for the church, with or without qualifications. It helps if they have a very clear contract of agreement with the local church. They should at least always be recognised and linked to the local body of Christ and be under supervision and training.

Counsellors come from a particular worldview and function from a trained academic perspective. They should not veer into areas in which they have not been trained or supervised. They are supposed to make this very clear when they take on a client. Pastoral carers will come from a Christian worldview (although there will be variation within that Christian perspective). They too should have a specific and clear role, whether it be to offer advice, support, prayer and/or the sacraments.

Counsellors have tight boundaries in a different way to pastoral carers, although pastoral carers should still have boundaries and ground rules.

Informality and working in different contexts makes pastoral care more complex than counselling and, in some respects, more dangerous. In a university setting as the chaplain and pastor of staff and students, I can go to the hospital, take someone to the doctor, visit strangers in need, challenge without the fear that I will lose my job (this is a prophetic ministry), have an open-door policy without appointment and be on call. All of this does, however, lead to some degree of messiness.

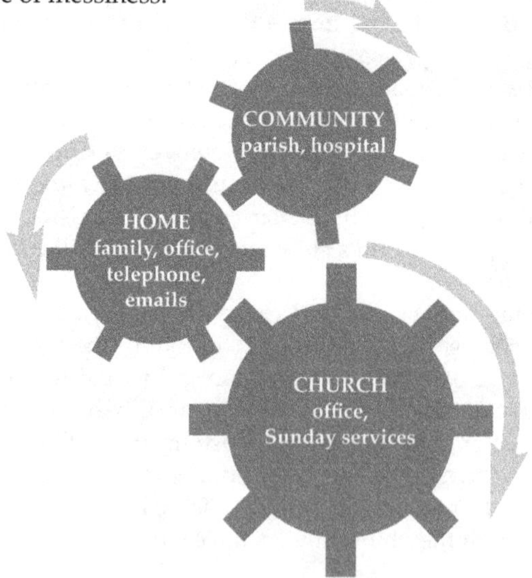

Figure 6: The Pastor's Work Environment

Sometimes it is said that counsellors do not direct, influence or have fixed views like Christian pastors. But I don't believe this is true. In a sense, just meeting another person influences them. When payment is involved it clearly changes the relationship: the number of sessions will affect the income of the counsellor. All counsellors bring with them their beliefs and worldview systems. It is why we have person-centred, narrative, psychotherapy, psychodynamics, etc. Counsellors are also required to represent the organisation they work for, along with its policies and expectations. This therefore should be no different to Christian organisations or pastors in general. When I work as a counsellor and psychologist I bring my bereavement, narrative, and play therapy knowledge with me as well as recognise the university and Church of England context in which I minister. Yes I endeavour to be truly congruent, self-aware and focused on the client, but my tools naturally influence the encounter. This is no different from the way a pastor ministers, bringing with them their Christian framework and particular skillset.

Counsellor or pastoral worker?

Here in the West, we live in a part of the world where counselling has mushroomed, leading to thousands of people being in therapy. This comes out of a society that has lost its roots in regard to whom and what it is meant to be. People live individualistic lives, often separated from their families and friends. This means that they don't have people that they can sound off to and from whom they can receive regular support. This only raises the degree of isolation and loneliness. People do not have safe enough friendships to be able to knock ideas, fears and hopes about. Clergy are often not seen as professionals in the listening/counselling world such that people would turn to them unless they were already in the church. Even then, people are often inclined to turn to so-called 'professionals' who charge rather than to seek help from a priest or voluntary pastoral worker.

We perhaps need to recognise that different levels of help are needed in our communities. Figure 7 (page 105) shows just how much overlap there is between pastoral care and counselling. What is key is making sure that both the carer and the client are absolutely clear about what is taking place.

There is first the everyday support that people need just to handle life with all its ups and downs. This is very much the pastoral worker's domain, and they should feel comfortable here.

The next level is support that goes deeper, where an individual seems to be stuck with a particular issue. This might be connected with a person's faith, their marriage relationship or work problems. Here the pastoral worker can use their counselling skills to help an individual or couple to work through their issues.

There are then more complex cases that clearly require more skilled or professional counselling support. This might be a sufferer of anorexia or someone who has been abused, or a person showing ongoing problems that require more expertise to engage with. We need to have a clear idea of what level we are able to work at and know when we should refer to others.

The simplest definition of counselling is when one person seeks to help another to grow in greater self-awareness. This simple definition doesn't seem any different from the role of a pastoral carer. Both involve a relationship that is beneficial to the participants. Both endeavour not to make a situation worse. Both set out on a journey not aware of what the end outcome will be. This means that there is no manipulation or hidden agenda. The counsellor and the pastoral worker need to be willing to be helped themselves, if they are to seek to help others.

Although the definition of counselling is broad, in reality and practice it is very specific, controlled and regulated. Counselling involves a clear contract between two people about what they will be working together on. This will involve clarity about the competence of the counsellor, the length of the sessions, the regularity of the sessions, the fees, confidentiality, supervision and boundaries about locality, touch, contact out of sessions, etc.

Counselling, when done well, is far from the advice or guidance that people think it might be. The Christian world is of course full of guidance and direction, and it is easy for a pastoral worker to fall into this domain. We might want to consider why counselling does not employ these guiding tactics. It is simply that a counsellor believes that only the person who knows best is the person themselves, and that they have to grow up into maturity by making their own choices. The person we are coming alongside will know of our Christian convictions already; we don't need to thrust our beliefs down their throats. A counsellor's ministry begins with unconditional love, regardless of whether the person agrees with our Christian stance or not.

The counsellor acknowledges that a person might well make very different decisions in their life compared to decisions they themselves might make. The counsellor has to recognise that only the client can decide what is right for their own life. Here, the counsellor has much to teach the pastoral worker. Carl Rogers, one of the pioneers of counselling, suggested the need to be truly genuine as we accept others and offer them empathy.[33] This is no different from a pastoral worker. After all, Jesus was the most genuine person who ever lived. Being genuine means being truly ourselves with others and not hiding behind professionalism. Accepting another means we recognise their worth as a human being created in the image of God.

Some clients might feel very negative about themselves; both counsellors and pastoral workers should express clearly that the person has value and worth. This might be the first time in a person's life when they feel they are being taken seriously and valued for who they are, warts and all. All of this leads to an empathetic response from the counsellor or pastoral carer as we attempt to get inside the person and try to comprehend what it must be like to be them right at that very moment. This giving of oneself at that moment enables us to grasp the significance of being where the other person is sitting. It requires the ability to develop a listening ear, as explained earlier.

All of these qualities are conveyed through the eyes, ears, touch, voice, mannerisms and belief systems. Simply conveying this is the first step to enable many to begin to love themselves.

Up to this point the two roads of counselling and pastoral care share the same tarmac. Counselling now veers off into an area of other skills, knowledge and psychological tools which the average pastoral worker will not engage with. There is a range of therapeutic skills that a counsellor can use to help people with particular problems, such as narrative therapy, psychosocial education, creative play therapy and many, many others.

A pastoral worker may see a person who then goes off to see a counsellor for a course of sessions. They may eventually return to the pastoral worker who will then continue their support. The pastoral carer's role lasts much longer and is not confined to the cost of therapy or to a specific number of sessions. Our work is an ongoing ministry to help a person function and play their full part in the life of the community and, hopefully, the church. This has no time limits in that for as long as someone is in our community they are under our care. We don't seek to reap short-term results but observe over a longer period changes in people's lives and, hopefully, in their families' lives.

We have the privilege of seeing people find themselves, find release from what bound them in the past, discover their gifts for themselves and others, and grasp the hope of being all that God has created them for.

---

33. C. Rogers, *On Becoming a Person.*

Areas in common

In my chaplaincy work I operate an open-door policy. This means that if the door is open anyone is welcome to come in and sit down, whether it be a student or member of staff. Needs vary considerably: sometimes a listening ear is required; others come seeking advice and guidance. But some come with needs that are on the border of pastoral care and counselling. At times I have to make a distinction and decide either to offer counselling sessions or refer the person to a counselling service. Because my counselling specialism is in the area of loss, I will offer a student counselling only if this is the issue that they want to work with (and if I have time).

Whether a person sees a counsellor or a pastor, there will be several things in common during the process. Work in any healing community has a few key aims to fulfil:

1. The first objective is an ability to communicate our true authentic selves. This is essential if we are to be congruent and at peace with ourselves. Here there is naturalness in the relationship without tension. There is awareness by both parties that painful things might be shared and that neither party has all the answers.
2. Secondly, we will seek to resolve areas of conflict and help people accept differences in life. This begins with an opportunity to tell one's story. Clarity develops in understanding the framework by which a person views their life and the world around them. The assumptions in life may or may not be Christian, but the aim is the same: to bring understanding of what that view might be. It is within this understanding that the counsellor/pastor might decide that they need to refer on to someone more skilled and appropriate to handle the situation.
3. Thirdly, we desire to help people accept themselves and through this be able to love others. Helping another must involve some kind of boundary clarification. This may be very precise in counselling and also needs to be there in the pastoral world. If we are not clear about what we mean when we talk about helping another, we are in danger of misunderstandings and creating further hurt. Here there is an opportunity to reflect upon the past, present and future and to consider whether we need to adjust our 'worldview' in order to lead to a more satisfactory and fulfilling life.
4. Fourthly, both approaches must resist the temptation of taking on the problem and making it their responsibility. Perhaps pastoral carers are more likely (through less training) to leap in

INITIAL STAGE

IN COMMON
Initiating a relationship. Hearing the story. Actively listening. Being genuine. Conveying empathy. Being self-aware. Making an assessment.

COUNSELLING
Very specific ground rules and boundaries – e.g. cost, number of sessions, length of sessions, supervision, contact out of session, clarification of type of counselling being offered – e.g. Christian? Refer on if appropriate and have no further contact. Use prayer if agreed beforehand. Specific confidentiality agreement. Meeting in appropriate counselling session. Counsellor is accredited and supervised.

PASTORAL
Location may vary from home, meeting room, church, etc. using prayer appropriately. Clarification of purpose of meeting. Agreeing either an open-ended approach or arrange another or regular meetings. No fee is involved. Sadly, confidentiality is often not clarified.

MEDIUM STAGE

IN COMMON
Developing the relationship. Focusing on the problem. Developing new aspects of the story. Understanding the past and present. Developing a new perspective. Staying with the issue yet not personally owning it.

COUNSELLING
Keeping within the framework of the contract. Regular supervision about the case.

PASTORAL
May have previous contact and history with the person. Use of Scripture and prayer. Flexibility to focus on current issues. Integrating the church into the situation. Developing faith. If referred on to another, still supporting.

FINAL STAGE

IN COMMON
Ending well. Awareness of the issues of closure. Reflecting together what has been achieved. Being 'good enough'. Referring on.

COUNSELLING
Reviewing the past, present and what has been achieved. Letting go with no further contact.

PASTORAL
Renegotiating the relationship and expectations. Passing on to others in the church for support and fellowship. Commending to God.

Figure 7: The Stages in Counselling and Pastoral Care

> and attempt to resolve someone's issue. However, we must learn to be willing to stay with someone's 'stuckness' and pain. People have to be responsible for their own lives. Our job is to encourage them to grow into responsibility. If we keep jumping in and fixing the fuse when it goes, people will never learn how to do it themselves.

God seems far better at this task than humans; he expresses a higher degree of allowing free will and seems far more patient with his people. God doesn't push his omnipotence upon us. We can model this responsible behaviour by not taking on other people's responsibilities. This allows us to remain healthy and to operate within clear boundaries. This might mean saying 'no' to someone, even if the consequence might be that a person may do something silly, like harming themselves. We'll say more about this in Chapter 55, Suicide issues. There is always risk in not taking on another person's problems, but in the end it is the only healthy approach for all involved. Too often we see a well-meaning person become overwhelmed with the burden and responsibility of a needy person. It then takes a more experienced pastoral carer to disentangle the situation, and help the hurt carer to understand the consequences of their own actions, whilst also encouraging the original hurt individual to begin to take responsibility for their own life.

Reflections

- How do you use counselling skills in your pastoral ministry?
- How can you make sure you do not just become a counsellor?
- Are there areas in your skill base that need developing?
- Can we see counselling skills being used in Scripture?
- When is it right to be more directive in offering advice or guidance?
- How can churches make greater use of the skills of people with counselling skills?
- What does pastoral care bring in addition to counselling skills?

See Appendix 2 for an example of a pastor's/counsellor's log.

Chapter 19
Counselling in church

The world can only change from within.
(Eckhart Tolle)[34]

The life of a church involves a great deal of organic development that is not always thought through clearly. This isn't a problem if it works, but a church can suddenly find itself doing things it hasn't really given enough consideration to. I once led a church that had set up an effective prayer ministry after each service. This led to a greater focus on healing; we put on teaching events and assembled the ministry team for prayer and training. However, we began to wonder whether some people needed something more than prayer, as we noticed that the same people came back for ministry week after week. A few of the ministry team received training from an organisation called 'Wholeness Through Christ', while others chose to train as counsellors. Eventually we developed a ministry that involved general prayer, extended healing prayer sessions and confidential counselling. All of this required carefully handling so that all involved were aware of the ground rules to ensure the safety of those to whom we ministered.

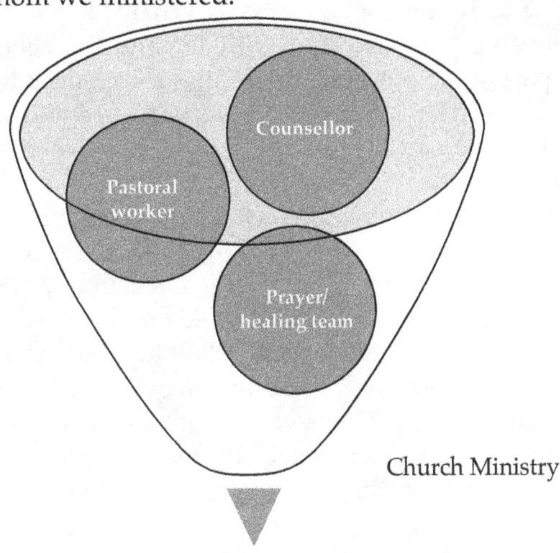

Figure 8: Types of Formal Church Care

34. E. Tolle (2003), *Stillness Speaks*, Novata: New World Library.

If we are going to offer counselling within the church, we need a clear understanding of what we mean by counselling and what type of counselling is to be offered. At its simplest, counselling is a conversation between two people, but it also involves so much more. A pastoral worker might find themselves involved in a kind of counselling situation, depending upon their definition. This can range from a casual conversation with a friend to a more formal counselling agreement to using specialised skills, as in psychotherapy, for example. This might be seen as similar to medicine where anyone can help to remove a splinter from a finger but only a highly skilled surgeon would attempt heart surgery. The key is to be aware of one's own training, ability and competence and to ensure an appropriate level of supervision.

In formal counselling, an agreement is made between two people where one is the counsellor and the other is the client. It involves very clear agreement or a contract concerning what is to take place, including times, payment (or not), supervision for the counsellor, confidentiality and safety issues. This creates a safe place in which the client can explore personal issues with the confidence that the counsellor will be congruent (totally present in the situation), offer listening and empathy and reflect back what is being communicated so that the client can work out how they want to deal with the situation.

Although there are various types of counselling, this is the heart of what is taking place, with the client being in control of the decisions and choices that they make. What is key in counselling is the relationship between the counsellor and the client. This is an essential part of the process. The feelings raised need to be explored sensitively. As the relationship becomes secure and develops, the client will be encouraged to share at a deeper level issues that they wish to work upon.

How should counselling be used in the church, and should a pastoral carer seek counselling training? This raises four questions:

Firstly, is a counsellor more professional than a pastoral carer? There is no doubt that anyone who learns counselling skills will understand themselves better and relate to others more effectively. But that is not to say that counselling is better or more skilled than pastoral care. Indeed, I believe that in an ideal world both are necessary and valuable. This usually means (since pastoral care is unregulated) that pastoral carers need to become more highly trained and supported.

Secondly, what relationship should there be between a pastor and a counsellor in a church setting? It certainly requires a great deal of skill for a person to be both a pastor and a counsellor in a church. It can very easily lead to confusion. Where the roles are filled by different people, there needs to be clear agreement about responsibilities, referrals and confidentiality if the two skills are to work together.

Thirdly, should churches even have counselling teams? Churches have evolved over recent years from having a prayer team to having a ministry team and now to having a counselling team. In the churches I have led, I have seen people develop their skills from praying with others, understanding the healing ministry, developing listening skills, growing in spiritual awareness and finally acquiring counselling knowledge and skills. All these skills are valid and needed, but we must be very clear about what we are doing in each situation. We also need to recognise that a person who is good at praying may not necessarily make a good counsellor.

In the church we meet the same people every week. How healthy is it to see your counsellor or ex-counsellor every Sunday? The knowledge that a minister/priest/pastoral carer accumulates about individuals is confidential and must always remain so. However, knowledge affects relationships, whether we like it or not. This might mean that it would be more appropriate for people to be counselled outside the church. In an ideal situation, an independent Christian counselling organisation in each town to which churches could refer people would be ideal. Here, the counsellor is separate from the church and is held accountable by the supervisory process. This allows the pastor to continue to provide ongoing support both before and after counselling.

Fourthly, should a Christian seek out only a Christian counsellor? Personally, I have always valued working with people who operate within a different framework to my own, and I have found that it has strengthened my faith rather than weakened it. I have appreciated counselling supervisors that I have had who came from different traditions to mine. I have had interesting discussions with atheistic supervisors who have helped me see things from a different point of view. What is there to fear? I think the more important question is, 'How good is the counsellor?' If a counsellor recognises that a client requires specific help from a religious/spiritual perspective then they will refer them on. This happens often in my university setting. We need to remember that a counsellor is not guiding or directing but simply helping another to reflect upon their position to come to their own conclusion. Any kind of religious or anti-religious coercion is very poor counselling and a supervisor should address the issue. So we shouldn't be hesitant to use a secular counselling organisation (the reality is that many Christians are to be found in such organisations anyway).

I agree that finding a counsellor is a tricky business. One can use the Association of Christian Counsellors (ACC) to direct you to someone in your area. But in the end it is like finding a good doctor or dentist: word of mouth seems to work best.

We need also to be aware of the danger of colluding with another who comes from a similar 'assumptive view' of life. It is very easy and comforting to find someone who thinks in the same way we do. This may simply reinforce our viewpoint rather than deepen our own self-awareness.

Supervision is an important part of the counselling encounter. Anyone who calls himself or herself a counsellor must have regular supervision and perhaps ongoing counselling for themselves. If a counsellor is not willing to be counselled then it can be argued that they shouldn't be in the counselling business. Supervision provides a safe place for a counsellor to be supported and kept in a safe, regulated practice. It is very emotionally demanding to be a counsellor, to hear difficult stories and to feel strong emotions that are transferred through the client. Supervision creates a safe place for a counsellor to become more self-aware, to raise issues from client sessions, to be checked for safe practice, to recognise transference and conflict issues, and to explore the unknown between the client, counsellor and supervisory dynamic.

Another important element of counselling is a commitment to continuing professional development (CPD). Whether the counsellor is monitored by a professional body or a health-care council, there is a requirement for CPD. In addition, it is vital to keep clear records and to function within the professional framework of recognised good practice.

One significant difference between counselling and pastoral care is that counsellors are often paid. With charities, people are often encouraged to make a donation according to their financial means. If payment is required and made, this clearly changes the relationship between the client and the counsellor, and pastoral care occurs on a very different footing. The church offers care as a form of grace, although this doesn't mean that pastoral care doesn't come at a cost. Some may carry out the role voluntarily while others are full-time paid workers, but there are costs to the church that need to be acknowledged. These include salaries, training, supervision and an awareness of the personal sacrifices that individuals make.

Reflections

- How can we counsel an individual and maintain confidentiality?
- How do you behave when you meet someone in church whom you have counselled?
- How can a healthy relationship be developed between counselling agencies and the local church?
- How important is supervision, line-management, spiritual direction, mentoring and coaching in your role? Whose responsibility is it to initiate the right support?
- What are some of the issues of offering counselling within a church setting?

Appendix 3 is an example of a pastor's/counsellor's one-to-one form.

Chapter 20
A ministry of tears

My eyes were glued on life, and they were full of tears.
(Jack Kerouac)[35]

Be a gardener, dig a ditch, toil and sweat, and turn the earth upside down and seek the deepness and water the plants in time. Continue this labour and make sweet floods to run and noble and abundant fruits to spring. Take this food and drink and carry it to God as your true worship.
(Julian of Norwich)[36]

God made human beings with the ability to cry tears. From the moment we are born until our final day on earth, tears have their place and fulfil an important role in our well-being. Human babies have not yet developed the ability to communicate clearly with their caregiver in words, so have to resort to crying to express when they are hungry, feeling vulnerable, uncomfortable with a dirty nappy or when they are tired and need help to get to sleep. Tears journey with us throughout our lives, particularly at times when we struggle to find words to express what we are feeling. At times of grief and loss, or when we are feeling angry, hurt, guilty, fearful, lonely, pain, relief or joy, tears will often follow. Yet it is strange that in the British culture we have developed an attitude that one should hide one's tears or not cry at all. This is particularly true for men; crying is seen as a weakness. However, modern science has enlightened us to the benefits of releasing tears. For example, we know that the chemical composition of tears shed early on in grief is different from the composition months later. This captures the developmental nature of grief and of the way it evolves and develops over time. Here the body is telling us something of the importance of releasing our emotions in a safe way through tears.

All of this is nothing new for the psalmists, who often expressed their prayers through weeping. Did they know something that we in the modern world have forgotten?

What is clear is that we can't engage in pastoral ministry without being able to handle other people's tears and therefore, hopefully, our own. It is hard to be relaxed with a person who is crying if we

35. J. Kerouac (2000), *Atop an Underwood: Early Stories and other Writings*, London: Penguin.
36. E. Spearing (trans) (1998), *Revelations of Divine Love*, London: Penguin Classics.

ourselves are uncomfortable with our own ability to cry. We need a ministry that allows people to express their emotions in a safe way. One of the ways God has created is through tears.

Tears of anger

Anger is a powerful emotion that needs to be expressed. We see that

- God gets angry (Exodus 4:14; Numbers 11:10); his followers became angry (Genesis 30:2; Exodus 32:19; 1 Samuel 20:34)
- Christ himself became angry on several occasions (Matthew 12:34; Mark 3:5; Luke 11:42; John 2:14-16)
- Christ's followers became angry (Acts 15:2; 15:38; 1 Corinthians 1:11; 2 Corinthians 2:4)

Anger is a natural response to things like abuse, neglect, manipulation, violence and evil. Jesus was angry with the Pharisees who abused and manipulated the poor, neglected the weak and oppressed the vulnerable. He wept passionately at the insensitivity of a community (Luke 13:34). People need to be able to express their anger without fear of judgement. Angry tears represent a safe way of expressing how we have been scarred in life.

Alas, although weekly corporate confession may take place in church, a large number of people still carry confused guilt in the form of shame. Often the most powerful confession is to another person. In true confession, tears flow (Psalm 51:3, 4). Tears alone do not bring forgiveness but they can be a sign that someone is on a painful journey that can lead them to forgiveness, release and a new beginning.

Pastoral workers should be of such standing within the church that individuals can identify them as suitable people to confess to. This means we need to be people who are known more for listening than talking and recognised as people who can keep confidences. This doesn't mean, though, that we are able to distribute grace and forgiveness cheaply like aspirins. The forgiveness that God offers us through Christ came at a great cost. To ease our disposition we can too easily rush to offer forgiveness without allowing a person to get to the depths of their confession. After all, to be contrite means to resolve not to walk that way again. That requires a change of heart and will. Some will shed cheap tears but for others it is a sign of how seriously they are taking their sin and confession. The pastoral worker needs to be discerning enough not to rush in but to allow a person to confess till they have emptied the cup. Only then should we minister God's grace.

We also need to be able to distinguish when someone is feeling false guilt for things they have not done. This is a characteristic of shame, where a person has been so traumatised with guilt that they feel guilty for just about everything in the world, and shame penetrates all aspects of their lives. A good pastor doesn't want to condone this attitude but to shed light on the truth of the situation.

Guilt focuses upon what we do or have done, while shame focuses more upon who we are and what has been done to us. Shame brings with it a feeling of being uncovered, embarrassed, unprotected and vulnerable. It is also contagious in the sense that a person can become ashamed of being ashamed. It can sometimes be passed on through families, be it consciously or subconsciously.

There appear to be three hurdles to overcome with regard to forgiveness. Firstly, it can be compared to a hurdle in a race. God is generous with his love and desires to forgive us. It is extremely costly to him but offered freely to us. All we have to do is to accept his offer of forgiveness and step over the hurdle. This is the easiest hurdle.

The second hurdle is like the high jump, which is forgiveness that comes from others. We can only ask for forgiveness here; the willingness to forgive is in someone else's hands.

The final hurdle is like the pole vault. Forgiving ourselves seems to be the highest one to jump. God calls us to love others as we love ourselves, but unfortunately many people today have such a poor self-image that they find it extremely hard to release themselves from their failures. Part of the answer is to help people to realise that they are just like all other humans, no more or no less special than any other. Here, forgiveness is more about discovering self-knowledge than doing something.

> I am more like those who have hurt me than different from them.[37]

As the person works this out, which can take some time, we are to reflect God's image and be a 'mirror of forgiveness' to the person.

> I am able to forgive when I realised that I am in no position to forgive.[38]

Alistair Ross suggests that four things need to take place here.[39] First, the story needs to be told and heard. Second, emotions need to be released. Third, there needs to be an encounter with another. We

37. Source unknown.
38. S. A. Pattison (2000), *A Critique of Pastoral Care* (3rd edition), Norwich: SCM.
39. A. Ross (2003), *Counselling Skills for Church and Faith Community Workers*, Maidenhead: Open University.

cannot always meet with the perpetrator or hear their request for forgiveness, but we can bring it to another, be it God or the pastor. Here there is an opportunity to bring a new perspective to the situation. Finally, there is an opportunity, a choice to release someone and forgive them. This involves letting go of the hurt and re-engaging with life and all of its risks and vulnerabilities – particularly the risk of being hurt again. Indeed, people do oscillate with regard to forgiveness, which is why we need to be reminded each week that we bring all things to God for forgiveness every Sunday. God's forgiveness is an ongoing commitment that we have to choose to receive and to practise all our lives.

Tears of failure

This leads us to another aspect that often brings tears: failure. I have seen more tears from men because of a sense of failure than any other experience. This is less related to whether we have actually failed than how we perceive that we have failed. Peter failed the Lord, but he didn't weep until the cockerel crowed three times (Luke 22:59-62). Jesus' ministry to Peter after the resurrection helped him to not exaggerate his failures into a universal one. Jesus quickly affirmed Peter with a new calling and ministry. We need to be aware when people turn their failures into a universal failure of their life; after all, failure is common to us all. The obsession to see ourselves as failures often ties into our self-esteem.

The ability to shed tears for our human qualities with all their failures can be a very releasing thing to do. It brings hope of something new, the belief that Jesus will complete all things in us (Philippians 1:6). This was Peter's discovery with Jesus that allowed him to re-engage with life without guilt, shame and failure.

Pastoral ministry will inevitably lead us to caring for people experiencing physical and emotional fatigue. Workaholics are common both in the Church and in local church leadership. Increasingly in today's digital, globalised society we are called to make every minute count. This brings its own pressures. Emails on mobile phones and tablets mean we 'follow the sun' and are available to others 24/7. Unless we learn to tame this we are all in danger of fatigue. Christian teaching about having a weekly day of rest, withdrawing for retreats and living a balanced life doesn't seem to have caught on with church leaders. They are good at preaching one thing and doing another, all of which sets the community the wrong example.

Pastoral workers need to set boundaries. They need to be people who are not driven but able to balance their work with self-care. If we are not careful, as we minister to those who are fatigued we will be in danger of becoming wrapped up in our own emotions. How can we minister to the exhausted if we ourselves are worn out? Fatigue and exhaustion bring tears readily to the surface. Ministering to people in this state requires us to have some knowledge and awareness of stress and its issues. Tears are a natural release to hours of tension and strain. An emotional, tearful release can refresh the soul:

> Weeping may linger for the night,
> but joy comes with the morning.
> *Psalm 30:5*

As well as physical and emotional fatigue, people can experience spiritual fatigue. Over the years a number of people have joined my church who have expressed that they didn't want to get too involved. Eventually they told me about how much they were doing in their previous church and how they were relieved to be away from the never-ending pressure of 'doing' that had bled them dry spiritually. This is not just a modern state of affairs. From Moses to Paul, people of faith have experienced exhausted, lonely moments. They have all needed a caring pastor to be near to understand and encourage them back to full health. This is something all pastors can understand and empathise with.

Tears of fear

'We promise according to our hopes and perform according to our fears.'[40] Fear can grab hold of anyone. The body goes into survival mode; blood rushes to the inner core, leaving the limbs cold to the touch. Living on 'full alert' mode is very exhausting. It can paralyse us to tears. We have a choice of three responses. As children we cry, scream or run away. As adults this becomes freezing, fighting or fleeing. Jesus experienced the power of fear as he wept in the garden with tears of dread (Luke 22:39-46), yet he was also able to move on with an inner peace that allowed him to face his destiny.

Pastors need to become skilled at helping people to face their fears and then manage them. It begins with our presence. After all, Scripture tells us that 'perfect love casts out fear' (1 John 4:18). All three reactions of freezing, fighting or fleeing may be helpful initially, but they don't help people to deal with the real problems. People begin to discover love when they see that they are not alone, and the pastor can play a powerful part purely by being a supportive presence.

40. François de la Rochefoucauld, (1613–1680).

The story of the young prince

It was before my time; it was before your time; in fact, it was at the time when birds built their nests in old men's beards. There was a kingdom with a valley, a road and a river running through it. And there was a king and queen who had a son aged thirteen. Now he was just an ordinary boy, except he was a prince.

Now the boy was not particularly brave; he wasn't a coward, he was just not particularly brave. The king and queen sadly died and the young boy was crowned king, but on that same day a fearsome giant moved into the valley and terrorised all the inhabitants. As they travelled along the road they would feel the ground trembling under their feet. The giant would rear up in front of them and they would hear 'Swish, swash, bang, boom, I am your nightmare, I am your doom,' followed by a splat as he trod on them.

All of the boy-king's subjects were frightened and went to see him. 'Sir, you're going to have to do something about this giant.' The boy-king thought to himself, 'I'm not frightened, but I'm not very brave,' so he decided to do as other kings did and sent his knights to deal with the giant. 'They can do the dirty work for me,' he thought, which is what kings have thought since time immemorial. So he picked his bravest knights, the SAS of knights, and he sent them down the valley. The knights thought this was all in a day's work, so off they went. But as they travelled along the valley they heard, 'Swish, swash, bang, boom, 'I am your nightmare, I am your doom,' and as the giant went 'splat,' the knights just managed to escape. The knights decided that this was too big a job for them so they returned to the king and said, 'There are some problems in life you just have to solve yourself, and this giant is too big for us. You're going to have to deal with it yourself.'

The boy thought, 'I'm the king. What can I do?'

The king had a special friend, a mentor, someone everyone should have. She was a wise woman called Sophia. So the king got on his horse and went to speak to the wise woman. He got to the house, secured his horse and went in to see her. She was sitting by the fire. The boy stood beside her, shaking with fear. 'Whatever is the matter with you?' she said. 'Sit down and count to ten.' So the boy sat down and told her his problem and how he wasn't brave enough to deal with the giant.

The woman said, 'Listen. I'm going to tell you a little poem: We run from what we do not know, and then it seems to grow and grow, and then it stands in our way until its name we learn to say.'

'That's good,' said the boy-king. 'Say it again and I'll learn it.'

'We run from what we do not know, and then it seems grow and grow, and then it stands in our way until its name we learn to say.'

'That's true,' said the boy-king. 'I don't know the name of this giant, but I now know what I need to do.'

The king thanked the woman for her wise words, got back on his horse and rode down the valley until he could hear the noise of the giant. 'Swish, swash, bang, boom, I am your nightmare, I am your doom.' As the giant reared up in front of him the boy dodged the 'splat.' He wanted to run away but the voice of the wise woman was whispering to him, 'We run from what we do not know, and then it seems to grow and grow, and then it stands in our way until its name we learn to say.' And even though his instinct was to run away, the king tied up his horse and took an enormous step towards the giant. And as he did so, the giant seemed to get a little smaller. He took a second step and then another, and with each step the giant became smaller and smaller until he was no bigger than the king's thumb. The boy looked down, picked the giant up in his hands, looked at him and said, 'What is your name?'

The giant looked straight up into the boy's eyes and said, 'My name is FEAR.'

Tears can result from other situations too. Some people cry from frustration as they begin to realise and accept the limitations of their lives. Others cry from gratitude, when they survive a disaster, avoid an accident or recover from an illness. The pent-up emotion that they have been carrying is suddenly released with feelings of joy.

Others cry because of loneliness, and you may be privileged that they might share this with you. Loneliness is something that is on the increase in today's society as more and more people live alone. Pastors can find themselves visiting someone who becomes emotional because of their loneliness. Here the pastor can bring value to the individual and offer openings in which they can gain confidence to re-engage with others. In this way the church should come into its own as it draws individuals into friendships and support structures within the church. It is in the church that we can find ways to use our skills, gain confidence, relate to like-minded people and learn to like ourselves.

Reflections

- Do you feel comfortable with tears?
- How do you react when another person cries?
- When is it appropriate or inappropriate to cry with another?
- How can you tell what is the reason for the tears?
- Can you detect when you are building up pressures that could be released by crying?
- When was the last time you heard a sermon about tears?

Chapter 21

Healing ministry

What happens when people open their hearts?
They get better.
(Haruki Murakami)[41]

Pastoral care and healing seem to go hand in hand. Many previous theological views on pastoral care have been rooted in the healing acts of Christ. Perhaps this is why a number of pastoral writers have been medical doctors. In recent years there appear to have been bursts of interest from within the Church about healing, which have continued after hearing well-known preachers such as David Watson or John Wimber focus on renewal and the Holy Spirit. Then it calms down and the emphasis becomes more on the counselling, caring role of the Church. We may be told that the movement of the Holy Spirit may come and go, but I am sure God's interest in healing does not wax and wane quite as much as the Church's. We minister in the belief that God is a creator God, constantly at work in his creation.

Bishop John Robinson, when he was near his own death, expresses this well:

> When two years ago I spoke at the funeral of a 16-year-old girl who died in our Dale, I said that God was to be found in the cancer as much as in the sunset. That I firmly believe, but it was an intellectual statement. Now I have had to ask if I can say it of myself, which is a much greater test . . . By saying God was in the cancer I did not mean that God was in it by intending it or sending it. That would make him a very devil. God is to be found in the cancer as in everything else. If he is not, then he is not the God of the Psalmist who said, 'if I go down to Hell, thou art there also.'[42]

At its heart, any pastoral ministry is dealing with healing, whether it is simply ministering in the name of Christ or praying for a specific healing in a particular context. Bishop Morris Maddocks said that all

41. H. Murakami (2001), *Norwegian Wood*, London: Vantage.
42. Bishop John Robinson, quoted in M. Wilson (1988), *A Coat of Many Colours: Pastoral Studies of the Christian Way of Life*, London: Epworth Press, p.163.

Christian healing is at its root focused on Christ.[43] Christ is at work through his whole creation as he seeks to bring salvation to humankind. Salvation at its heart is all about healing. So when we are involved in general visiting, worship or teaching, we are crying out to God to be in the healing business. As pastors we are more specifically seeking healing through our prayer ministry, special healing services, the laying on of hands, anointing with oil and through the Holy Communion service.

We are following a good tradition. Any glance at the Gospels will see that Jesus spent considerable time bringing healing to individuals and families, whether by pastoring those who were ill, disabled, demon-possessed, bereaved or by opening people's minds and hearts. Jesus then taught his disciples to follow in his footsteps as they travelled from village to village. The commission is now passed to us as his followers.

We can, of course, feel that this healing is totally the responsibility of the local health service. However, it is healthy for the Church to recognise that Christians through the centuries have been promoting healing and have played key roles in medical developments.

We may feel very inadequate to engage in the healing ministry. We may feel it is presumptuous or arrogant, or simply that we do not have the faith to believe in healing. Perhaps we need to broaden our understanding of healing. Any pastoral work represents Christ and the Church. This means that we stand for forgiveness, reconciliation and wholeness, whether it is physical, emotional, spiritual, relational or social. So when we are involved in listening, counselling, guiding or praying, we are seeking to bring healing.

Once we acknowledge to ourselves that we are in the healing business, we can begin to acknowledge it openly. This might at one level simply be letting someone know that we are praying for them. Others will be more confident and ask for permission to pray openly for the person and the situation.

Be gracious to me, O Lord, for I am in distress;
my eye wastes away from grief,
my soul and my body also.
For my life is spent with sorrow,
and my years with sighing;
my strength fails because of my misery,
and my bones waste away.
I am the scorn of all my adversaries,

43. A *Time to Heal: A Report for the House of Bishops on the Healing Ministry* (Church House Publishing, 2000).

> a horror to my neighbours,
> an object of dread to my acquaintances;
> those who see me in the street flee from me.
> I have passed out of mind like one who is dead;
> I have become like a broken vessel.
> *Psalm 31:9-12*

When we are praying with a person, we can feel unsure what to say in our prayers. I find that the safest way of handling this is to ask the person in question what they would like us to pray for. Often a person will ask us to pray for others rather than themselves or for something that they are worried about rather than for physical healing. If we do not check out what the person wants, we might find ourselves praying for a person's healing when in fact they are ready to die and would prefer us to pray for their family.

If the person would like you to pray for physical healing, you have the choice of either using a formal prayer (from prayer books from your tradition) or to pray extemporarily. A very simple prayer could be something like, 'In the name of Jesus Christ, the Son of God, (name) be healed, Amen.'

You may feel it appropriate to reach out and touch the arm of the person as you pray. There is no reason why we cannot lay hands on a person's head as we pray, or anoint them with oil on the forehead in the shape of the cross (Mark 6:13; James 5:14, 15). However, it is always appropriate and proper to ask permission first and to explain why you want to do this.

On our next visit, we mustn't be afraid to ask how the prayer has helped the person. We can be shy to ask in case nothing has happened. But whether the person identifies any change or not, we believe God is at work. By asking, we are raising their faith and ours. The very thought that someone cares enough to pray can be very uplifting in itself. Even at the point of death, we can pray for a healing that takes a person into God's kingdom, and we know that God cares for those who are widowed and bereaved.

We need to be aware that we are representing the front face of the Church in this ministry. When we pray, we do so in the name of Christ and the Church. It can be helpful to let the person know this and to give them the choice of whether they would like others in the local church to pray for them. We must obtain a person's permission before putting their name in a news sheet or prayer sheet. Some churches have prayer chains, which enable a broader Christian community to engage in support. It also allows others to exercise their ministry while at the same time supporting and praying for our work.

Some pastors keep a record of people they have visited and the prayers offered. It can be very encouraging to look back and see how issues have been resolved. The notes need to be kept confidential and locked away, however.

Praying for the sick can be very emotionally draining and tiring. We need to recognise that after we have given out, we need to take stock and refresh ourselves physically and spiritually.

Finally, we need to acknowledge that this is a ministry that demands humility. It is God's ministry, not ours; we are but a channel for God to work. We also need to practise what we preach and be willing for others to pray for us as we pray for others.

Reflections

- How comfortable do we feel in acknowledging that we are in the healing business?
- Have you had experience of others praying for you? What benefits have resulted?
- How would you answer the following questions:
  - How much faith should I have to be healed?
  - If God loves me, why has he allowed this suffering?
  - Am I ill because I have sinned?
  - Why does suffering exist?
  - Do I have to pray for healing?
- What should you expect after a prayer for healing?
- Who would accompany you with this type of ministry?
- Is there a wider network of people in your geographical area where prayer, training and good practice can be shared?

Chapter 22
Deliverance ministry

Out of suffering comes the serious mind; out of salvation, the grateful heart; out of endurance, fortitude; out of deliverance, faith.
(John Ruskin)[44]

Our Father, who art in heaven . . . deliver us from evil . . . Amen.
(Matthew 6:9-13, RSV)

When I was a curate, my training incumbent was the diocesan exorcist. As part of my training he often took me into all kinds of strange, complex and at times scary situations. Eventually I was allowed to be the lead minister and to carry the responsibility of assessing a situation.

On one occasion I went with a colleague to the home of a couple who believed there was an evil presence in their home. I remember it well. It was a Saturday morning as we ventured into the large Victorian house. We didn't know the people involved, so we followed the usual pattern of explaining what we did, listening to the family's story and then coming to some conclusion and action. The couple had been bequeathed a range of eastern belongings and furniture. Ever since they had taken possession of the articles, there had been a 'disturbed' feeling in the house. The family had trouble sleeping and one room had become particularly cold, despite heating being on in the house. After going through our usual procedure (see below) I decided to do a salt and water prayer around the house. My colleague would pray quietly (often in spiritual tongues) for protection as I went from room to room praying out loud and sprinkling holy salted water over the room. I came to one particular bedroom, opened a window and then worked my way around the room. I had been taught to specifically look out for dark corners and cupboards. I casually opened a door, briefly prayed, sprinkled water into the corners and turned to close the door. In that split second, I felt a rush of movement over my left shoulder, which instantly froze up. The woman of the house, who was standing watching, screamed and fell to the floor. My colleague, who was quietly praying, became aware of a movement that went past her and out of the window!

44. J. Ruskin (1819–1900).

You can't be involved in pastoral care for any length of time without becoming aware of the reality of evil in this world. There may be a wide spectrum of what we mean by evil, but there is no doubt that the world is full of evil acts. For most of us it takes the form of knowing that we are surrounded by sickness and darkness. But sometimes we find ourselves encountering situations that are hard to understand and are far darker than we can imagine. We will all formulate our own theological perspective of what is evil and how we understand it. Some will be fascinated by it and intrigued to find out more about exorcism and deliverance. Others will not want to accept the concept and shy away from the mere thought that evil exists. I personally rarely talk about the subject, but when I do, I am very cautious about what I say. However, we do need to be aware of the issue and be clear about how we will handle a dark, evil situation.

The first thing we need to acknowledge and believe is that Jesus is Lord. If we have Christ, have we not overcome all things? I believe Christ is Lord of all, so ultimately we are safe in his care.

Secondly, we need to understand our gifts and limitations in ministry. We are all called to stand up against evil when we encounter it and be accountable to God for our actions. But this doesn't mean we have to go looking for evil. A few are called to engage in deliverance ministry, those who are given the faith, maturity and gifting to handle such situations in Christ. However, I suggest that the majority of pastoral workers would do well to know their limitations and be quick to refer on when they encounter something that they feel uncomfortable with. Every Christian organisation will have a regional exorcist who is trained and experienced in assessing and handling unusual situations. If in doubt there will be a Church of England diocesan representative from whom you could obtain advice and direction.

Thirdly, we need to recognise that Christ has not left us unprotected and has equipped us with tools for every situation. We have the armour of Christ (Ephesians 6:13-18) to put on. This is a passage of Scripture that pastors should almost know off by heart and say regularly before beginning their weekly ministry. We are also given the considerable tools of prayer, intercession, speaking in tongues, water, oil, salt and light, the laying on of hands, Holy Communion and the call of the Holy Spirit. These are tools with which we need to be well acquainted in everyday ministry, well before we encounter anything of the demonic order.

Let me point out some guiding principles so that we can minister safely within clear rules. Look out for situations where you feel extremely uncomfortable. This might be in a particular location or with a particular person. We can feel uncomfortable for lots of reasons, often linked with our own psychological make-up. However, as we develop discernment, we can become experienced in identifying an oppressive situation, separate from our own issues. It may be a room that is cold in the middle of summer or despite the heating being on. It may be a person who gives off negative vibes that makes you feel vulnerable and threatened. I don't mean people we simply don't like but those that cause a reaction within us such that spiritually we feel uncomfortable and threatened. Someone may invite us to their home or office because there is a room that is cold, or they are having strange dreams disconnected with their lives; perhaps strange occurrences are happening in someone's home, such as objects being moved, or they are seeing a presence in a room, or maybe they have dabbled with a Ouija board.

We need to always remember the story that Jesus told of the man who swept his house clean of evil presences only to fail to fill it with something better and so left a vacuum for more evil to return (Matthew 12:43-5). Therefore we need to always begin by calling people to confess, repent and turn to God, and to worship every Sunday and receive bread and wine. If someone were not willing to engage in this Christian direction, I would hesitate to get involved. James 4:7 is very clear that we are to submit to God and to resist evil by turning to God.

All Christians are involved in spiritual warfare, whether we like it or not (Matthew 4:4). We are told that the Holy Spirit comes and goes and that evil wanders the world looking to bring turmoil (John 3:8; 1 Peter 5:8). Personally, I have always found Lent to be a time of spiritual oppression in which relationships become tense or minor things become complicated and blown out of proportion. Easter becomes a day of release and joy. One might argue that this is just psychological self-induced perception. I can only say that, as a psychologist, I believe it is more spiritually based and something that seems to come upon me rather than from within. We therefore need to be aware of the seasons of life and learn to recognise times of spiritual attack.

Always have a policy that two are better than one. I would never see someone that I felt uncomfortable with or enter a house where there may be some evil involvement without taking a colleague. This should not be just another member of the church to keep you company; rather it should be an experienced person who is mature in the faith and willing to simply but powerfully pray during the ministry. The person who leads in situations like this is more likely to come under spiritual attack, hence the need for a colleague to be praying for protection and guidance at all times.

Always be ready to take any issues straight to your supervisor or line manager. If you feel that perhaps your supervisor wouldn't understand the issue, report it to another experienced Christian (who is under Christian authority) and seek their advice. It is vital that you do not proceed in this ministry in any way until you have appropriate support and guidance.

Be very willing to pass difficult situations on to those who have more experience, training and supervision. If you feel reluctant to let a situation go, ask yourself what it is that is making you hold on to the case. It may not be from God.

If in doubt, commend the person to God, assure them of your prayers and leave the situation till the person is a regular worshipper at your church. At this point refer them to a regional adviser.

Reflections

- Have you experienced seasons of doubt, oppression and spiritual attack?
- Are you clear about when you would refer a situation on to another?
- Are you clear about to whom you would take difficult cases?
- Have you a spiritual director who can pray and support you in your ministry?
- How well developed is your theology with regard to the concept of evil?

Chapter 23

Referring to others

When every hope is gone, when helpers fail and comforts flee,
I find that help arrives somehow, from I know not where.
(Mahatma Gandhi)[45]

If you have a healthy Christian community that nurtures and heals, then it is inevitable that you will attract people with needs of one kind or another. The church community should be an environment where people should be upheld and cared for as they develop into rounded, mature Christians who can contribute as well as receive. If we create this environment early on in a pastoral ministry it will be realised that we cannot support, care or counsel everyone. The sooner we grasp this and set into motion some parameters for the care team and guidelines for referrals the better. Being in charge of the pastoral care in a church certainly doesn't mean you have to do it all yourself. Sharing the work brings a healthier attitude, and this can make your expectations more modest. Hopefully this will encourage you to develop a facilitator role within the community.

The primary questions when someone asks to see us should be, 'What is the problem?' and 'How and where can this issue best be resolved?'

Sometimes the person will want you to solve their problem, but it is not your task to do so, although you may play a part in the solution. Others are not expecting you to know the answers but are hoping that you may know where they can go to obtain the most appropriate help. In other situations you may begin to support a person but very quickly realise that you are out of your depth. Far better to realise this early on and be wise (and humble) enough to refer the person to someone who can give more specialised support than become overwhelmed and possibly do damage to the person and yourself.

We cannot overestimate the role we play in people's lives. They will come to a pastoral worker often at significant times of change. The circumstances of their lives may have changed such that they have lost their orientation. They come to the church because they believe they will find understanding, comfort and support. This is

45. M. K. Gandhi (1927), *An Autobiography: The Story of My Experiments with Truth*, London: Penguin.

often well before they engage with a doctor, counsellor or a mental health worker. This puts us at a primary point of intervention where we can help to make a positive difference at a turning point in their lives. When people encounter a pastoral worker their stance is very different to how it would be when visiting a health professional. They will either know us personally or will have heard about us in much more detail than what they know about an NHS consultant. We may have been an early visitor when they gave birth to their first child, for example, or we might have been involved in the liturgy of a baptism, wedding or funeral that they were connected with. This relationship tends to make people far more open to hearing what we have to say, and our guidance is therefore more likely to bring about a significant change.

We need to be aware that it will not always be a primary order of change that someone comes to see us about. We may expect that the issue is something like redundancy, illness, bereavement or divorce. However, it is often secondary order change that causes confusion and needs untangling – the confused feelings that come after a primary change that people struggle to identify with and adjust to. These issues may seem small compared to the major loss, which is why the person will only raise them with someone they can trust. Skilled pastors will find themselves dealing with more secondary order changes than primary.

We need to develop willingness and the ability to discern when it is necessary to refer people on to other support agencies. Firstly we need to recognise when an issue is beyond us and not see it as a personal failure. If we are never referring people on to others then there is probably an issue with our ministry. The most obvious time to refer on is when our diary is simply too full. We need to agree with ourselves the number of hours we will work each week and stick to it, otherwise an open diary will be filled with the world's problems. It's no wonder that burnout is common in ministry.

We need to be aware of the areas where we have not been trained, and perhaps have little interest in. We can't be experts in everything. The danger for church leaders is that it can seem that the congregation expects you to be just that! Perhaps we collude with this when we fail to say, 'No, this is not my area of expertise.' This might be in bereavement work, marriage guidance, drug issues or mental health problems. Recognising what we will not focus upon frees us to focus on areas in which we are more skilled. And the first skill we need to acquire is to be willing to pass people on to others who are more trained than ourselves in particular areas.

A church should be a place that has up-to-date knowledge of what is available within the community. We need to know where the women's refuge is, for example, or at least have their contact number readily available. This applies to a range of support agencies.

There is in some churches debate around whether we should refer on to non-Christian agencies. The reality is that many Christians are working in such agencies. Just because you have referred on, it doesn't mean that you cease supporting the person or are not able to contribute a more Christian perspective.

Some people are hesitant when you mention referring them on as they may have been hoping that you would be, or provide, the solution to their problems. We need to give people time to think about going to another agency. There is often hesitancy, perhaps because they feel that they don't want to have to share the story again, or it might not be accepted as readily. However, we delude ourselves if we simply give in to this reluctance. Part of our role is to educate. This means we need to convey to the person the importance of receiving the right support. It might also mean that they leave disappointed. We have to learn to live with this. If the issue is serious enough they will come back when they are ready to tackle the problem. Sometimes this is part of God's timing. We can't rush people into healing; it has to be at their pace.

Reflections

- Have you a clear policy with regard to whom you report and are accountable to?
- What understanding is there within the church for referring on to secure bodies?
- Has the church a working relationship with the local medical centre? Mental health trust? Counselling agency? Social services? Care of the elderly?
- How proficient are you at recognising that you are out of your depth?

Chapter 24

Pastoral care to the church as a whole

Pastoral care: a pattern of corporate, responsible, sensitive acts motivated by a compelling vision.
(R. A. Lambourne)[46]

I was once challenged by a very learned member of my church that, as a fairly new vicar, I should be careful when offering to visit the sick and the needy. I think he thought I would be consumed by it. Rather, he thought I should spend my time preaching and offering pastoral care through the word. I accept that *good* biblical preaching can change hearts and minds, but is this the only way to minister in Christ's name? Wilson suggests that a series of logical arguments is like forming a chain.[47] One broken link and the sense of the argument is lost. But if you convey meaning by using story, argument, exposition, case study and parables, then your communication is more like a rope with many threads. A break in a thread doesn't lead to losing the meaning of the message. However, many of us need more than one rope to secure and anchor us.

The Church historically has had a monopoly on social care within the community. The Church on the whole is recognised as a place of care, particularly for one-to-one encounters. We need to seek to bring our pastoral care not only into one-to-one situations but also into small group dynamics, as well as the larger church community as a whole. This means creating a community where problems and issues can be resolved.

Much of a pastor's ministry is to help people where there is conflict and disagreement in the family. But how does the church model this? Some churches view conflict and disagreement always as negative. In such a church, either things are brushed under the table or people become frustrated at not being heard and eventually leave the church. However, conflict can be seen in a more positive way. Groups that have a healthy understanding of conflict tend to produce a more cooperative community. Here, conflict is seen as a

46. R. Lambourne (1975) in *Contact*, No.35.
47. M. Wilson (1988), *A Coat of Many Colours: Pastoral Studies of the Christian Way of Life*, London, Epworth.

way of expressing differences rather than a clash of ideas. When people are encouraged to share their views and be fully heard, there is less likelihood of anger simmering away under the surface.

As pastors we need to be encouraging the leadership to have a positive attitude towards those with differing views. To agree to differ in love while recognising the role of leadership involves working together to understand each other's differences. Here, differences are seen as a process to be worked through rather than a problem to avoid. We need to represent maturity where we don't take other people's views as a personal attack on the leadership. But it is important to be willing to face anger when it arises. This means allowing ambiguity to exist in the church. It does not mean we change what we believe but it does mean we recognise that there are other points of view than our own within the kingdom of God.

The pastor needs to be open to the possibility that God will speak to the church from an unlikely quarter. Willingness to admit to our mistakes from the pulpit might be necessary, bringing a greater degree of humility and humanity to the church. This is a church that does not rely solely upon the religious leaders to interpret God's will.

Unfortunately pastors can find themselves picking up ongoing issues within the life of the church that simply reflect systemic problems; there can be a lot of lingering, unfinished business. These can range from personal disagreements that continue for years, unresolved issues around power and authority, finance and how money is spent, differing views of mission, doctrinal issues (such as baptism), social issues (sexuality, abortion, role of women, etc.), differing age groups, and problems handling change where there is tension between those who want to hold on to the past and those who want to try new things. It is easy for a pastor to be consumed by these drip-by-drip problems and lose sight of the need to have a more focused process within the whole church.

We tend to assume that a church community is a safe place where conflict can be resolved peacefully. However, churches are often not well equipped to handle anger and may even see any sign of frustration as a sin. This leads people to push down their feelings and frustrations or deny that they even have such feelings. However, they have to surface somewhere, be it via alcohol as a form of self-medication or anger outbursts within the home. Eventually someone in the church will be hijacked by their feelings such that they will struggle to control their rage. It usually results in someone storming out of the church and leaving confusion in their wake.

Another common problem pastors get drawn into is when the church carries secrets that only a few trusted people know about.

Here people are sworn to secrecy about another member of the congregation. Alas, secrets are rarely perfectly kept, which means that suspicion and gossip arise in such a way that the real problem can't be addressed. A skilled pastor can play an important role here in bringing resolution. They can use either debriefing skills or the Quaker technique of resolving problems. Both involve clear ground rules:

- A person who doesn't take sides and remains 'un-anxious' about the issue should act as a facilitator.
- The problem is expressed and an attempt is made to resolve the issue. This simply gives time for people to name and express what they see as the problem.
- Everyone present is given a time-controlled opportunity to speak about their view of the conflict and how they feel about it. People can clarify what they are saying but not contradict or challenge others' views.
- Once everyone feels that they have been heard, silence is held to give people time to reflect upon what has been said. This might mean going away and thinking about it without talking to anyone about the subject till the group meets again.
- An opportunity is given for people to express whether and how they have gained a different perspective of the issue.
- People are encouraged to share where they might have been wrong or mistaken or where they want to confess.
- Consensus is then sought that both sides can agree on. This might require a mature Christian on each side speaking in such a way that encourages others to follow their lead into reconciliation.
- When a conclusion is reached, it is read out three times to allow people to take it on board. People are given time to raise any final alterations without going over old ground.
- Once all agree to the conclusion, it is acknowledged that the matter is closed and that all will stand by the decision and trust the conclusion.

The role of the pastor can be very important in these situations in keeping both parties engaged in the process. Clearly such developments will stand or fall by a willingness of the church leadership to fully participate. Again, it may require the pastor to support and encourage the leadership to hold on to the process and commit themselves to the conclusion.

Often the pastor is not the overall leader of the church. This means that we have to fit into someone else's model of ministry, and this will clearly affect our style of ministry in the church. The leader of the church may be authoritarian, collaborative or consensual in their leadership style. Each style affects the pastor in different ways. Working with an authoritarian leader may mean you know exactly where you are and what is expected. The disadvantage is that the leader may not appreciate your role or the responsibility that you carry. With a consensual leader you may seem able to share your ministry with the leader, yet it may involve a lack of urgency with regard to making decisions and lead to stalemate with some issues.

A collaborative approach allows a pastor to share when appropriate and set clear ground rules about who will make final decisions concerning important pastoral issues. The approach you are comfortable working with will depend upon your personality. What is important is that you recognise your own style and compensate for areas of frustration with additional support elsewhere.

Reflections

- How can pastoral issues be expressed and discussed in a church?
- How can sermons be more pastorally orientated?
- Can church problems be tackled from the pulpit without condemning or accusing?
- How can the church be a pastor to the leadership team?
- What would a pastoral policy look like in your church?

Chapter 25

The seasons in church life

For everything there is a season, and a time for every matter under heaven:
a time to be born, and a time to die;
a time to plant, and a time to pluck up what is planted;
a time to kill, and a time to heal;
a time to break down and a time to build up;
a time to weep, and a time to laugh;
a time to mourn, and a time to dance;
a time to throw away stones, and a time to gather stones together;
a time to embrace, and a time to refrain from embracing;
a time to seek, and a time to lose;
a time to keep, and a time to throw away;
a time to tear, and a time to sew;
a time to keep silence, and a time to speak;
a time to love, and a time to hate;
a time for war, and a time for peace.
(Ecclesiastes 3:1-8)

When we enter into pastoral ministry in a church community we need to recognise that the church has a life cycle all of its own that we are dovetailing into. Just as we have the seasons, churches have periods of autumn, winter and spring. Our task is to make sure that the community stays healthy. Much has been said in recent years about what makes a healthy church.

The first task is survival, which might focus upon increasing numbers, bringing in more finance or repairing the building. But surviving does not mean that a church is healthy. We might like to think more in terms of gardening analogies. The garden is a living organism that might need to be watered, given nutrients, need to combat fungi infections or require a time of fallowness. If we are to be holistic pastors we need to look beyond individual care and look at the needs as a whole. A church leadership team needs to regularly ask:

- Does the church need a rest from over-activity?
- Does the church need fresh teaching input?
- Does the church need support for what's already going on?
- Does the church need to tackle an ongoing problem?

- Does the church need to focus on one section of its 'garden' – perhaps the young or the elderly?
- Does the church need some time to play and enjoy a summer period?

All of these questions will have an impact upon our pastoral work and where we place our emphasis. Our aim is to bring balance to the church community. A gardener doesn't just rip up plants without thinking about the impact this will have on the neighbouring plants. If we are to bring a gardener's healing touch to our ministry we need to think about to which part of the garden we should bring it. It might be through:

1. Special services, anointing with oil or Holy Communion.
2. Prayer individually or in groups.
3. Teaching programmes in the services and through home groups for different age groups.
4. Calling on individuals and families, both in the church and in the wider community.
5. Specific counselling, guidance and spiritual direction sessions as well as retreats.
6. Outreach within the community after finding out what the specific needs are.

All of these activities send us one clear message: we can't do this work alone. There needs to be a range of gardeners at work, some general hands and other specialists for particular tasks. We may well find that our calling is solely to support all of these workers, helping them to not burn out. In the end our task is to produce a church where members are helped to live abundant lives. This is perhaps a good question for the pastor to be constantly asking the leadership team as they think about the future direction of the church. What aspects of church life do we need to focus on to bring about abundance in all its colours?

As the seasons change in a church, some will struggle with such changes and seek out the pastor for support. This can sometimes be awkward to handle. Often when a new leader arrives in the church and introduces change, the pastor can be caught between the way the previous leader managed the church and adapting to new ideas and styles. Sometimes people will try to use the pastor to get their message across to the leader. Here the pastor is caught between loyalty to a new leader and caring for those who don't want change (or the type of change that is being introduced) whilst still having to handle their own thoughts about what is happening. Yet the skills of a pastor who understands conflict management can bring healing to the church. Helping the church individually or corporately to think through change in a non-threatening way can be liberating.

There is a range of questions we need to reflect upon as the church journeys through its seasons. The first questions to ask are whether the proposed change is necessary and, if it is, how can the change be clearly explained and understood by the church? The pastor will play a key role here in picking up people's questions and feelings.

Then we need to ask how quickly this change needs to take place for the leader, congregation, fringe and outsiders of the church to grow healthily. Again, the pastor will be helpful in knowing how people are likely to react and what impact this will have. It will then be the pastor's job to help to make the change complete in the most caring way so that people are carried along in the process.

It will take time to discern when the change is complete and to be able to assess the change and evaluate it. A caring hand will be needed with those who have been hurt by the process or are about to leave the church because of the changes.

If the change doesn't go as planned, how will we accept failure in such a way that it leads to all-round healing? The pastor may be caught in a dilemma, wondering whether to keep quiet about injustices or to speak out. Pastors need to reflect on their own limitations in all of this process. They can find themselves in conflict with the rest of the leadership team if they get caught up with opinions of individuals rather than focusing on the overall vision. It is good to have an external support system that allows the pastor to have a place where they can think away from the situation. However, if all of this is handled carefully, the pastoral role can enable a church to move through turbulent waters to a more healthy position.

Reflections

- In the church, who controls the seasons of a church's life?
- Can you recognise seasons within your own personal faith journey?
- In your diary, do you forward plan times of quiet, refreshment and holidays, and do you recognise times when it will be very busy in ministry?
- Can you recognise your role in times of change in the church?
- Are there people in the church who have still not adapted to previous changes in the life of the church? How can you help them move on?

Chapter 26

Pastoral care in the workplace

We have too many people who live without working and we have altogether too many people who work without living.
(Charles Reynolds Brown)[48]

In a university setting, I am constantly informing people what the word 'chaplain' means. The word is not used internationally and many British people are unsure of its meaning. It goes back to the days of a Roman Centurion called Martin de Tours who saw a beggar dying in the snow. He offered the man half of his cloak (cappa), which then became a symbol of a religious person who supports others through the storms of life. This is where the shepherd analogy can seem weak in today's society. The Christian tenor of pastoral care is a willingness to care for all individuals equally, including those of a different persuasion from oneself. It is too easy today to think of a shepherd only caring for his small, like-minded flock. Jesus, of course, constantly challenged this approach.

There is an increasing need for chaplains within the workplace. At a time of diminishing full-time paid ministers, this means that there is an opening for lay workers who have developed pastoral skills.

Christian work in secular organisations has its own particular characteristics. Some people, including some in the church, think chaplaincy is about putting on a carol service every Christmas, getting Christians together to form prayer meetings and trying to convert the managers.

Chaplaincy work is quiet, subtle and has a long shelf life. After all, what is the point of reproducing what happens in church on a Sunday in an office, factory or school? Those who go to church know what they want and what they will get. This works fine, except for the fact that about 95 per cent of people do not relate to this. Chaplaincy must offer something different if we are to provide anything of value in the workplace. It is very much about good pastoral care. Initially it involves getting alongside people, understanding their pressures and having a laugh with them. In time, trust is formed and individuals will turn to us for pastoral support. In the university, I have been used for funerals, weddings,

48. C. R. Brown (2012), *The Gospel of Good Health (Classic Reprint)*, Hong Kong: Forgotten Books.

baptisms, counselling, religious advice, support during redundancy, as well as running stress and self-esteem courses, among other things. It is a costly ministry that begins with an open-door policy. Our church language and creeds have become so remote that people just don't grasp any longer what we are about. We are so busy preaching and answering our own questions that no one is asking why we have become meaningless and irrelevant to most people's lives.

We have to get back to grass roots and seek to be part of the community before we have the right to speak. The speaking comes out of what the workplace community is asking. This is slow, patient work, but it can be so rewarding. The surprise so often is that we find that Christ is already working in the community before us. Living a life of genuineness, trustworthiness and empathy becomes a powerful witness to those around us.

There is a wide variety of chaplaincy styles in the community. Some are totally voluntary while others are totally financed and supported by the organisation involved. The chaplain is a kind of mistletoe, only functioning because of the organisation they are attached to. But at the heart lies a pastoral ministry, journeying with people through their trials, tribulations, joys and pleasures. The chaplain is there to be a signpost, directing people in the right direction. It is recognising that it is their journey and not ours. We encourage people to take a step towards God. This is not drawing them into our own belief. We are there to nurture and enable people to work out the right direction for themselves.

Chaplaincy occurs in many different contexts so we cannot generalise. However, in most pastoral roles there is a general conflict between:

- Breadth and depth, in terms of role
- Activity and reactivity – finding a balance between being available with time on one's hands compared to being very involved in the organisation and having a full diary
- Individual gifts and fulfilling a particular organisational requirement
- Accountability between the organisation and the religious sponsoring body
- Line management, appraisals with clear goals and having the freedom or autonomy to be prophetic.

There is much the local church can learn from the way pastoral chaplains are managed in secular organisations. Where the role is taken seriously and valued, the chaplain is well resourced, supported and line managed. All of this leads to a more professional service that proves to be a Christian witness to the community. Chaplaincy only survives in a secular setting if it is adaptive and keeps itself relevant to the organisation. This is the challenge the local church must face if it is to be relevant to the local community.

Reflections

- Does your church recognise those who are fulfilling a chaplaincy role in work locations?
- Could the church offer a chaplaincy role to local businesses?
- How can the pastoral work offered by the church be more relevant to the local community?
- How can we keep our pastoral ministry open to change and development?
- What can we learn from chaplains for our ministry in church?

An example of a chaplaincy protocol is in Appendix 4.

Part three

Ministering safely

Chapter 27

Ground rules and boundaries

Boundaries are to protect life, not to limit pleasure.
(Edwin Louis Cole)[49]

Church life has developed naturally over the centuries. It has always been a sharp contrast from the way of the world. However, that doesn't mean that there are not developments in the world that the church could learn from. One area that the church has always been rather casual about is the issue of clear boundaries. We all need boundaries in life: they are there to protect us from harm, from over-stretching into a dangerous area of ministry. There are times when we have to learn to say no, that this is not my ministry but someone else's, even though we might not know who that other person is. Indeed, we have to learn to live with the fact that there may not always be someone who can step into the breach. It still doesn't mean that we have to fill the gap. Boundaries enable us to know where our responsibilities lie and what is beyond our domain.

Jesus seemed to work within his own framework rather than be pushed into someone else's agenda. We see this with a number of one-to-one encounters that he had with people. He was clear and direct with people without taking on their problems or robbing them of their own responsibility.

- What did Jesus say to the rich young man that reflected Jesus' boundaries? (Mark 10:17-27)
- What did Jesus teach blind Bartimaeus? (Mark 10:46-52)
- What did Jesus expect of the man at the pool of Bethesda?(John 5:1-9)
- What did Jesus show in regard to his own needs? (Mark 1:35; 4:37-41)
- What did Jesus teach about discernment and priorities? (Mark 1:29-31; 5:21-43; John 11:1-6)

All of this reflects the need for ongoing discernment in pastoral work in order to develop an awareness of when to respond to a need

49. E. L. Cole (1995), *Winners Are Not Those Who Never Fail but Those Who Never Quit*, London: Honor Books.

immediately, when to defer and when to refer to another. Some of us are good at responding spontaneously to an emergency situation; indeed we get an adrenaline rush which gives a buzz to the calling. But this doesn't necessarily mean that the response is right. Others are less adapted to crisis ministry and will more naturally delay any action. All of this shows how important it is to be as self-aware as possible so that we can control our natural temperaments. What marks our ministry out from other types of workers is that we soak our ministry in prayer, Bible study and fellowship, allowing the Holy Spirit to direct us and attune us to his will.

Today there is perhaps greater confusion of boundaries owing to the fact that more lay church members are actively involved in pastoral care. Previously the dog collar was a mark of identification and gave clarity to what was expected. But a lay minister turning up in a pastoral situation can be confusing unless there is an openness in stating what one's role is in such a situation. A uniformed ministry is neither better nor worse than someone in plain clothes; both bring their own benefits. But both can be equally confusing. Today there can be a positive or a negative reaction to someone in priestly dress. This is something I personally have grappled with in a university setting. At times I dress very casually to relate to the students, but increasingly I find that the university staff prefer me to wear my dog collar as they feel it instantly brings a religious presence. With or without the collar, I still need to be aware of my boundaries and be able to communicate clearly what I do in this context to remove any confusion or bias.

Boundaries are very clear in the counselling world where we have written and verbal contracts with people. But pastoral care has a greater number of grey areas to its ministry. Sometimes I find myself going from a pastoral encounter with a student or staff member to having to identify that we seem to be heading into a counselling situation. Then I clarify the difference and negotiate what the person wants. Both forms of support are acceptable but there needs to be clarity as to whether it is counselling or pastoral support that is taking place. This can be confusing for those who are pastors and counsellors, but for those who are purely pastoral workers there is less of an issue. Here you are caring and supporting, perhaps using counselling skills, in a supportive role.

Pastoral workers need a clear understanding of their boundaries. This requires clarity from the church as to what they think you are doing and clarity as to what the individual thinks you are involved in. There are a number issues to consider. For example, we need clarity about the use of our time, the number of hours we work per week. What is expected on Sundays also needs to be clarified as this can be seen as a grey area. It can be very hard for a staff worker to just worship without people wanting to talk about work issues.

We need to be very clear before we begin working with an individual about knowing when to end a session.

All workers with the church must be covered by insurance and be CRB checked.

There should be agreement in the church as to what is expected when working alone and in what context that should take place. An alarm button offers a greater feeling of security. Dress code should also be discussed.

It needs to be clearly communicated about how people gain access to your ministry, whether it be via the office, a telephone number or just on Sundays. This protects the pastor's family members and their privacy right from the beginning of the work.

Confidentiality within the staff team needs to be understood and clearly defined, otherwise it can become a gossip shop where a pastor becomes uncomfortable talking about people without their permission. Many pastors have dual roles within the church and the community – for example, the pastor may also be the local dentist, GP or local policeman, or may fulfil other roles within the church.

An understanding about what is acceptable physical touch in ministry needs to be talked about. Some churches are very touchy-feely at the sharing of the Peace, whereas others are far more reserved. The key is to make sure that the person being ministered to is at ease and has a choice.

In many professions today, touch has become unacceptable for fear of misunderstanding and potential legal accusations. Yet touch is something that has been at the heart of Christian expression over many centuries. We have touch when putting bread and wine into people's hands, the laying on of hands for healing, handshakes and hugs at the Peace in Communion, foot-washing on Maundy Thursday and simple physical contact at the end of a church service. A sensitive touch is an important part of the healing process for many who are ill or bereaved. This brings to mind a vicar who decided not to stand at the church door at the end of the services. He felt awkward and not sure what to say. However, a few weeks later an old lady expressed her sadness at not shaking hands with him. Eventually she expressed that he was the only person she ever touched or had physical contact with each week. We mustn't undervalue the contribution that the church makes in allowing healthy physical contact. The key is to make sure the contact doesn't violate a person's own boundaries.

There has been much negative publicity about the church in terms of sexual abuse and we need to be very clear about our parameters. It is easy to delude ourselves that our physical touch is for the other person's good when in reality it might be giving us erotic pleasure. Since ministry is often from a position of power, it is easier for a pastoral worker to initiate touch than someone who is feeling hurt and powerless. We need to ask permission of the person, whether it be a hug, laying-on of hands or a blessing. A person's right to choose not to be touched is sacrosanct in this situation. We must respect a person's right to say no for whatever reason. This includes passing the Peace in Communion.

When touch does take place, we need to develop a sensitive approach that leaves the person in a positive state rather than feeling alarmed. One can lay hands in a gentle way or in a way that is forceful and pushy. A hug can be given in a safe way that does not crush but rather brings the sensitive care that is needed. We have all received handshakes from people who decided to exert their masculinity and crush every bone in our hand. A disastrous thing to do if someone has arthritis or brittle bone disease! All of this shows how easy it is to abuse someone without realising. We therefore cannot be cautious enough in this area.

Counsellors are encouraged to be cautious with regard to self-disclosure with clients. Ministers find themselves in a world where they are often preaching and sharing stories from their own experiences. This can encourage them to be rather relaxed with one-to-one encounters. We need to ask ourselves why we have the urge to suddenly share a personal story. Personal disclosure can bring a degree of equality and help a person see that their experience is not unique. But disclosure can be used as a form of manipulation, coercing a person to a particular viewpoint. It can lead the other person to offer sympathy back and to be drawn into wanting a deeper relationship and over-involvement in your life.

Bear in mind also that the pastor works with an understanding of confidentiality and will not divulge what a person shares with them; however, this person is under no such restraints and might feel free to share your story with anyone. This might feel fine to you but there is a danger that a story will get twisted and misunderstood. If we ask them to keep it secret, we are confusing the roles of the pastor/carer and client/parishioner. A sensitive parishioner might pick up the vulnerability that is being shared by the pastor and want to offer affection in return. If the pastor has a need for attention, warmth and love, they may subconsciously use the parishioner to meet their own needs. This has led to a number of ministers' marriages breaking down and damaging individual lives as well as the church. If confused feelings are arising in such pastoral encounters, it is vital to quickly find confidential support and guidance. This is another reason why regular supervision is essential in the pastoral role. Warning signs must be heeded, such as when the pastor finds themselves preoccupied with thoughts and fantasies of a parishioner, finds excuses to visit someone, divulges more and more personal information, exchanges gifts, seeks physical contact and deliberately does not tell other colleagues who they are visiting.

A pastor can feel caught between a rock and a hard place when they begin to minister in the church. This is because they have often come out of the church's congregation so there is a confusion of identity. Is the pastor my friend with whom I can chat at any time or a professional who is distant and objective? The question a pastoral worker often asks is, 'How can I be real in this role and also be a real person?' We need to always remember that our role is primarily for the church community and not for ourselves. As we gain experience we learn how to journey with others and to use ourselves in the process. This requires a growing awareness of our own journey to wholeness that is separate from those for whom we care. As we understand our own wounds and hurts, realise where we are making adjustments because of our past and become knowledgeable about our personality type, we are better equipped to know how to use our 'presence' in a situation.

It is important to have discussed how a pastor would handle issues that arise relating to sexuality when visiting. There needs to be a discussion with a line manager to help identify when we are visiting people for our own benefit rather than theirs.

Finally, what we mean by confidentiality needs to be clarified. The art of learning to hold confidentiality and then knowing how and when to share information with others is essential. Leaks of confidentiality are fatal in the church. It is easy for a Christian to say to a friend, 'Don't tell anyone as it's confidential but do pray for X because they have Y problems.' Before you know it everyone knows this confidential piece of information.

The ACC has set out a very helpful ethical policy for churches with regard to their pastoral care policy (see Appendix 5). The Church of England 2003 Guidelines for the Professional Conduct of the Clergy can also be helpful.

Records

Electronically we are all governed by the Data Protection Act 1998. Records should not contain details of individuals without their consent. Information needs to be relevant and up to date. It should be kept safe and locked away securely. Information should not be passed to a third party without the person's permission.

Keeping notes is an important issue for pastoral carers. It helps us remember the names and details of the many people we meet. Notes kept should be as basic as possible. If any detail is included it should be coded so that others can't identify it. Counsellors use a coded technique which separates people's names from their details. This is then locked away separately.

If we hear an account of abuse or bullying, we need to keep careful account of what has been said, with dates. One day these notes may be required by a court.

It is good practice for a pastor to make an agreement with a colleague as to what to do if the pastor is moved on or dies in post. A written living Will should exist, authorising a person to destroy all of their records and notes. When a new person is appointed in a pastoral care post, the previous person's notes should not be passed on. We need to enter relationships without prejudice or influence from others.

Reflections

- Are your ground rules and boundaries identified and written down?
- With whom do you discuss these issues?
- How regularly are they reviewed?
- Have you ever had a negative experience because of the lack of clear boundaries?
- How do boundaries keep you safe in your ministry?
- How comfortable are you with touch in a church context?
- What is your church policy about records?
- For how long do you keep data?
- Where do you keep your records? Are they locked away?

Chapter 28
Endings

Endings are not bad things, they just mean that something else is about to begin.
(C. Joybell)[50]

As a play therapist, I found myself supporting a teenager who had an eating disorder. My original contract was to support the girl for ten weeks as we focused on building her self-esteem. However, after the sessions, there seemed to be no way forward for the teenager and no other offers of help or support. Her parents seemed desperate so I agreed to continue on an open-ended agreement. However, it soon became clear that if I wasn't clear with my boundaries, I would still be counselling the girl into adulthood. There had to be a point when I said enough was enough. I wasn't her saviour, nor was I the only person responsible for her. She and her parents also had responsibility, along with the NHS. After talking to the girl and her parents it was agreed that the sessions would end. I passed on to the parents suggestions of ways forward for them as a family. The choice was now theirs. I took the issue to my supervisor as I grappled with leaving a situation so incomplete. Sometimes you can only do so much and have to recognise when it is time to call it a day.

We have all sat through sermons that should have ended ten minutes earlier. Instead it feels as though we are hearing two or three sermons that seem to have no link and don't know how to end. Endings are rarely discussed in church. Hence we have well-meaning schemes still ticking on long after they should have closed. This applies equally to some charities and churches themselves. Somehow we seem to think that because something has started by God's encouragement it cannot come to a natural and timely closure. This equally applies to one-to-one ministry.

Unfortunately, many people in our society never experience what is a called a 'healthy ending'. We as pastors can bring both education and healing by implementing a positive closure of a relationship encounter. However, we must recognise that for some people the problem is that they have had repeated encounters of

50. C. Joybell (2010), *The Sun is Snowing: Poetry & Prose*, London: AuthorHouse.

relationships ending sourly and painfully. The last thing we want to do is to increase their negative experience by closing an encounter without a lot of thought and consideration. But inevitably all relationships come to closure. Therefore, right at the beginning of our ministry with someone, we need to put into place a procedure of how we will end the relationship. This might be to explain at the outset how many times we will visit the person and then keep to that contract. If it is to be extended, we should be clear how long the extension is for. Otherwise we can get trapped in a never-ending ministry that is leading nowhere and with no sight of the closing horizon. When we are approaching closure, we need to remind ourselves that this final stage may well be painful for the person but this is no reason to delay or defer. Just because something is painful, it doesn't mean it is not healthy.

In some instances, we may have to be big enough to take a person's anger and resentment towards us. It is their choice and if they choose to carry this with them afterwards, so be it. We have to maintain the position that it can never be healthy to just continue in a pastoral role endlessly. If we can't let go then we must recognise that perhaps we have a personal problem and need to take it to our line manager or supervisor or even seek counselling ourselves to get to the bottom of our own insecurities. Our ministry is always a part of the jigsaw of someone's life. We need a 'good enough' attitude to our work to be able to relinquish the contact.

Part of closure is to explain:

- Why the ending is appropriate and reflect upon what has been gained through the relationship
- How the final session might end and discuss other lines of support that are available
- How the boundaries will change such that we can meet and relate to the person in a natural way in church on Sundays without either party becoming dependent on each other. This needs to be discussed and agreed.

We must help those we care for to own their story and to grow and develop. If the person can see this, then they can hopefully see the ending as an achievement to be proud of. The person is beginning a new chapter of their lives, and we will always be a part of the previous chapter. Hopefully our good work will be carried forward as the person moves into new relationships.

We may need to acknowledge that we ourselves experience a reaction of grief, hurt, anger, guilt and closure just as much as the parishioner. We may need space to reflect spiritually, to refresh ourselves and give ourselves time before we fill the gap with another pastoral situation. Resistance by the parishioner is no reason to refrain from ending.

Reflections

- What is your experience of endings?
- Why do we find endings so difficult?
- How can the church face endings and be an example to the congregation?
- Why is it healthy that the church acknowledges someone when they step down from a position of responsibility in the church?
- How can you prepare for an ending when you first start a new ministry?

Chapter 29

Child protection

Who says I'm not under the protection of God?
(Adolf Hitler)[51]

One day I was asked if a respectable charity could rent out one of our church rooms. It was a charity that specialised in caring and supporting young boys in primary schools who seemed to have low self-esteem. Having checked the references and history of the charity, it was agreed that the organisation could use our premises. Unfortunately, weeks later I had the police at my door informing me that the leaders had been charged with assaulting children. Even though CRB checks had been carried out and the individuals had respectable jobs and references, children had been put at risk.

We hear so much about the subject and the need to have regular CRB checks that we may think it is all over the top. We also hear of stories of people who have been CRB checked who later on are found to be abusers. No system is perfect, but it is a step in the right direction. The history of the Church is that it has had an open door to all in the community. This means that the Church cannot ignore the issue of abuse or fail to take appropriate action when it has any concerns. Experiences like the one above show that sooner or later we will have to deal with a safety issue concerning a child or a vulnerable adult. Far better to have a clear policy beforehand and to be aware of what we would do in various situations than to wait for it to raise its head and catch us unprepared.

We need to acknowledge that all children are potentially vulnerable to abuse. Since the Church attracts children from a wide range of backgrounds it is inevitable that abused children are more than likely to be in our midst and that at some point in time adult abusers will be attracted into the congregation. This means we need to be even more cautious and aware. A church's policy for children should begin with a clear statement that it seeks never to leave a child with a legacy of emotional, psychological or spiritual damage. Any harm we may cause a child not only leaves lifelong issues for the child but undermines the credibility of the church and our personal ministry.

---

51. A. Hitler, from a speech in March 1933.

We need to reflect upon our own ethics and be well trained in church guidelines on this subject. Most church authorities offer regular training on this and will also offer examples of guidelines and policies. It is easy to think that we'll do it when we have a problem, but this is invariably too late. Problems arise when we are not appropriately trained and are unprepared.

The church needs to be as professional as possible when it comes to safety of the young and of vulnerable adults. It is recognised in law that, in regard to public interest and the prevention of harm, confidential information can be shared or ordered by a court. Clearly, if we believe a child or a vulnerable adult is being abused or mistreated, it is our responsibility to inform both our supervisor/ manager who should bring in the church organisational regional child safety adviser and either the police or social services.

If the church does get itself involved at whatever level with a child safety issue, it needs to seek to bring the love of Christ into the situation for all concerned. This means providing the appropriate support for children and their families. But it also means providing independent support for the abuser. This is challenging for any community but the church needs to be willing to go the extra mile in its appropriate care. Any priority must be with the child first, then their family. But if we can provide separate care for the abuser too, then we are bringing the gospel of hope and redemption. Many abusers have been abused themselves as children. This doesn't justify their actions but it does challenge the pastor to see the abuser in a broader light. It is essential that whoever is involved in caring for the child and family is not the same person who seeks to care for the abuser. Church members can very quickly take sides when issues like this arise so it is essential that the leadership of the church gives a clear statement so that gossip is restricted and the congregation are given confidence that the issue is being appropriately dealt with. This can stop people from meddling in issues that they are not trained in.

We need to keep sharing information about a situation to a minimum. Sharing objectively is permissible, but subjective accounts should remain confidential. This is known as the Chatham House Rule, where participants are free to share the information received, but the identity of the people involved remains secret.

Disclosure rules need to be clear. The history of the Church is not good here. Years ago priests believed that whatever was shared with them would remain fully confidential. This was a mark of a true priest.

Traditional canon law said that it was an offence to share anything that had been shared in a confessional situation bar treason.

Unfortunately, this has been used as a cloak to cover bad practice and evil. We need to be totally clear either at the beginning of an encounter or when a particular issue arises that concerns us about where we stand on the subject and the actions we will take if a serious disclosure takes place.

There is still some confusion as to whether law courts would respect a priest's silence on a particular disclosure in a confessional situation. For those of us who are priests, we need to have clarity as to whether someone is talking to us in a confessional way or in a more relaxed pastoral context. The key is to be clear with people about what we will or won't do with any information given. More is said about abuse in Chapter 52.

Finally, we need to be aware of the society in which we live, where litigation is now common. Any pastoral work involves an element of risk. The local church needs to provide appropriate insurance cover for all of their workers and have the policy on view. For their own protection, pastoral workers need to clarify with the church what this insurance covers.

Reflections

- How can your church make sure that religious abuse is prevented?
- Is the church too secretive with its policies and issues?
- How can you protect yourself from abuse?
- How do you or your church cope with grey issues rather than black and white approaches?
- Are you up to date with your regional authority and their protocols?

Chapter 30
Authority

We work for peace every time we exercise authority with wisdom and authentic love.
(Jean Vanier)[52]

Alice, the pastoral worker, has been informed by a church member that a couple have started to worship within the church that she should know about. Alice is hesitant to listen to gossip but finally hears the story of a couple with a chequered history within churches. Years previously the husband, who was a curate at the time, was accused of abusing a girl in his youth group. The church in question didn't believe the accusations so the girl and the family involved left the church and now worship in Alice's church. They are now alarmed, eight years later, to see this couple in the building. Over the last few years the couple have changed churches several times. The man was later accused in a different church and finally lost his licence to practise as a priest. He is extremely bitter and has been trying to exercise his ministry ever since. When asked why they had left their church and were now worshipping at Alice's church, they said they wanted to belong to the nearest church to where they lived. At the end of an evening service the situation became a confrontation between the man in question and the family who had been so affected by him years ago. Alice got caught in the middle and told the newcomer that perhaps he should go back to his old church and work through his issues. The man became very aggressive and was not far from physically attacking Alice. The leaders of the church met to decide what to do. Despite Alice feeling vulnerable and anxious whenever she met the man, the leaders felt that everyone should forgive each other and all be able to live together in the church. This infuriated the couple that had been in the church for eight years and left Alice feeling undermined.

There are at least two issues that come to mind with the dilemma above. First, who in the church will provide protection for those who are vulnerable and feel threatened? In other words, when someone behaves badly, is there ever a time that is appropriate to tell them that they are not welcome in the church? Some people seem to go from church to church causing problems and are not

52. J. Vanier (2008), *Essential Writings*, New York: Orbis Books.

willing to be under any church discipline or authority. Unless the church has clear parameters of what it will and will not accept, an individual can cause no end of harm in a congregation.

It is very honourable to hope that people can resolve their issues and get on in life as if nothing has happened. However, we have to be very clear what we mean by forgiveness. The 1662 Anglican service uses the language of contrition. This means that forgiveness is not just saying sorry but doing all that is required by the injured party to make amends. This might mean not worshipping where you have inflicted previous injury. It is one thing expecting people to forgive; it is another to expect people to sit in the church feeling insecure and unprotected. For Alice, it seems she lacks a leadership team that is willing to respect and protect their workers.

Secondly, how do we recognise inappropriate use of power and authority in a church? The word 'authority' brings with it a sense of power, which can either be a good thing or have negative connotations. We have all observed people who have exerted power with sensitivity and humility while others have lorded over people with their authority, and in a sense simply bullied people. The church, like any organisation, is open to both extremes. One might initially think that pastoral care has little to do with authority and power; after all, we simply want to help other human beings. But the question is how we bring about this care, and particularly how others see us exercising our ministry. It is easy to underestimate how powerful we are in our work. Sometimes our own insecurities make us project ourselves more forcefully upon others to enhance our diminished self-esteem. Our ability to receive constructive criticism is a good test of our own sensitivity. All of this is very important when we are dealing with people who often have low self-esteem. The very fact that you have been given by another the role of a pastoral carer gives you power.

- Reflect on times when you have seen power correctly and incorrectly used in the church.

One of the key tests of a good pastoral worker is how much the worker encourages empowerment in another person. The example of John the Baptist when he met Jesus is a wonderful example of someone knowing his or her place in life (John 3:30). John saw that his role was to nurture others until he wasn't needed any more. He willingly released his disciples to follow Jesus. This helps us to understand the role of a pastoral worker: our role is to help the less powerful person to nourish their self-awareness so that they grow in their own freedom and competence. Remember, our role is not to develop people to be dependent upon us; rather we are helping them to grow into healthy adulthood. This means we are to relate to people as equals, regardless of their maturity in faith; we are to draw out their unique strengths and gifts for the good of the church and the community.

To be able to do this we need to get in touch with our own feelings of times when we have felt vulnerable and powerless. It is by sitting here that we can begin to understand how people want to be treated. There are enough dictators within oppressive regimes in the world without such behaviour being present in the church.

The misuse of power and authority has been played out over history through the gender differences. We need to recognise that both the sexes may use power and authority differently, but both are equally capable of abuse of their position. One common misuse of pastoral care in both sexes is the need to be needed. By being a person who has something to offer another, it puts us in a position of authority that can stroke our ego. There are a number of people in the church who just can't stop taking on a caring role. They believe that to stop would somehow diminish their persona. If as a child a person only gained attention by helping others, it can easily become a habit driven not by love but by deep need. Some people desperately need to know everything that is going on in a church to feel secure. This is difficult to address when we are encouraging Christians to be caring. People who do far too much in a church will often quote Scripture to back up their excessive behaviour. They see themselves as part of the minority that set the example for others. However, those with eyes to see perceive that this is in fact not gospel driven but need driven.

When should you tell someone not to be caring? I guess the answer is when that care is carried out for one's own selfish purpose and creates a dependency upon the carer. Not that a person might see this initially. Perhaps a warning sign is when a person finds it extremely difficult to say 'no' when asked to do a job in church, or when a carer is upset when a person no longer requires their help or support. Of course, caring for others is very rewarding and fulfilling, but it must never be driven from inner insecurities. We can only help others to become self-aware, independent and mature if we are well along the road in our own self-development.

In churches it can often be thought that pastoral work is female work. This unfortunately diminishes the full impact of the church's ministry to people. The danger is that we are assuming pastoral ministry is a feminist role due to women's ability to sense and feel situations more than men. However, this is not recognising individuality and diversity in human beings. If we are going to care for the whole person, we need to have a ministry that reflects both the masculinity and the femininity within people.

Another aspect of authority being misused in pastoral care is when we use our role to either manipulate, dictate, harass or abuse vulnerable individuals. It may be a way of forcing our own particular Christian stance, arrogance that we know best or a way of boosting our ego. This is where we need clear job contracts and descriptions of what is acceptable behaviour. A disciplinary policy is important to prevent long-term problems in the church. A small church doesn't have to invent these guidelines; they are readily available from support agencies. Individuals need their voice to be heard if they are to be empowered in their lives. Equally, we have to recognise that the pastoral worker also needs their voice to be heard if they are to be protected from abuse, be it from church leaders or members.

Reflections

- How do you see ministry being expressed in your church?
- Are men and women treated equally?
- If there is stereotyping within your church, does it prevent individuals from using their full gifts?
- What benefits can be gained by men and women working together in pastoral care?
- Who controls those who become workaholics in the church?

Chapter 31
Discipline

Discipline is the refining fire by which talent becomes ability.
(Roy L. Smith)[53]

Discipline can be seen from two perspectives. There is the discipline of the church that you work for, be it paid or voluntary, and there is our own discipline that we exert upon ourselves. No one should work in the Christian kingdom without allowing oneself to be under another's authority. This might involve a line manager, having a clear contract of expectations, goals and annual targets and goals. This then allows for an annual appraisal and lays a foundation in case any difficulties arise during the year. It is important to have more than one person supporting the pastor in case relationship difficulties arise with the line manager. There should be a policy that explains disciplinary procedures in case of serious issues.

However, we also need self-discipline within pastoral ministry. We have already talked about ground rules and knowing our boundaries, but there is also the discipline that keeps us spiritually healthy, sane and growing in our ministry. This was modelled well by Jesus who would take himself and sometimes his disciples off to a place of reflection, calm and nourishment.

> 'Come away to a deserted place all by yourselves and rest awhile.' . . . And they went away in the boat to a deserted place by themselves.
>
> *Mark 6:31, 2*

Our self-discipline should involve a number of key components. It begins with a growing awareness of oneself. This comes about through personal reflection and is often fed by additional learning. We know that often our own presence gets in the way of our ministry. It is easy to have traits, behaviours and habits of thinking, speaking and acting in such a way that they form a block to our ministry. The Johari window is a simple way of understanding how we can enlarge our own self-awareness and push back the blind spots.

53. R. L. Smith (1960), *Towards an Understanding of the Carpenter's Son*, Nashville: Tidings.

Johari window	
Things I know about myself Things others know	Things others know Things I don't know
Things I know Things others don't know	Things I don't know Things others don't know

Figure 9: Johari Window

As we develop in our ministry, hopefully we will grow in our self-awareness. Figure 9 shows us how this opens up our self-knowledge: we are moving from areas unknown about ourselves to a growing openness where we become very self-perceptive and comfortable within our own skin.

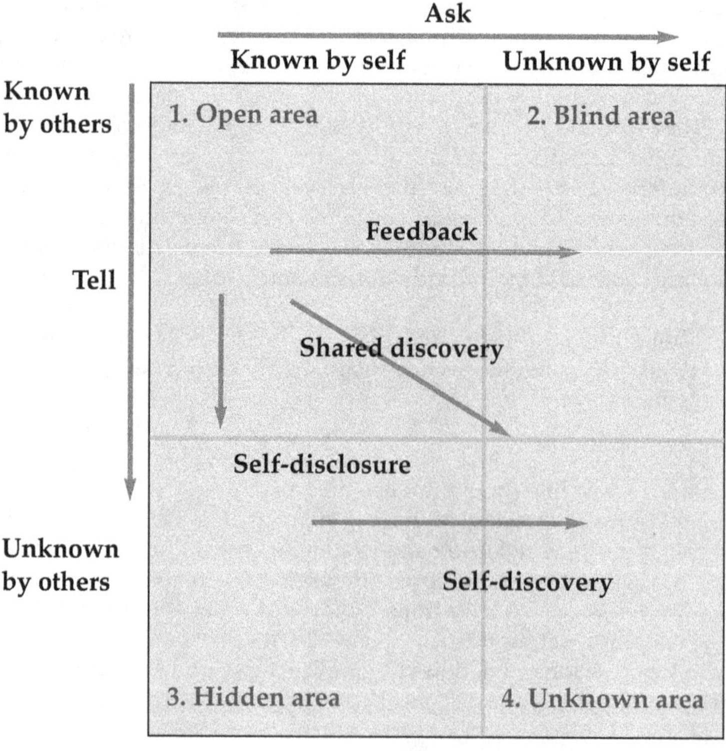

Figure 10: Developing our Ministry

Booking regular retreats that allow us to pray and reflect are essential to prevent us from becoming spiritually dry in our ministry. This might involve trying out new ways of praying or reading Scripture, for example. Choosing to sign up for retreats that might be slightly outside our comfort zone can be very rewarding and can induce spiritual growth.

Regularly checking the balance of our workload and how we are spending our time can be revealing. Work often tends to come at us and before we realise it we are spending a lot of time doing things we never intended. The computer was supposed to reduce our administration time, but in fact it has increased it with the ever-increasing number of emails we need to attend to. We need discipline to ask the questions about whether we have the balance right.

I have always endeavoured to study a different subject every year. It might be just reading a couple of books on a subject I don't know much about or actively going on a course. If we don't make a clear effort to focus on a new topic we will easily find that work just fills our time. This means that our ministry is increasingly relying upon all of our past training, but this may now be more and more out of touch for the current generation and situations that arise.

Reflections

- Do you acknowledge that the church has a right to discipline you?
- What would a disciplinary policy have to have in place to make you feel safe and comfortable in your role?
- What can you put in your diary to ensure that you have appropriate spiritual disciplines?
- What model and example do you want to set for the congregation in terms of your behaviour, use of time, balance of life and priorities?

Chapter 32

Dangers in pastoral care

Back where I come from there are men who do nothing but good deeds all day. They are called good deed doers.
(The Wizard of Oz)[54]

There is a great attractiveness in being engaged in pastoral care. Yet this appeal has its dangers as it supplies us with power that we can use to cloak our own deep personal needs.

Caution necessary

Although most ministers experience a clear sense of a spiritual calling into their work, psychologists have identified particular characteristics in the make-up of ministers. For many, there is a deep need to be loved. This can naturally produce ministers who are workaholics; they just can't stop going the extra mile to have the attention of the flock.

However, it is not just clergy who have this tendency. Any caring organisation can attract people who enter the role because of a deep personal need. I find that students who choose to study psychology at university often come with considerable hang-ups, which they are seeking to resolve within themselves. This is just as true for those who engage in pastoral care. Now there is nothing wrong with this as long as we recognise it within ourselves. Once truly acknowledged, it should provide us with the ability to assess others without our personal needs getting in the way. There are at least two ways of knowing whether we are aware of ourselves: an ability to self-reflect in a situation and a willingness to ask others for their perspective. The fact that we recognise our own frailty and vulnerability can be beneficial in helping us to remain humble and approachable to others. We are humans who depend upon the eternal God for our very existence. We will never outgrow God's care; we will always require pastoral care from our heavenly Father. We are therefore just like the one we reach out to care for. It is one needy person reaching out to another.

---

54. F. Baum (1982), *The Wizard of Oz*, London: Puffin.

The danger is when we see people who are unaware of what is driving them into the pastoral care business. Here a caring act can do damage as it can lead to dependency and deepen the need and drive within the carer.

Pastoral care provides a wonderful opportunity to care for individuals. However, it also opens up the door to all kinds of abuse, manipulation and power games. People who need to be needed often find themselves drawn to a church's care ministry. Of course, pastoral carers reap the reward of caring for others and this must not be denied, but when people minister to others mainly out of their own emotional need, this cripples both the carer and the cared for and creates an unhealthy church. In this situation no one is the winner; all are weakened to some degree or other.

A basic knowledge of transactional analysis might be helpful here. This looks at the ways we behave with others, particularly whether we behave in a childlike, parental or adult manner. One particular aspect of this approach is the drama triangle, which is common in churches. This is where people perform a particular role ranging from persecutor, rescuer or victim. Victims present themselves as being unable to cope by themselves, appearing not to have the resources to handle their problems. Feelings can overwhelm them such that they are unable to think clearly or act in a practical way. Along comes the rescuer who is genuinely concerned to help the victim. Unfortunately the rescuer begins to take over the situation and takes full responsibility for the problems. This might seem initially to help the victim, but in reality it still leaves the victim helpless. In the end, only the victim can solve his or her own problems. The rescuer can feel rewarded for intervening and feels needed. However, they need the victim to remain a victim if they are to keep receiving this false reward. This means that the rescuer is focusing on the victim rather than tackling his or her own personal needs.

Often a persecutor is also involved. The persecutor is someone who is very self-absorbed and uses others to fulfil their needs. This means that they often act in a way that diminishes others, particularly people who are prone to be victims. Again, for a persecutor to lift themselves up they need to keep the victim in their place. This gives power to the persecutor. These three roles are not fixed, and people can find themselves swapping roles.

A victim can keep on demanding the support of a rescuer, who might then begin to feel a victim. The rescuer will then begin to resent the victim and so start to persecute the victim. They then begin to feel guilty and seek sympathy for themselves, just like the victim.

A persecutor can feel guilty for pressurising a victim and can flip into rescuer mode or seek sympathy as a victim, claiming that no one understands their pressures.

If you reflect on any leadership committee meeting in a church you may well have observed this kind of unhealthy behaviour. It reminds me of the story Jesus told about the unclean spirit wandering restlessly (Luke 11:24-6). It keeps looking for a resting place and when it struggles to find peace it returns to where it has resided before. Unless we fill our lives with a new spirit and awareness, we will find that people will constantly pull us back into this negative game.

What all of these positions have in common is that no one wins or moves on in a healthy way. One of the three must take responsibility for handling and changing their own difficulties and encourage the other two to do the same. This is easier said than done, as the other two are very likely to try their best to keep the person in role to bolster up their own position. Sometimes it takes a fourth person to intervene and break the triangle. With the right intervention, all three people can find themselves in a win–win position.

A victim can acknowledge that they are vulnerable and that they have the power and ability to do something about it by seeking appropriate help to release them into independence and growth.

A rescuer can learn to empathise without taking over. They now become an effective carer, releasing the victim to grow and develop independently. The rescuer is now more in touch with their own feelings and needs and can therefore strike the right balance between giving out and taking in. Many church people are very good at giving out to others but they find it very difficult to receive. This imbalance needs to be addressed in the church with carers who are just as capable of being cared for themselves.

A persecutor can begin to recognise their own needs and give themselves some priority time, such that they don't need to bully or minimise others. They can become assertive in a way that is not damaging to others, and will now be able to negotiate and listen to a different point of view without feeling threatened.

Stephen Karpman provides a helpful picture (overleaf) of what a healthy position should look like.[55]

The example that Jesus sets us is one who was able to allow us to make our own choices. He didn't rescue us by force, persecute us or make us into victims. There was no control or manipulation of people; rather a healthy respect of the autonomy that God has given to human beings. So often it is our fellow man who chooses to persecute, victimise and indulge in rescuing.

---

55. I. Steward & V. Joines (1987), *TA Today: A New Introduction to Transactional Analysis*, Melton Mowbray: Lifespacing Publishing.

Victim – vulnerable	Rescuer – carer	Persecutor – assertive
I acknowledge my suffering.	I can empathise with others and be aware of my own needs at the same time.	I can get my needs met while respecting other people.
I can solve my problems.	I can decide how much to help without feeling guilty.	I can change things for the better.
I have the resources or can seek appropriate help.	I can find out what people want before taking action on their behalf.	I can be assertive without putting other people down all the time.
I can feel and think at the same time.	I can give myself priority.	Others have the right to disagree with me.
I can attune into my feelings and work out what they are telling me.	I can allow other people to do their own thinking.	Others have the right to do things differently to me.
I can assess the situation and what I need to do next.	I can allow other people to make up their own minds.	There are more ways to solve problems than my own way.
I am OK.	I am OK even when I'm not doing things for others.	I am OK and don't need to get my own way all the time.

Figure 11: The Healthy Drama Triangle

Picking up someone else's baggage

Getting involved in another's life can be highly rewarding, but also very dangerous. We are invited deep into the soul of another that others rarely see. Yet the close encounter can also release imaginary thoughts and desires so that both parties can be engulfed and destroyed. It is not necessarily the obvious visible sexual attraction that is the danger, but the nakedness of someone who reveals all to you and to you alone. This intimate encounter can unleash a legion of thoughts, desires and fantasies.

A recognised occurrence for counsellors is something called 'transference' and 'counter-transference'. However, it is just as likely to be present for pastors filling this role within the community. They can find themselves with a vague sense of hopelessness, guilt, resentment and a spectrum of other feelings resulting from a pastoral visit. These feelings can seem hard to pin down, and it can be even harder to identify the cause.

Pastoral relationships can evoke memories from childhood relationships. This is particularly true of authority figures in our lives. When this happens we might suddenly feel helpless, vulnerable and childlike. It can be an embarrassing situation to find yourself in. As a young adult I would often find myself blushing for no apparent rhyme or reason. It was only as I worked through my childhood experiences that I began to understand what was at the root of this reaction. Some situations were taking me right back to an emotional memory that was in my deep subconscious and triggered the glowing red face.

Other reactions that pastors might find themselves having are daydreaming when they are with individuals, reducing contact time with people, withdrawing into their home, or forgetting appointments. Others become intensely involved with parishioners, continually going the second and third mile and become unable to switch off from their ministry. Their faith justifies their behaviour, and this action is often then affirmed and encouraged by the parishioners.

All these reactions can simply be automatic responses to the dilemmas we find ourselves in through our involvement in Christian ministry. Ministry is costly and often seems to attach itself to our inner emotions in a way we struggle to understand. We find ourselves struggling to control our feelings and fail to predict how we will react in new situations. This is counter-transference, where we tune in to all the pain, feelings and confusion of those we minister to and then project them back to the person. If, in a pastoral encounter, I find myself feeling confused, agitated, restless, frightened or angry, I must ask the question, 'Are these my own uncomfortable feelings or am I responding to the other person's experience?'

We all have our own transference issues that hook us. When I was a maternity hospital chaplain, I was at the stage of life where my wife and I had one child and my wife was pregnant with our second. All of this hooked me into the dilemmas of parents of neo-natal babies. I could very quickly identify with parents as I reflected on what it would be like for my wife and me to have a premature baby. This assisted me in the care of others but it also influenced my thoughts concerning my family.

I have a number of other 'hooks' that I have to be aware of that affect me in ministry. They have evolved over time and reflect my own life experiences – for example, people with headaches, those in their fifties who are ill, drug issues and, since many of my relatives have died of cancer, just the very word can have a subtle influence upon me. We have to realise that it is normal to get 'hooked'; the danger is where we don't recognise the vague gnawing feelings of discomfort that reveal that we are 'hooked'. If we are unaware that we are hooked, we are unable to take appropriate action. My own life experiences can be a great boost to my awareness of another's story, but I also have to be aware of when they interfere with my work.

It has been recognised that this reaction is particularly true when we are dealing with illness and death. If the person we are caring for mirrors our own past experiences of life, or the person reflects what could occur for ourselves in the future, or if we see similarities that correlate to our own age group, then we are more likely to attune into their situation and experience their pain.

One of the great challenges for ministers is how to be truly present with people as they struggle with fear, emptiness and trying to make meaning of their lives in the midst of tragedy and pain. As Christians, we look to the example of Christ who manifests the depth of what it is to share in the world's sufferings. As church workers, we seek to identify with Christ's suffering as we draw close to those who are suffering in our community. It is only as we empathise and draw close that we are able to bring a new perspective to the situation and a glimmer of hope. But this is not easy, which means that we can have a tendency to retreat into our professional objective skin. Here, we can appear to be aloof and distant. It is easy, for example, to slip into the mode of discouraging a person from shedding tears. This is the opposite of what many grief specialists would recommend. A healthier practice is to encourage a person to go deeper into the tears by inviting them to share their thoughts about the tears. It is here that we can begin to get a handle on understanding what the tears represent and therefore where we can offer appropriate support.

Lament is well represented in the Old and New Testament. It constitutes addressing God, complaining, petitioning and bringing motivation to a situation. The Psalms are full of prayers crying out in difficult situations (for example, Psalms 22, 74, 126 and 143).

At the heart of lament is an ability to give rise to the telling of the narrative about the pain and suffering. Here we are allowing the subconscious suffering and pain to be experienced in our consciousness, where its power can be diminished. By allowing a person to express their pain and suffering we can help them in several ways.

Firstly, we allow someone to put up an umbrella of safety, to lay out their complaint in a safe, managed way that can allow movement and healing. It places the cry in the context of another and of God himself. As we accompany a person in their pain, we help to reduce their loneliness.

Secondly, we make sure that the complaint is not minimised but rather given its full weight of merit. It is very hard for anyone to move forward until they have been truly heard. Here we provide a safe space for the person to formulate his or her own language of expression.

Thirdly, we bring a painful situation into a relationship dynamic, both with ourselves and with God. Relationships are never static; they are always moving in one direction or another. Hopefully this relationship will be one that goes from pain to pleading to final praise. However, this can be a long, drawn-out relationship journey with many twists and turns along the way.

I think of Jesus in the garden of Gethsemane (Mark 14), where he felt alone in the pain he was bearing. The disciples journeyed with him in prayer as they tried to understand what Jesus was going through, but they seemed to struggle to go all the way in comprehending Jesus' burden of pain. There seemed to be an attitude in the disciples of wanting to 'do' rather than 'be' with Jesus. It's a tendency that all professionals can slip into very easily.

To sit with someone when they are at death's door or in deep pain and not be able to 'do' anything can be frustrating. We can find ourselves fidgeting, looking at our watch, frowning, tapping our foot or hand and are likely to feel relieved when we are dismissed. It is very hard for us to be with people when all we can offer is our presence, so we can easily slip into evasion, false assurance, denial, avoidance and flight. All of these strategies provide a way of protecting us from being overwhelmed by feelings of our own mortality, anxiety and stress and, ultimately, burnout. So, armed with our education, skills and techniques, we find ways of engaging purely with our head and bypassing the heart. Pastors are encouraged to wear the whole armour of God as they minister (Ephesians 6:10-20). Unfortunately, we can also put on a defence uniform that might protect us initially, but in the long run doesn't help the parishioner, ourselves or the kingdom of God.

The pastor's armour of defence

Emotions experienced	Our reaction	A positive response
Helplessness	• We become over or under-involved. • Clock watching. • Thinking about other things when with the person. • Thinking of reasons why people don't need a visit.	• Being willing to acknowledge our helplessness. • Sensitively enquiring whether this is also how the person is feeling.
Embarrassment	• The problem can seem so great that we protect ourselves by not fully 'seeing' the person.	• Seek to engage in order to empathise more fully.
Denial	• Hoping the situation will just go away. • We don't talk about the issue, thinking that we will just make it worse. • Offering misguided advice. • Reassuring the person that the problem isn't so bad.	• Recognising the feeling of wanting to run away. • Acknowledging that we haven't any easy answers.
Anger	• We might label the person as a 'problem'. • Sarcastic comments. • Putting the person down.	• Recognising and acknowledging to the person that the situation makes us feel angry. • Sharing our feelings with another person who will listen.
Sorrow	• Withdrawing into our own deep sorrow and feeling sorry for ourselves. • Becoming the sufferer, rather than the one we are visiting.	• Recognising that as we feel sorry for another, we are also feeling sorry for ourselves. • Making sure we do not become a burden to the other person.
Restlessness	• Wanting to bring good out of the situation such that we become pushy or dictatorial, seeking some positive outcome that makes us feel better.	• Staying with the person's agenda and not our own. • Taking our restless emotions to a counsellor or supervisor to talk through.

Figure 12: The Pastor's Armour of Defence

When we learn to attune into these feelings, we can develop an awareness of how to handle them appropriately. This might mean we convey what we are feeling back to the person in such a way that it leads to a deeper discussion of the situation. However, it is not always appropriate to place this discussion on the shoulders of someone who might be already overwhelmed by their situation. We need a protocol of deciding when to share and when to choose to take our reactions to a colleague, counsellor or supervisor.

Firstly, will the information be of benefit to the parishioner? Will it raise information that is new to the person or bring clarity to his or her own feelings? In some situations it can lead to a deeper, more open discussion about how a person is truly feeling. This can enrich our theological discussion, inform our prayers and allow a person to feel more fully understood and supported.

Secondly, if I share my feelings, will it lead to a change of focus away from the person to myself and my own needs? A common mistake in pastoral visiting is to become more focused on ourselves, our stories and our opinions rather than on the parishioner concerned.

Thirdly, could we cause harm by sharing our thoughts? Have we the time, experience and confidence to handle what might result? Could the situation become so upsetting for us that we might be unable to continue in the relationship? Perhaps the person already has others who are supporting them from this open emotional perspective. The person may not be looking to you for that kind of support or encounter.

Fourthly, is this the right time to share and disclose our own feelings? We may prefer to just allow our feelings to educate us as to how the person might be feeling. We also have to be ready to acknowledge that we could be on the wrong track and have totally misread the situation.

Finally, when we have recognised the feelings that are rising within ourselves, we can, without disclosure, raise open questions as to whether the person is experiencing feelings of deep pain such as helplessness, confusion, anger, despair, etc. In this way, the person is free to engage in this line of discussion or not without fear of rejecting our personal feelings.

I recall visiting a dear member of my church in a nursing home. The lady had recently fallen and was now unable to care for herself. All through my hour-long visit, the lady begged me to take her home; she was convinced the staff were punishing her. I had a duty to check that she was being properly cared for, but once assured, all I could do was to sit with the lady, offer my presence, pray with and for her and share our common humanity. I had to fight the urge within me to excuse myself and run; I had to control my fears and feelings of helplessness, control my guilt about being unable to change this lady's perspective and control my anger at the mess of it all. Perhaps I was picking up all her inner feelings of fear, guilt and anger. I had a choice: I could either see these emotions in myself as an obstacle and so go and do something else that made me feel better, or recognise them for what they were – an opportunity to stay connected with a person in their suffering.

It is as we listen and feel another's story that we are able to reflect upon what the situation tells us about the person's view of the world, of God, of the Church, of their family and of the professionals who care for them.

When we reflect upon Jesus' ministry, we see that he may have helped people with his miraculous interventions, but what took place first of all? Jesus was exposed to people who brought him their shame, rage, trauma, anguish, loneliness and hopelessness. Jesus seemed to be able to draw out of a person how they viewed their illness or dilemma. Jesus at no time gave the impression that he was overwhelmed or uninterested in a person's story. Indeed, he seemed to be able to get beyond people's avoidance techniques. This seemed to come about through the way he developed an intimacy with the person by his compassionate understanding of the situation. Intimacy can be a scary word. We tend to keep it for marriages and very close relationships. Here I am using it to mean 'coming close to a person such that we accept the state of being of that person'. This can be a powerful position to be in and can raise all kinds of feelings within, be they physical, emotional or spiritual.

In the end, the more time we are willing to invest in our own healing, the greater we will be able to 'be' with a person in their suffering. It is here that we find the beginning of the road that leads to hope, change and acceptance. At the very least, we will be able to offer a person the assurance that they are not alone in their pain.

Reflections

- When have you felt vulnerable in a pastoral situation?
- Can you reflect upon the past week and notice when you have been child-like, parent-like or adult-like?
- Are you aware of church members who 'rescue' people?
- Can you recognise when you are picking up other people's feeling and emotions that tap into your own story?
- Have you had situations that have prevented you from relaxing and having a peaceful night's sleep? What does this say to you?

Chapter 33

Supervision

Supervision is an opportunity to bring someone back to their own mind, to show them how good they can be.
(Nancy Kline)[56]

My wife and I were looking for a church to settle into, having recently moved to a new area. We were invited out for a meal with a couple who had also invited the local curate and his wife. As we listened to what the church was like, it soon became evident that the curate just wanted to complain about the vicar.

John was a middle-aged, new curate in a well-established church. However, only months into the training post it was clear that all was not going well between the vicar and the curate. After the first year the curate had gathered a few disgruntled members of the congregation to support him in his moans and groans about the vicar. Whether they were justified or not, it caused a division in the church. Before long, a few people were praying for the vicar to leave, no doubt hoping that the curate would take over. My wife and I wondered whether this was the type of church we wanted to settle in and began looking elsewhere. In the end, the curate left his training early.

What lessons did the curate learn about authority, submission, respect and being a deacon called to serve? What did the vicar learn about training curates, clear contracts and working agreements? What did the church learn about true Christian leadership, humility, service, accountability, gossip and respect?

This story is, sadly, not unique. Christian leaders are given an incredible amount of autonomy. This may provide great innovation and creativity but it can also leave room for pride and stubbornness and lead to unchristian behaviour. I can think of two curates in one church I knew who used to argue and compete with each other about who was more senior. On Sunday mornings they would compete as to who would walk out first behind the vicar to show their superiority to the congregation. Alas, sometimes the church fails to be a light to the community.

Appropriate supervision is an area in which the church could learn much from professional, even secular, organisations.

---

56. N. Kline (1999), *Time to Think: Listening to Ignite the Human Mind*, London: Cassell Ltd.

When we engage with individuals we can quickly find ourselves engulfed by a person's problems. It can be hugely demanding to carry confidential information and serious issues that are taking place in people's lives. We can easily become so wrapped up in others that we struggle to see the wood for the trees. It is not uncommon for a person's problems to raise issues in the pastoral carer's life, either from the past or present. It can be hard to put aside one's own needs to listen and support another. This is why all pastoral carers need a supervisor that they can see regularly. This is not their line manager in the church, but someone from outside who can support them in confidence. The supervisor needs to be someone who is trained and experienced in counselling skills and who is particularly aware of transference and counter-transference issues.

To practise as a qualified counsellor, a counsellor needs not only to have qualifications and training but also to be willing to be counselled themselves as well as have regular supervision. This ensures that the counsellor is safe to practise ethically, with another experienced counsellor who can challenge, guide, correct and, if necessary, report to a professional body for malpractice. We may feel that the pastoral worker is not trained to that level of responsibility, but should the church not be aiming high for its workers? Regular supervision has given me a sense of safety in my practice. I have learned much from supervisors who practise in different ways to the way I practise and who have at times enabled me to see where I was failing to see a situation correctly. I wonder how many situations that develop in churches could be nipped in the bud if appropriate supervision were in place. It enables an outside, objective body to say challenging things that allow the pastor to self-reflect. It also allows things to be said in confidence, knowing that they will not get back to the congregation. This prevents issues from simmering and helps pastors to reflect on more appropriate ways of handling situations within the church.

If a pastoral worker is encouraged and expected to have an internal line manager, an external supervisor and a spiritual director, they are far less likely to burn out and to feel valued within the church. In this way, in the end, everyone wins.

Reflections

- What kind of supervision does your church provide?
- How do you think supervision would help you?
- Should the church pay for supervisors and spiritual directors?
- What problems might have been prevented in your past experience if you had had an external supervisor?

Appendix 6 gives examples of issues that ought to be addressed in a pastor's contract.

Chapter 34
Training

I never teach my pupils; I only attempt to provide the conditions for them to learn.
(Albert Einstein)[57]

In an ideal world, a person would be trained and then gain experience before they themselves train others. Alas, life is never quite that simple. However, all pastoral care workers should be concerned about their own training and also be willing to engage in training others to work alongside them.

Church organisations ought to have various protocols in place to provide a balanced training experience. We hear many stories of trainees leaving posts early because of disagreements which perhaps could have been prevented if the appropriate protocols had been followed. This is a large subject, but there are three main aspects to be considered if pastoral care is to be performed effectively. Issues that apply to a trainee may also relate to lay pastoral workers.

Firstly, it is very important that the trainer and trainee are clear about what will be involved. Too often I have heard of Anglican curates going to posts that were just not suitable for them – there was simply a mismatch between the curate and the church or with the incumbent. Both parties have to take responsibility for this. There is a pressure for students in their last year of training at theological college to find a curacy post, and it can be understandable in the circumstances if they think that a particular post is 'good enough'. Not enough time and consideration are taken to understand and appreciate the intensity of a working relationship between a church leader and a trainee. It is not just a job but also a way of life, and a belief system that, when it goes sour, can have long-lasting effects. To demonstrate proper care of a trainee, there should be careful consideration by the church leader and the church lay leaders about the appropriateness of a particular trainee and whether they would fit into the life of the church. If a church chooses to train a person who comes from a different cultural background or Christian belief system, extra provision should be introduced to

57. A. Einstein (1879–1955).

support them, as they are very likely to encounter problems during their time with the church.

Clear job descriptions need to be produced so that there is clarity as to what is expected of the trainee. Too often potential church leaders are treated as glorified youth workers, and they inevitably become frustrated and disillusioned. Equally, it needs to be made clear from the beginning that the trainee is in a 'training post' and is not the leader of the church. Potential leaders are not always easy to train! But true leaders must learn what it means to be humble and to be under authority, as Jesus' disciples discovered. Many people today would have walked out on Jesus because they didn't like where he was heading. If a person takes a training post for 3–4 years, the church leaders need to make it very clear that they will not tolerate a trainee causing any divisions in the camp. This kind of behaviour is not a sign of Christian leadership. Trainees need to be helped to realise that, even if they don't like what is happening in the church, they can set a godly example by sticking to their agreement and using the time to learn from the negatives as much as from the positives. Unless trainees learn to work through issues, they simply echo today's society where people seem to bail out of any relationship when it becomes difficult or uncomfortable.

If the trainee is married, there needs to be clarification about the role and expectations of the partner, both by the church and by the couple. Some couples enter ministry with the belief that they will share their ministry, but the church may have no expectations of the spouse. Unless these issues are made clear at the beginning, misunderstandings can arise that may cause resentment from the partner for what they see as over- or under-involvement. There also needs to be a discussion about how both parties view confidentiality within a marriage. Some couples enter ministry with the belief they will share everything. This can be disturbing if there is a lack of confidence by the church in the ability of the husband or wife to keep things confidential.

Secondly, it is important to think about the ongoing pastoral support of the trainee while they are with the church. I have already talked about the importance of supervision. This certainly applies to trainees: they need both a line manager within the local church and someone external who can help them work through issues of a work or personal nature.

There needs to be acknowledgement of issues that might arise if the trainer and trainee are of different genders. Issues of power, assertiveness and recognition of different forms of leadership styles need to be aired and discussed. If the trainee is of the opposite gender to the trainer, the church needs to provide an additional person from the church of the same gender as the trainee to support them.

One of the purposes of a trainee post is to help an individual to identify their gifts, strengths and weaknesses. This requires an open, honest and safe relationship such that the trainee can feel both encouraged and affirmed while exploring areas to develop.

It can easily be assumed that a trainee will work all the hours God sends or will simply copy the hours that the church leader fulfils. This can be an area for considerable conflict. It helps if this is clarified before the appointment is made. A church needs to recognise that there is more than one way to work in church ministry, and a trainee needs to be given the grace and freedom to not copy the failings of the church leader. It is important that we are all enabled to find our own way of developing a fulfilling ministry that is honourable to God and the church. To achieve this there needs to be a discussion with the lay leaders as to what is expected of a married or single person, recognising that each will have their own particular pressures. The church can easily fall into the trap of following the world's concepts of good working practices.

- What is an honourable number of hours to work?
- What would set a good example to the congregation and community?
- How much time should a leader have to nurture their family?
- What are the particular needs of a single person having to look after their own home and have time to develop friendships and other interests?
- How many hours should a person work in a day?
- What constitutes 'work' in a church?
- Is entertaining a friend in the church, work?
- What is acceptable as appropriate holidays / retreats / days off?
- What are the boundaries with regard to answering the telephone, emails, etc?

Unless these issues are raised and discussed right at the beginning, they are just time bombs waiting to erupt.

Thirdly, the church needs to recognise that a trainee is simply that – someone who has come for training and may eventually move on. This means that they have particular requirements that the church needs to support.

This affects at least three areas. For the trainee, there is the complexity of making friendships knowing that they will be moving on and will have to let go of most of these attachments. Trainees need to be encouraged to maintain previous friendships outside the parish that they can preserve in the long term. Otherwise they will find it very difficult to move on when the time comes and will be constantly coming back to the church, which will not help new trainees to settle in, lay people to learn to let go or the ex-trainee to settle in a new parish. The alternative is that some will go through ministry with no significant attachments and friendships. Lonely ministers do not make good leaders, as they will become distant from the congregation. Trainees need to be helped to understand this dynamic and to reflect on how it is affecting them.

The trainee needs to be trained for the good of their long-term ministry and not just to fulfil a particular need of the local church. This means that some clarity is required about how the trainee will be given a variety of responsibilities over the duration of their training. They need an opportunity to chair leadership meetings, to see projects through from beginning to end and to reflect upon them, to lead significant events within the life of the church, to be encouraged to engage in ongoing educational training and actively encouraged to read. A wise pastoral tutor encouraged me to make sure that every year in my ministry I would embark on some specific training or active reading in a particular area. I have found that this approach has served me well in keeping me fresh in my faith and ministry. People often ask about how we are to find the time for such things, but I believe it is to the detriment of our ministry if we don't. It is unfair to ourselves and the church to allow ourselves to run dry on outdated thinking, sermons and pastoral tools.

Continually repeating the style of ministry that you were given as a trainee is no way for the Church to grow in today's ever-changing world. God's kingdom is never static, which means that our understanding of Scripture, of the Church and of God's kingdom needs to be viewed with fresh insight for every new generation.

The local church has a responsibility not only to train a person for their church but for the wider Church. This means that when a trainee is coming to the end of their placement, there needs to be a clear review about what additional training the person requires to be a rounded Christian, let alone a significant leader in the church. Problems and issues that are not faced in the first three years because of inadequate training, poor review procedures or fear of conflict result in ministers simply repeating the same failings time and time again. Issues should be tackled early on in the local church in such a way that allows the trainee to feel safe enough to reflect, change and grow. Once they are released into their own leadership, it is difficult to rein in maverick leaders. A local church may recognise that it is not capable of providing the full rounded training required and may need to release the trainee for a short placement elsewhere to complete their training.

The old concept of apprenticeship, where a craftsman passed on their skill and learning to a trainee, is one that still operates in the church. This was the model that Jesus used with his disciples. However, a common factor for trainee pastors is that their line managers (usually church leaders) are often not very pastoral themselves. This means that they either train inadequately or in the wrong way. In the end it is up to the trainee themselves to take responsibility and shape their own training. This might be with other capable lay members of the church or with other trainees in other churches doing similar roles.

A vital aspect of training that we can so easily miss is not related to professionalism, knowledge or skill base; rather it is how to be Christlike as a leader. Jesus showed us how to balance power and leadership alongside a sense of vulnerability. This is a unique trait to Christianity that we need to foster in our leaders. Jesus began and ended his ministry in a state of helplessness. As a baby he was as vulnerable as any other baby in the world. Days or weeks later, many babies and young children were slaughtered. At the end of Jesus' life he endured the death of a common thief, stripped of all pride, dignity and respect. During his life he lived a simplistic lifestyle with an ability to relate to all types of people from different backgrounds and cultures. The apostle Paul put it well when he said that,

> God chose what is weak in the world to shame the strong.
>
> *1 Corinthians 1:27*

Jesus constantly identified with the weak, whether it was the lepers, the blind or the outcasts. Yet he also empowered them through his healing. He used his power to draw out the best in others so that they might reach their full potential. He shared this power with others as he equipped the disciples to go out and do likewise, yet in a humble and simple way. The disciples were able to see this strength in action in the way Jesus related to people in authority who were seeking to push and manipulate him. He challenged people's misuse of authority and beckoned others to use their power for the good of others. This strength and vulnerability was supremely expressed in the example Jesus set us when he knelt down and washed the disciples' feet. Jesus was certainly not a doormat to the parishioners' needs and fancies; neither did he just lord it over people to the detriment of their well-being. This balance between being in leadership with responsibility and authority and offering this ministry with humility and dignity is an art that needs to be taught, mirrored and encouraged in all trainees.

In the end, churches can be all too pleased to receive an additional worker and see it purely from their own perspective. But what better ministry can a church have than producing good, rounded leaders who will have long and full ministries in the Christian church, all because the local church people provided wise and carefully thought-out training?

Reflections

- Were you trained appropriately before you engaged in pastoral ministry?
- What do you feel you lack that would equip you more fully for ministry?
- Is there a church budget for your ongoing training?
- How can you make sure the person who replaces you receives the appropriate support and training?
- What aims do you have for the forthcoming year to develop your ministry?
- How can you ensure your ministry is Christlike?
- How can the whole church be responsible for an apprentice's training rather than just the leader?

Chapter 35

Staff meetings

Even though I walk through the darkest valley . . .
your rod and your staff – they comfort me.
(Psalm 23)

Many people think it must be wonderful to be working as a Christian in a Christian organisation. There is the assumption that the usual issues and tussles that develop in a secular environment won't happen in a Christian charity. It is true that it is something very special to work with like-minded Christians who support, pray and want the best for your ministry. Unfortunately, however, when you get a group of people together, Christians or not, there is sometimes a tendency for people to veer off course from how they should behave.

Christian staff meetings are no different. They tend to occur once a week and begin with a morning office or Bible study and prayer. Some are brave enough to talk about the Sunday service, although this can be difficult with the preacher/leader of the service and/or music leader in the meeting. Diaries are checked, future planning is discussed and then personal issues are raised. You would think that there is very little that can go wrong. Yet I have heard from a good number of Christian workers who hate staff meetings. This could be because they become gossip shops, where people are talked about without their permission, or everything under the sun is discussed except the real issues in the church. Sometimes people are afraid to raise a particular issue in case it is seen as personal criticism, or lots of things are discussed and then the leader does their own thing and leaves everyone else in the dark.

Pastors need to recognise that they will pick up vibes from staff meetings and may be expected by individuals to pastorally sort out various situations. We need a clearly thought-through perspective to prevent us from drifting into complexities with fellow workers.

Staff meetings are the responsibility of all members of staff, not just the leader. It is very easy to criticise and yet not be willing to contribute and play a fully committed part. It is easy for staff members to dump their problems on to the pastor. Individuals need to be encouraged to take responsibility for themselves at meetings rather than expecting someone else to behave as their shop steward.

Beware of the game that people play called, 'Everyone thinks . . .' People are quick to claim to know what everyone else thinks as a way of gaining ammunition to get what they want. It is a sign of insecurity and needs to be firmly challenged.

Recognise that groups need time to say hello and chat about the weather before they engage with an agenda. They also need time to chat before they part. However, if there is no control, people will chat about minor things all day. Time management is essential. My experience is that Christian workers love talking rather than getting out there to evangelise, pastor or do what they are paid to do. Sin lurks at the door of every staff meeting. All members of the group need to acknowledge this, discuss these tendencies and be clear about what is expected without making the leader out to be a 'baddie' who expects too much.

Sometimes a person might choose to share very little at a staff meeting but then may want to spend time with you later to tell you everything individually. This might be because of insecurity or lack of confidence, but it should be discouraged. It undermines the staff meeting and doesn't allow the person to take responsibility. It is also an unnecessary use of your time, unless, of course, the issue is particularly confidential.

When should you talk about others at staff meetings? This has been a real dilemma for me for many years. If you don't share with your colleagues, they feel you don't trust them. But when do we have permission to talk about others behind their backs? We have to balance the tension of sharing in a confidential way yet knowing that the people we are talking about are often friends of the staff team. In the counselling world, clear procedures have been developed with supervisors who generally don't know the clients at all. The church context is quite different. Nevertheless, we need to be very careful what we share in a staff meeting. It can too easily become nothing but a gossip shop. We need to ask:

- Why am I sharing this?
- Is this for my good, for the person in question or for the staff?
- Do the staff need to know?
- Is there a question of safety?
- Can I share anonymously?
- Do I have the person's permission?

Only after we have weighed up these questions should we carefully divulge any information that we deem to be appropriate. This also applies to times of prayer, which can subtly be used as a way of communicating news. If a congregation is to grow in confidence with the staff team, they need to know that staff meetings are handled with care and with clear ground rules.

We need to remember that Christian staff meetings are no different from any other grouping. They go through the normal group dynamics of

- Forming – each person working out where they fit in
- Storming –people trying to change and adjust the group
- Norming – tensions being recognised and settled
- Performing – taking on roles and working to a task
- Adjourning – withdrawing from activities.[58]

At least once a year it is helpful for the staff to discuss how the group is working for them. Are people committed to the group? Are creative ideas discussed and taken up? Are individual skills identified and used appropriately? Does the group achieve the task objectives?

The pastor may well be the first to observe a dysfunctioning group. This might be through the observation of frustrations, unhealthy competition, body language, dishonesty, leaders cancelling, members not turning up or where individuals lack personal development. This may be due to inappropriate behaviour, hidden agendas, dysfunctional members; maybe the group has become too comfortable, or facilitation is poor, or the group is inappropriate, unnecessary and needs to be disbanded.

When a church staff group works well, there is no better place to be supported, appreciated and encouraged to blossom.

Reflections

- How effective do you find your line management?
- Are there hidden expectations of you in staff meetings?
- How can individuals feel appreciated?
- What would improve your staff meetings?
- How might you prevent issues developing in the future?
- How might the group have a group sabbatical?
- What do you bring to the staff meeting?

---

58. J. Heron, *The Facilitators' Handbook.*

Chapter 36

Living on site

Love begins at home, and it is not so much what we do . . .
but how much love we put into that action.
(Mother Teresa)[59]

Living in the heart of a city, in a small terraced house, my wife and I had a range of people coming and going in our home. The youth group of about 60 teenagers would pass through, the front lounge would be used as a counselling room and my desk and office were in our bedroom. My wife was expecting our first child just six weeks after I was ordained. Being in a city we had already started to get tramps calling at the door. Naively, I helped one with money for a bus ticket. He started to come back and we gave him food, which he took reluctantly. As a keen young curate I began my ministry by working all hours, leaving my wife at home by herself as she settled into a new way of life. The tramp kept returning when I was not at home and my wife had to handle the situation. He became more and more aggressive, demanding money, and when he wasn't given any he would sit outside the house and wait for my return. This left my wife very upset and tearful. On one occasion, when I eventually returned home, we had a confrontation with the man, who threatened violence. The traumatic situation was enough to make my wife go into labour and we rushed off to hospital for the birth of our first child.

It took a few years in ministry before I realised that I needed to protect my family. Once the church office telephoned me while we were on a holiday abroad and I was expected to return home for the funeral of a key member in the church. This and other expectations all cost my family dearly.

It is a noble task in being willing to engage in pastoral ministry.
1 Timothy 3:1 (RSV paraphrased)

There are joys and sorrows along the way, but our responsibilities are to care for ourselves and our families, and to set a good example to the congregation and community. To do this we need to be clear about the level of our workload, making sure we have proper days

59. Mother Teresa speaking at her Nobel Peace Lecture, 11 December 1979.

off. If we live in a tied house or live on site, this needs to be carefully managed. No one will look after your health and the well-being of your family unless you do.

There has been a tradition and a kind of collusion among ministers and their congregations that it is impossible to be a pastor without working at least six days a week. It is strange how all other forms of work in our country manage with five days a week. This might well be because of both a Christian work ethic as well as the biblical concept of having only the Sabbath off for rest. However, I don't think the Genesis story really puts expectations upon us to work morning, noon and night. In the story of creation, the concept was to work in daylight and sleep in the dark. Today we have done away with the twilight zone and therefore can easily find ourselves as pastors working three sessions of the day.

Being a workaholic may be commendable to some, and it is true that most church members will applaud your hard work, but it certainly won't help your health or your relationships. Worst of all, it will set a negative example to others about what it means to love your neighbour as yourself. It is too easy for the church to simply reflect the world in terms of employment and expectations. That is not to say we shouldn't go the extra mile, but you can't do this every day without harming yourself.

A clear contract that clarifies expectations, days off and holidays is essential if we are to prevent misunderstanding, abuse or burnout. This means being clear about when your day off is, and letting people know – including all the local funeral directors. A good relationship with a funeral director will mean that you will have an arrangement between you as to what is expected if there is a funeral on your day off, or if the need arises to book a slot in your diary. It is easy if a secretary in the church is employed as they are likely to know your diary and plan things accordingly. It is helpful to have someone in the church who is in charge of organising funerals and liaises with the funeral director, so that whenever a funeral is arranged, this person will take responsibility to make sure the right people in the church are informed. In this way, a professional approach is maintained in regard to caring for the community.

The use of answerphones is a great help, unless you are someone who stands over them listening to the messages as they come in. This is a great way of keeping your stress levels high. If you have an answerphone, let it do its job and pick the messages up on your next working day. If you don't have an answerphone, simply unplugging the phone is the best way of getting peace and quiet. If there is anxiety about family being able to contact you, have a cheap pay-as-you-go mobile that your family and friends know about that they can ring (but guard the number carefully!). In this way, you are in control of your day off and are more likely to enjoy it.

Pastors are always worried that a significant event will happen on their day off and people won't be able to contact them. The truth is that this rarely happens, but if it does, and it is that serious, people know where you live. We need to realise that we are just one part of the church and it will function with or without us. It has for centuries and will in the future.

We need to give a healthy message to the congregation: that our physical and emotional as well as our spiritual well-being are important. By setting this example, we are encouraging others to follow. Jesus found time to wander off by himself without the disciples when he needed a break. Who are we to think we can do better than Christ?

Reflections

- How can you live with the ambiguity of working and living in the same house/parish?
- How can you give priority to your family over your work?
- In what ways can you differentiate between work and socialising?
- Who decides the ground rules in your home for answering the phone? For not entering the office? For closing the office door? For working on a day off? For doing a funeral on a day off? For returning from holiday because of a church issue?
- How can you protect your family and your personal life?
- How can you bring clarification of the expectations of your family within your work?
- How can you regularly check that your family is satisfied with their lifestyle and the way it interacts with your work?
- What are the tensions of working in confidential situations and not sharing your pastoral work with your partner?
- Who looks after the spirituality of your family, which is often challenged because of your work?

Chapter 37

A word for those living with a pastor

I asked my wife what it has been like living with a pastor for the last 32 years. She laughed and said immediately, 'Extremely hard work!'
(Abridged comment)

And whoever does not provide for relatives, and especially for family members, has denied the faith and is worse than an unbeliever.
1Timothy 5:8

I do not call you servants any longer, because the servant does not know what the master is doing; but I have called you friends, because I have made known to you everything that I have heard from my Father.
John 15:15

Now as they went on their way, he entered a certain village, where a woman named Martha welcomed him into her home. She had a sister named Mary, who sat at the Lord's feet and listened to what he was saying. But Martha was distracted by her many tasks; so she came to him and asked, 'Lord, do you not care that my sister has left me to do all the work by myself? Tell her then to help me.' But the Lord answered her, 'Martha, Martha, you are worried and distracted by many things; there is need only of one thing. Mary has chosen the better part, which will not be taken away from her.'
Luke 10:38-42

The pressures placed upon church leaders have been more recognised lately and there is greater awareness within congregations of the demands put upon the vicar/leader. But what about those who work in slightly less prominent roles within the church? The dangers of burnout, marriage breakdown, problems with children and the loss of faith are just as possible. Like many pressurised jobs, we can have a tendency to bring work problems home, which goes with the tension of being aware that the job of ministry is never done. There are always more people with more needs that can't be instantly solved and who come to church with ever-increasing expectations. There is also the tension for the family of seeing their partner or parent care for others all hours of the day and perhaps not being at home as much as the family would like.

So there exists a tension between the demands of the church leadership, the demands of the congregation, the needs of one's family and the need to find space for oneself. 'Serving the Lord' can sometimes seem to be just too costly. But does it have to be like this? Does ministry have to always come before one's marriage and family commitments? We have to find a solution to this otherwise burnout and broken relationships will result. I have observed a number of models of how people attempt to make this work.

Firstly, there are those who try to juggle and satisfy both family and role. This is rather like having two part-time jobs that turn out to be two full-time posts. It can be a very uncomfortable fit to be serving two masters that results in neither side being satisfied with what they receive.

Then there are those who accept that ministry and family life don't fit together and so decide to devote themselves totally to the one and neglect the other. This usually means people give more and more time to the ministry because this is where they receive the most strokes and encouragement. The worry here is that the pastor might eventually find someone outside the home to share their worries with and, if they are not very careful, they find themselves in a sexual relationship.

Bringing the ministry into the home each day can cause the rest of the family to becomes burdened with the pastor's ministry. This can then lead to family members, particularly the children, becoming extremely stressed and burdened with guilt.

Others find that the ministry takes them in a particular spiritual direction which leaves their partner behind. As time goes on, they can appear to develop a very different perspective on their faith, which in turn causes tension in the marriage.

There are no magic solutions to this dilemma. Any ministry is costly and comes with its own pressures and disappointments. The key is to recognise that engaging in ministry is a journey which will lead to change. That change needs to be acknowledged from the beginning and worked through, both in the job and in the family context. It is when there is tension between the family and the church role without open, ongoing communication that problems arise.

When my wife and I went to theological college, we embarked upon it together. Alas, my wife then had to go out to work to support us financially. From that moment on, I was trained on my own, even though we thought our ministry would be a partnership. But what happened when I came into a parish, with all the confidential information that was passing my way? In the end, my wife stayed at home and brought up the children, playing her part in the church by releasing me. She used her catering skills as we entertained, and eventually she began to help run various women's groups. But it wasn't quite how we had envisaged it originally. I guess, in the end, we each had our own ministries and a ministry that we shared together. I know other couples who work far more closely together and others who have a very clear divide. The key is being clear about what you expect of each other and what expectations the church might have. We are back to the boundary issues of being clear about what you will share with your partner and what you will maintain a silence upon. There is nothing worse in a church where everyone knows that the minister's partner can't keep a secret; it gradually strangles the minister's ministry.

Pastoral ministry leads us into very close relationships. It is understandable that we end up making friends within the church that we share with and perhaps rely on. But there is a need for caution. There can easily be a confusion of role in these relationships. When are you pastor and when are you friend? Can you be both? I recall having a meal with a couple who had invited my wife and me one evening in the week. We were talking about what it was like being a pastor and I happened to express that it wasn't easy to know when I was or wasn't working. I went on to say that even that evening was a form of working. I have never forgotten how the husband's face dropped. It was as if I had insulted his friendship. We were never invited back. But the issue is a real one. How will others in the church feel if you become especially close to a few individuals?

Relying too much on one individual or couple in a church is certainly unwise and can do damage to the church as a whole. This is why we need to formulate healthy relationships both inside and outside the local church, with clear expectations. An example of this is when people in the church do paid jobs for us. We all want jobs and tasks done as cheaply as possible, but what happens if the job is poorly done? Unless we are specific about expectations at the beginning, we can end up with disappointment all round.

If we draw close to people in the church we need to be aware of the emotional, psychological and spiritual demands that can be put upon us. If these people are also our friends and visit us in our homes, we may find that we have nowhere to retreat to. We can end up with an escape mentality that leaves us drained and emotionally withdrawn.

Figure 13: Relationships in Church

In all of the contacts listed in Figure 13, some will be relationships that are developing and strengthening in friendship; others will seem static and yet more will be diminishing.

Issues in the home

Let me now draw attention to some potential issues that can arise in a pastor's home.

Firstly, we need to recognise why we are in the ministry and clarify that the family understands the calling. Any ministry begins and ends with the desire to love God. Ephesians puts it this way,

> Therefore be imitators of God, as beloved children, and live in love, as Christ loved us and gave himself up for us, a fragrant offering and sacrifice to God.
>
> *Ephesians 5:1, 2*

But this life of love begins in the home. Before we enter into ministry, we need to have good communication within our home about how this work will impact upon the whole family. We won't be aware of all of the issues but if we at least begin with openness about the fact that there will be issues to think about along the way, we are more likely to keep talking about them. We mustn't forget that our commitment to our family is lifelong, which might not be the case in regard to our ministry. A key rule is to agree that any member of the family is allowed to raise it as an issue when the ministry begins to impact upon their lives in a detrimental way or they become anxious about the person doing the ministry. This open line of communication can prevent all kinds of issues from being brushed under the carpet until it is too late.

Secondly, the family needs to recognise that having a minister in the family will affect how people in the congregation relate to the family. There is often a tension in regard to how much a family member can talk in the church without appearing to betray the family and the pastor's work. We need to see that it is also strange for the congregation, as they may feel cautious in sharing openly with the pastor's family in case the information gets back to the pastor and consequently the staff team. This uneasiness can make the partner of the pastor find church a difficult place to be.

Pastors' children can suddenly find that there is a hidden expectation that they are to be perfect young people. At times the pastor can almost collude with this assumption, not wanting any negative reaction to return to him or herself. I recall in one congregation a few people muttering how terrible it was that one of my children had holes in their jeans (when it was fashionable) and fancy the vicar allowing him to come to church on Christmas Day looking like that! There is no easy way of handling these tensions except to be honest about them.

Historically, pastors kept their private lives totally separate from the church. Today there is a more open attitude, which brings joys as well as tensions. Ministers can be as guilty as the congregation in sharing inappropriately. Sharing things in a church context without the permission of the rest of the family is very dangerous. The rule of, 'Do I have a person's permission to talk about them?' applies just as much to our family context. Supervision would be a more suitable place to talk about family tensions with work, where there are at least clear boundaries of confidentiality in place.

The family needs to recognise that the pastor's role is one that involves deep emotions. Christians can often be divided about emotions. By the way they behave we could almost believe that some church leaders don't have emotions. Others can appear to be upset by the least little thing and will let everyone know their feelings. The fact is, we are emotional beings, created in the image of God. By denying the presence of our feelings, we are doing damage to ourselves physically and not portraying a holistic image. King David was a good example of a leader who could express his feelings. He danced with joy, and he expressed his weariness and anxiety (Psalms 55, 69, 94 are but a few examples). Jesus himself seemed at ease with his feelings as he wept in public and shared his heartache with his close disciples.

Clearly, a pastor dealing with all kinds of problems in the community needs opportunities to release the emotions of the day. Here the family can be a great source of strength, provided the pastor doesn't simply burden them with all the issues. A staff meeting and/or a one-to-one meeting with one's line manager can also help. It means that the raw emotions of the day can be shared with the family and/or partner but the details can be saved for the professional context. This allows emotions to be expressed but not unleashed to the damage of another.

It is strange how having a staff meeting is natural and common each week at work, but couples seldom give time each week to discuss their marriage. If we can set aside time each week, this can allow both the pastor and their partner to share their feelings. It can be easy to think that only the caring pastor has emotional trauma to share, which can make the partner's needs seem trivial.

A worrying issue is when a pastor presents one image to the church and community but is very different at home. Pastors are human. Sadly, though, this means that in some homes, pastors take out their anger and frustration on their family. The family can feel obliged to maintain secrecy while the pastor grapples with guilt, which only pushes them further into anger and rage. Abuse of whatever kind has to be dealt with, otherwise it simply spreads to the next generation. There are times when loyalty is important in a family if people are to respect each other, but we are first called to be true to God and ourselves. No pastor is perfect, but there is no excuse to take out frustrations on one's family. If it continues and the pastor is not willing to address the issue, then family members have every right to speak to someone in higher authority within the church until the matter is taken seriously. The outcome might result in something that no member of the family wants – perhaps the loss of a job, a marriage break-up, a family divided – but ultimately an abusing minister should not be in leadership. If the family members take the pain to themselves they can think they are doing the right thing, but this cannot be right in God's eyes. Sooner or later the abuser will find themselves abusing outside the family, and our silence effectually will condone this. However, with the right support, a pastor can begin to acknowledge the problems and, with counselling, the ministry and family can be rescued. In the end there is a time when it is necessary to speak the truth, in kindness, to redeem a situation.

Another issue that often arises is in regard to the complex relationship a church has with the pastor's family. Some people play up to the family, wanting to be close friends, while others seem to avoid the family and have nothing much to say to them. It is a strange but common dynamic. I recall early in my ministry, after the birth of our first child, we asked a family from within the church we had just joined to be godparents. They were pleased to support us but we were amazed by the reaction the couple received by others in the church. Many times they were asked the question, 'How did you get to be chosen to be godparents to the new curate's baby?' At the time we had no idea how many eyes were upon our actions.

From the point of view of the congregation, what do you say over coffee to the wife of the pastor who has just preached a challenging sermon? Or how do you talk to the husband of a pastor who has been emotionally supporting you? It's complex from both sides.

It is not uncommon that the partner of the pastor finds that someone is rude to them. This can happen for various reasons. Sometimes the pastor or partner is seen as a potential threat, taking over what are considered to be other people's ministries. Others are simply jealous that they are the pastor's wife, husband or child. At other times people can use the family as a way of getting at a church worker. They don't feel they can criticise a member of the church team outright so they do the next best thing: attack their partner or children. At such times, these people are not seeing the pastor as a person but more as an object to obtain what they want. This is a sign of an unhealthy church and needs to be tackled before such negative behaviour causes damage. Other elders of the church need to be drawn in to handle this in a calm, caring but firm way.

Naturally, the church attracts people with damaged backgrounds and childhoods as well as those with complex or malfunctioning families. When they come into the church they can slip into unhealthy and unchristian behaviour. We mustn't be afraid to address this issue if we are to lead the church into healthy concepts of family. It is an issue that needs to be generally addressed in sermons and pastorally handled over a period of time. However we handle it, we need to make sure we do not address the issue alone with the person in question. This will give them ammunition to attack us with things we didn't say. It is important to always make sure another person is with the pastor in order that they can clarify what was said, if necessary. If I believe a situation might become confrontational, I find it helpful to write a few brief notes about what was said, when and where immediately after the meeting. This is invaluable if at a later date we have to give account of the situation.

We also need to be careful when our family want to share in our ministry. This might be fine in the right context but there must be clear ground rules in place. The leadership of the church needs to agree such involvement. A pastor's family member should have no more right to ministry than any other member of the church. We need to be careful that we do not find a role for a family member by exerting our position. This can cause resentment within the church. The employee will have a job description, but the partner's role is usually unclear, and there is plenty of room for confusion to result.

Another issue in a pastor's home is how his or her children behave. One of the hardest lessons in life is to love and love your children until you give them away into adulthood. The problems very often lie in that in-between time when we are letting loose our hold on them and allowing them to become themselves. We naturally want the best for our children. I won't repeat what has been said under the chapter about children but I will clarify the difference for a pastor's family and the rest of the congregation. In a perfect world there would be no difference, but we all know that church leaders have greater expectations put upon them by their congregations. 1 Timothy 3 states clearly what is expected of a pastor in regard to their children, but this is only half the story. Jesus showed considerable love to individuals but acknowledged that they also had free will to choose how to live their lives. Growing teenagers heading into adulthood also have that freedom. While other members of a church can keep quiet about their children's problems, it is much harder to do this when we are involved in up-front ministry. The pastor's child deserves the right to an upbringing that has privacy. After all, they didn't choose to be in ministry with a church congregation looking on. A church needs to be respectful in this regard.

Pastors are human, and simply reflect the congregation. In the end we cannot make our children obey us or believe in what we stand for. Otherwise the story of the prodigal son would be meaningless. I have seen terrible examples where a pastor has shamed their child by writing about their 'unchristian behaviour' in a Christmas letter or in a sermon denouncing their child. I cannot imagine what harm that does both to the child and to the church as a whole. Which one of us can throw the first stone? The pastor needs people they can trust to support them and offer wise advice through difficult times with their children. This might be people inside the church or outside. Hopefully, in the end, our own family struggles will help to make us more sympathetic to those we care for who are going through similar situations. Perhaps later in our ministries we can talk about our experiences in a generic way that preserves the confidentiality of our children but helps the congregation identify with us in our struggles.

Financial issues

Financial implications for church workers is a subject that is not often talked about in church. Many people who end up working for the church in a pastoral way do so in a voluntary capacity or with a small salary. This is often seen as part of someone's 'tithe to the Lord'. However, issues can arise when the demands of the post in terms of time and energy are realised by the family. This can create a great deal of friction within the family relationships and a degree of resentment towards the church. If a family or partner feels that the church is taking a parent away from them and they feel that they are being neglected, it can create spiritual problems within the home. This needs to be acknowledged and talked about both within the family and with the church leaders. It is not unusual for someone to start working voluntarily and part-time only to quickly find themselves snowed under and working full-time hours without full-time pay. The pastoral worker has to be willing to keep communication open with the church so that they can reassess the post and recognise when it is far more than a voluntary post and needs remuneration for the work being done.

The Church as a whole struggles with the complex dynamic where it mainly functions in a voluntary capacity but chooses to employ and pay a few individuals. There is often confusion with congregational members when they are asked to do voluntary work such as youthwork when the church always asks for finance for the paid youth worker who is responsible for the task. Clearly, the church will function best if it has a healthy balance between a small number of paid workers and a larger voluntary workforce. The key is making sure that we do not take a person's goodwill for granted and almost abuse their generosity. This is where it is helpful to have short-term contracts for both paid and voluntary workers where the work is regularly reviewed and assessed. This would prevent any long-term resentment building up within families and the church generally.

The church, along with the pastor's family, needs to look out for any signs of potential depression. With the high level of demands placed upon pastors who are constantly dealing with other people's problems, it is not uncommon to find them being overwhelmed with the world's problems. As the psalmist puts it,

> Turn to me and be gracious to me, for I am lonely and afflicted.
> Relieve the troubles of my heart, and bring me out of my distress.
>
> *Psalm 25:16, 17*

Pastoral workers are good at putting on an act when they go home to their loved ones, but it is usually in the home that the first signs of 'cracking' appear. It is important that the family are given permission to make comments when they observe issues that concern them and that they feel they can also have a say about the activity of the ministry. After all, the ministry probably wouldn't take place without the generosity of the family releasing the parent into ministry.

Tensions

There are at least three areas that might cause pastoral workers to find themselves becoming depressed. There is the volume of work, which never seems to diminish. There are the serious issues that they face alongside people who are ill and experiencing terrible suffering. There is also the pressure that is caused by church members who are allowed to grumble and moan in such a way that it can feel as though it is a personal attack. All of these things are accumulative and can result in a worker feeling down in the dumps for no particular reason. Such frustrations often surface with irritability in the home. An alternative way that some people try to cope is to use alcohol to reduce the pain inside. It is at such times that the husband, wife or children need to have permission to comment on the situation. This is not to engage in a process of nagging, as this will just heap coal upon the fire. Turning to alcohol is a symptom, not the problem. The family needs to find a way of speaking out that is not critical but recognises the need and encourages the person to begin to acknowledge that all is not well. Without the family's support, the situation will just get worse and cause serious health problems to develop.

Finally, as previously mentioned, we can't engage in Christian ministry without being on a spiritual journey that leads to spiritual development and perhaps even a shift in our beliefs. Hopefully the journey leads to a deepening of faith, but this is not always the case. The dichotomy between the beliefs in the family home and the pastoral worker's changing views can eventually cause tension. The more open a worker can be with their family about the issues they are facing, the more it will help the family as a whole work through the issues together. The pastor's heart often wants to protect their family from the daily issues that they face, but ultimately this is short-sighted. The more the family understands the issues, the more they themselves can mature in the real world.

Reflections

- How can you protect your partner from burnout?
- How clear are you about expectations in the church/parish?
- Is there pressure for you to share your partner's faith?
- How can you reduce the stress in your relationship?
- How can you cast out the fear within you that your partner might have a sexual affair with someone in the church/parish?
- How can you make sure your marriage is not neglected?
- How can financial issues be discussed in a safe way with the leaders of the church?
- Where can the family go if they need spiritual or personal advice outside the church?

Part four

Pastoral ministry in the church-linked community

Chapter 38
Singleness

The best thing about being single is the time I have spent alone.
The worst about being single is the time I spend alone.
(Source unknown)

In the early days of my ministry, a deacon who was single at the time joined the team. At first, I felt she wasn't pulling her weight and perhaps not giving the same amount of hours I was giving to the post. It was my wise wife who opened my eyes to the reality of singleness. I had a partner at home to care for the children, do the shopping, cooking and release me to go out and serve the church. My colleague, however, had to organise all of her own provisions. She had no one to offload to at the end of the day to release the stress of the job or to just talk about things other than church ministry. To maintain contacts and friendships she needed time to venture outside the parish. I ate humble pie and my admiration and respect for my colleague grew immensely. I also began to appreciate my wife and realise that perhaps I needed to give more time to home provision!

Singleness in church comes in different guises. There are those who are young and enjoying the single lifestyle. There are those who are entering their late 20s and 30s and enjoying life to the full, or perhaps concerned about being left 'on the shelf'. Then there are those who have been single all their lives and those who become single through bereavement or separation.

Being single can have a stigma attached to it that other people fail to recognise. Putting on an event for 'single people' doesn't mean that they will attend or want to be identified in such a way. The subject needs to be handled with sensitivity.

There is often a need in a church's life to put on social events, trips and occasions where all church members who attend can enjoy friendship and fellowship. The events need to be open to all, allowing everyone to attend and enjoy full church membership. This needs to be right across the age ranges.

It is usually easier to be an older single person in a church that has a number of older single people, simply because there are usually more members of that age range. Being single in a church becomes more difficult for those who are in the minority. Small churches, particularly in the countryside, can find it difficult to provide the appropriate care for younger single people. A way around this is to continue to encourage church worship and membership and to also link them up with other church groups where a regional event can take place.

Today, many people find social groups across the world through the internet, although they may need support in helping to keep these contacts safe. In a town there is usually a choice of churches where one might meet more single people.

If someone has a personality such that they do not make friendships easily but rather have a tendency to antagonise people, there is not much one can do. But even these people like to journey with others, even if it is at a distance. Sometimes all that is required is to just get people together. They themselves often do the rest.

Issues that a single person may raise with a pastor range from loneliness, sexuality issues such as masturbation or homosexuality, finding a sense of purpose and direction, self-esteem issues, struggling to find the right partner, grieving past relationships to grappling with their faith in a God who has not answered their prayers.

One issue we may need to work through with a single person is to reassure them that a single person is fully human, complete and can be fulfilled by remaining single. The Bible says that it is not good for a person to be alone (Genesis 2:18), but this doesn't mean that marriage is the only way. The Apostle Paul saw that singleness was a preferred state for his ministry and commended it to others (1 Corinthians 7:8). The church is a family and can meet many of the needs of an individual. This will involve helping a person to think through their relationships, identify their passions, talents and gifts and help them to lead a purposeful life.

There needs to be caution from church leaders who mustn't just assume that single people have more time on their hands and will therefore be able to carry out more responsibilities in the church. A single person can have a life as colourful and busy as any married person, if not more so. A person can feel resentful if they sense that the church is using them.

In the end, working with single people should be no different to any other ministry. Some people love being single; others learn to live with it, while others find it a real difficulty and become sensitive even talking about it. Whatever attitude the person has, they still need to be treated with all the sensitivity and wisdom that a pastor has to offer.

Helping someone work through his or her own narrative such that it gives direction and meaning to their life can be very rewarding. Single people need friends and pastors who will journey with them for years. It is a demanding but rewarding ministry. In larger churches, home groups can offer particularly valuable support. But in the smaller, perhaps rural churches, a pastor's role can be life transforming.

A final note for those who are single in ministry. It is easy for a church to think they will gain extra hours of work from the pastor. After all, there is neither partner nor children to look after. But it is easy for a church to abuse a single person in regard to what is expected of them. Single people not only have to carry out all the daily tasks of living by themselves, but they also need to have time to nurture friendships and to socialise. They need to find friends both in the church and outside to offload, let off steam and with whom they can be emotional. This might particularly mean they have extra weekends off to relate outside the parish. Despite being surrounded by people and having a full diary, one can feel very lonely in the ministry, particularly as a single person. As they care for everyone else, they begin to wonder whether there is anyone who cares for them. It is important that a church helps individuals to put in place a well-structured support network with a spiritual adviser, counsellor and prayer partner.

Reflections

- Can you recall what it was / is like to be single? How did / does the church treat you?
- How can a pastor effectively support single people?
- How can churches in a region work together to support single people?
- How can we journey with single people to help them play their full part in the life of the church?

Chapter 39

Caring for those getting married

Now that your love has brought you to marriage,
let your marriage keep you in love.
(Dietrich Bonhoeffer)[60]

We now live in a society where people enter into stable relationships at a later age. How do you decide on the person with whom you will settle down? Love can be a confusing thing for young and old alike. We can get confused by what is love, romance, overwhelming desire for physical contact and being so idealistic that no one comes up to scratch. The reality is that love is something to be learned; it brings with it joys and sadness, hopes and disappointments, tension and fulfilment, deep longing and moments of hostility, gladness and pain. When a couple realise this, they are in a better position to work together and overcome problems.

A pastor can help couples considering marriage to think through issues concerning what they are entering into. Indeed, working with engaged couples and those already married could easily be a full-time role in any church.

Thinking through issues relating to relatives, religious faith, money, sex, children, careers, home responsibilities, recognising irritabilities, areas of common interest, do they both want the same things for the future etc. before marriage can help to prevent problems further down the line? In this way we can help people realise that any commitment is a risk, but by talking through the issues we make it a reasonable, manageable risk.

Couples find themselves in communities today where many simply don't bother with a recognised ceremony of commitment such as marriage.

These days it is very easy to get married in a secular way. If the Church wants to engage with doing church weddings it needs to wake up to the reality that it needs to enter the world of marketing. One thing that the Church is able to offer is a unique pre-marriage course. The Alpha marriage course is popular, but a range of alternatives is available. There is clearly a need to have one or two meetings about plans for the actual wedding as well as a rehearsal.

60. D. Bonhoeffer (1953), *Letters and Papers from Prison*, New York: Touchstone.

But the key contribution the Church makes is in its engagement with the couple to talk about what contributes to making a marriage a success. In many churches a married couple runs the marriage course, rather than a pastoral worker. That doesn't mean, though, that there is not an important contribution the pastor can make. If there is some engagement with the couple early on, there is more chance they will turn to the Church for support if and when difficulties arise. It is when closeness and intimacy break down that problems evolve.

Staying married

The pressures of married life are very different from those of 50 years ago, in many ways. People live for many years longer today and it means couples have the potential to be together for many more years. This can be a blessing and a strain.

Many couples have to move house due to job relocation and often live a long way away from close family and relatives. This means they have less of a support structure around them.

Today, in many marriages, both the husband and the wife have to work in order to earn enough to pay for their overheads. This affects the timing of when they have children and adds extra pressure to life in the home.

The Equality Act 2010 and changing attitudes in society mean that women have greater independence. This is both a blessing and a challenge for how a relationship is maintained.

We live in a very 'now' culture where people live in debt rather than saving patiently. Today's culture can't wait to reap results. This means that couples can easily think about bailing out every time they hit a difficult time in their marriage.

Many people are in what is called a 'patchwork family'. This is where the children may live with a parent who is not their own. The complexity of multiple past relationships influences the current relationship. Many couples today come from homes where divorce and separation are the norm within their family. Following in their parents' footsteps makes it easier to part when the going gets rough.

All of this places great pressure on marriage relationships and it is no wonder that many give way to separation. Marriage is perhaps something we don't pay enough attention to in our churches. It is only when we hear of a couple separating that we think about the issue.

Ministering to married couples

What kind of ministry does a pastor need to relate to married couples? We are clearly not marriage guidance therapists, but this doesn't mean we can't play a key role in a family's life. Perhaps the main difference in this kind of work is that we are dealing with two people, and each have their own stories. All the skills we bring to bear when dealing with one person can equally apply with a couple. We provide the ability to care for and communicate equally with both parties. Perhaps this is the key to success in dealing with marriages. It is easy to hear one side of the story or to take one person's side at the expense of the other.

As pastors, we obviously bring our own biblical picture of what is 'normal' within marriage and family life. It is clear that we bring our own baggage from our childhood and from what we think is normal for marriage into our relationships. There is clearly a divergence between denominations about what Christians think about headship, but the Scriptures are clear that both husband and wife have a high calling. In the Anglican Church we use the words, 'husbands to worship their wives' and 'wives are to obey their husbands'. But in reality this is a play on words. After all, Abraham showed what it meant to worship God by his obedience to his calling. The two words have very similar meanings and equally require diligence to achieve. A loving relationship requires both members to give of themselves wholeheartedly.

We need to recognise that any ministry to couples involves three generations. This involves the couple's own generation and perspective on life (it is said that when a couple goes to bed, several other couples get into bed with them – i.e. their family tree), as well as the influence of their parents' generation and their family within the marriage. After all, we gain an understanding of what is normal within marriage from our childhood, as we observe our parents make a good or bad job of it. It also involves any children within the marriage and the effect that the marriage is having upon the children.

This love is certainly not passive but requires ongoing action and repair;

- Spending time together
- Expressing loving words
- Acts of daily kindness
- Being generous with gifts
- Maintaining physical touch
- Practising forgiveness
- Having common goals, aims and interests

- When failure occurs, casting the fear out of the partner that you will do it again by asking them what would reassure them. Then fulfilling this requirement.

The pastor may not run the marriage course or be involved in the weddings, but we can keep a diligent eye on people's relationships. We can keep marriage high on the agenda of the church, making sure the church has yearly renewal of vows, maintaining a marriage course, remembering people's anniversaries and offering support to individuals and couples when it is needed.

Today, many churches are filled with middle-aged couples and individuals. One might think this is the prime time in life. However, increasing pressure means that people in their 50s are now finding themselves supporting ageing parents, children that still need financing, a pension that is not secure and the threat of redundancy well before the mortgage is paid. It is also a transition time in which we look back with regrets and look forward with uncertainty. Early ambitions may have not been fulfilled and our Christian faith has had to cope with a few knocks along the way. The conveyor belt of life is speeding up and we find ourselves heading in a direction that feels uncomfortable.

Yet at such a stage of life we still have so much to offer the Christian Church and the wider community. This is a stage when we can be wise about our limits and also aware of what we can offer. It may well be people in this category who offer themselves to do pastoral care within a community.

Reflections

- How can you protect yourself when you feel a sexual attraction to someone you are ministering to? Is there someone you can confidentially share this with?
- How can we support either Christians marrying young, which reduces sexual pressure, or those who wait and struggle with sexual desires?
- What can the church do to maintain and support marriages?
- How can we raise relationship issues so that the church community can be more honest and genuine?
- How can the church have a confidential scheme that encourages couples to seek help with their relationships?

Chapter 40

Separation and divorce

A divorce is like an amputation: you survive it, but there is less of you.
(Margaret Atwood)[61]

Today, a large proportion of the people in a church are likely to have had long-term relationships which resulted in separation or divorce and have remarried.

If we are supporting a person to grow through these transition points, we need to be aware of the dangers of remarrying or committing too soon. The Church is very good at wanting people to be married and can increase the pressure to tie the knot when in fact it might not be wise. If issues have not been resolved in a person with regard to what went wrong in the first relationship, they will simply bring past baggage into the new relationship.

Once past issues have been clarified, reflected on and learned from, there needs to be a period to begin to visualise what a new relationship should look like. This might include clarification about several things. We need to have a clear understanding of what the issues were in previous relationships. I'm amazed at how many new couples do not talk about why a partner's previous relationship broke up, bar a general statement. We need to clarify whether the emotional baggage from previous relationships has been expressed and released. Has the partner recovered emotionally?

There may be financial implications, with commitments to an ex-partner and children, decisions to be made as to how funds will be shared, who will own what in terms of property, possessions, etc. A relationship with a previous partner does not simply disappear, particularly where children are involved, and there needs to be some understanding of how the relationship with an ex-partner will be handled. There are also legal expectations with regard to support of the children. Recognising the fears, worries and loyalties within children can help to prevent problems from developing in the future.

Other areas include helping separated people to understand and organise their time commitments and expectations with different friends and people who are known in the wider community. We mustn't be embarrassed about raising issues around values and beliefs. This should include an understanding of religious and

61. M. Atwood (1973), quoted in *Time* magazine, 19 March 1973.

spiritual expectations. It might be the only time when people have the chance to talk about such personal subjects in a safe, non-judging context.

For the church, there needs to be an understanding of the intense problems that can arise when a couple in the church split up. It is natural that church members will take sides. It is usual that it is just too painful for both parties to remain in the church, but who should leave? Often there are wider family members in the church who try and influence who stays, understandably wanting their relative to stay even if this person was the one who initiated the split.

How should a church react when a person returns to the church with a new partner, perhaps with plans to remarry? This can stir up all sorts of hurts and pain in the ex-partner. It is possible that this is done innocently, but often it can be a form of malice and revenge. If the church is not clear with regard to its policy, then such situations can cause real division within the church. There needs to be an agreement between both individuals and the church about who will stay and who will go. This usually means that the one with the children stays in the church and the other parent will be helped to find another church. Once the decision is made it should be agreed verbally and in writing that the person who is leaving will not return as a regular worshipper as long as the ex-partner and children worship in the church. In this way the church is safeguarding issues in the future. There needs to be recognition that there are consequences to a breakdown of relationships and, although forgiveness is always available within a church, we still have to live with the consequences. A sign that someone is repentant and contrite is to obey the decision of the church and be willing not to create more pain for a former partner.

A sensitive pastor might see that a person needs not only the divorce paper to arrive to accept a separation but also needs to experience some spiritual liturgical rite. This provides an opportunity to acknowledge failings and regrets in the relationship. To mourn what was hoped for – lost dreams, plans and expectations; to confess and to commend the other person to God, releasing the range of emotions of anger, blame, shame and loss of one's own self-image. This provides a person with a clean sheet so they can begin to pray for a new beginning with a fresh perspective.

Reflections

- How can the church make divorced people welcome?
- Is it possible to have a strategy that supports both partners when they separate?
- Should the church become skilled at mediating for separating couples?
- What are the advantages/disadvantages of having a church leader who has been divorced?
- In what ways can we prevent ourselves from jumping to wrong conclusions and taking sides?
- How can we communicate that divorce is not an unforgivable sin?
- What would you include in a piece of liturgy to bring healing to a divorced person?

Chapter 41

Care of children

Children must be taught how to think, not what to think.
(Margaret Mead)[62]

The birth of a child causes major changes within a couple's life. The responsibility can seem enormous and it can put tremendous strain on a marriage relationship. For families who don't regularly attend church, the first contact is usually with a request for dedication or baptism. Although this is usually managed by whoever manages the liturgy service, it is a good opportunity for a pastor to enquire how the family is coping. Issues of fatigue, sexual tension, financial strain, work issues, accommodation space and any previous hurtful issues in the relationship can surface. If we have the opportunity it is good to reassure couples that it can easily take six months before things settle down into any kind of normality, and it can also be a time of finding deeper healing within the relationship. If we maintain an open door with the family, they are more likely to seek help from us if things get tough at any time.

In today's community we are more likely to encounter patchwork families. This brings additional pressures to bear upon the family dynamic. In all of these varieties of 'normal' family life, we will encounter unrealistic expectations. It is an opportunity for a pastor to bring reality into difficult circumstances.

However close a couple might be, they are never totally attuned to each other. There is always more that can be done to bring deeper harmony.

A partner can never be all we need in life. Although we may look to our partner to provide us with friendship, give us love, to be a playmate, a sounding board, an emotional support, a sex partner and someone who is always on our side, along with many more things, the reality is that no one can do all of these things all of the time. We cannot always expect the right support (even if we know what that should be) from a partner always when we want it. That is why we need friends, wider family and a supporting community to contribute to our lives too.

62. M. Mead (1973), *Coming of Age in Samoa*, New York: First Quill.

It is normal to have disagreements in relationships, particularly in regard to bringing up children. The key is to learn how to resolve conflict so that past disagreements do not linger into the future.

The way a couple functions before the birth of a child cannot realistically be expected to continue post-birth. The presence of a third distinctive person in the relationship affects all the ground rules previously assumed in a partnership. These need to be freshly discussed and agreed at various intervals over the months and years.

The presence of a baby must not replace the intimacy of what existed beforehand for the couple. This can often be an issue for the husband who can feel pushed out now that his wife is devoting much of her time, energy and affection to the baby. Time needs to be planned on a weekly basis for the couple to maintain and enjoy their relationship without the baby's presence. This means that right from the beginning some babysitting provision is required. This creates a healthy reality that the baby is in fact a very special 'lodger' who will one day move on into adulthood and leave the couple by themselves once again.

Both partners need to nurture their own wider family relationships. It is unfair to expect only one partner to handle all of the relationships within the family, especially the in-laws.

In every relationship each individual maintains a degree of privacy. However close a couple might seem to be, there will always be areas that are not fully disclosed. Our thought processes are always private until they develop enough that we are ready to share them with others.

Families exist as a safe place for children to gain their identity, to know that they are special and loved and to learn the appropriate skills for life. It is a springboard into adulthood. Within this safety net, children encounter a whole range of emotions for the first time. They begin by learning about trust and mistrust. Can the parent be trusted? There is a tussle between power and fragility – the desire to be independent yet needing someone to pick them up when they take their first ever step and fall flat on their face.

Then there is the discovery of powerful emotions such as guilt and shame. Pushing the boundaries in a world of dos and don'ts develops the concept of conscience, which can easily be oversensitised. Children try to do things in an environment where it seems to them as though everyone else is able to do the same things with ease. Self-doubt and self-blame can lie just under the surface.

We then move into the teenage years with the discovery of sexuality and effervescing hormones. Love and failure are encountered and can result in a deep loneliness. For some, this is a time when no one seems to be trustworthy, including parents and God. Added to the mix is the psychological dilemma of finding one's identity or concluding that they are a 'nobody'. During this journey a teenager can flip from either becoming attached to an authority figure such as a youth worker and engaging actively in religion or rebelling and rejecting all that their parents hold dear. Parents and youth workers have a responsibility to handle these ambivalent feelings patiently. It is like holding a dove in one's hand. Too much space and the dove flies away; too much constriction and the dove is damaged. What is required is consistency of care that encourages a young person to formulate his or her own views and beliefs. This means that a parent needs to remain calm when their child kicks against their belief system. Parents so often want their children to share their beliefs without recognising that their child's experience is very different from theirs. Jesus didn't tell the story of the prodigal son for no reason.

Pastoral workers often find themselves listening to parents talk about issues they are having with their children. An awareness of how children develop physically and emotionally can be helpful. An understanding of how faith develops in young people can also bring a valued insight to parents. We need to be aware of appropriate and inappropriate expectations upon young people.

The ability to listen without judgement and to ask open questions that encourage the parents to see life through their children's eyes can help. We might also find ourselves listening to a teenager, although they are more likely to have such a conversation with a youth worker. Parents are clearly under considerable stress these days. The church can become a helpful ally if it conveys a message that it is not there to judge but to support. This encourages parents to be more honest about their struggles rather than to just put on a face every Sunday morning. We also need to recognise that some of the issues parents have with children not only challenge what the children think but also what the parents think (even if they don't acknowledge it at the time). Through the use of careful open questions a pastor can allow parents to begin to adjust their own belief systems.

Ultimately, the parents' task is to work themselves out of a job. This doesn't mean that a parent ever stops loving, caring and being there for the adult child. But their task is to let go and release the child into the world. The alternative is suffocating, controlling parents who can be destructive to young people's growth. I meet this in university work with students who come to college with huge hang-ups with their controlling parents. It is therefore not surprising that many choose not to enter into marriage but rather to remain single and cohabit. If we convey a message that marriage is the only way to live, regardless of its pressures and pains, we are missing the point of parenthood. If we respect the children we have produced, we need to be willing to allow them to go their own way – in terms of their career as well as socially, sexually and spiritually.

This raises a dilemma that pastoral workers often find themselves in when asked about how an adult child should behave in a parent's home. Usually the issue revolves round sex. Should a child be allowed to sleep with a partner in the parent's home?

Before attempting to answer this, perhaps we need to broaden our perspective of what is happening today.

The Church has found itself in a real dilemma about sex. We have cast out homosexuals for something that might be genetic while we seem to ignore the fact that 90 per cent of young people these days sleep around, including Christians, and focus on the tiny number of homosexuals that we have issues with. I have been in churches both as a vicar and as a member of the congregation where one thing is preached from the front while some of the congregation quietly do something else. This highlights that the issue of sex and young people is something the Church struggles with. Perhaps that's why they have deserted the Church in their thousands.

In a university setting I see a diversity of behaviour in young people. Some see university life as a time for free experience and enter a range of relationships. Others, for whatever reason, do not feel ready to enter into close opposite-sex relationships. There are also keen young Christians who get involved in the Christian Union: some pair up very quickly and get married when they graduate. Years ago that would have seemed normal and would reflect the behaviour of the general public. Who am I to say that it is wrong? I did just the same thing 33 years ago.

My concern is that the world is a very different place today, for several reasons. First, people are living much longer than before, which changes the dynamic of marriages. Secondly, the role of women has been revolutionised. Today's 'average' woman has a career. Thirdly, young people often live miles away from their family support structure. On top of this, some psychologists have noticed that adolescence, which used to end at 21, now seems to go on till around 28 or 30 years of age. It seems to take this length of time for a young person to work out their identity, settle into a career, work out their sexuality and enter into a long-term relationship. Adolescence is a tough time when a young person tries to work out who they are and find a framework within which to place their lives.

All of this simply means that there is more pressure on young relationships that was not there 50 years ago. So why do Christians get married so young? Is it the pressure to have a full sexual relationship? If so, is this a good enough reason to enter into a life-long relationship? I don't know the statistics with regard to Christians marrying young today, but I do seem to meet a large number who fall at the first hurdle. This could be because people are less willing to work through problems, because there are additional pressures on marriage generally with both partners working, or because they live in a world where there are so many choices that it is hard to stick with one person. Either way, we need to recognise the problems, even if we don't have any easy solutions. Pastoral workers are likely to find themselves supporting the parents at such difficult times as well as the children.

So how can pastoral workers help? Perhaps we can at least remind people of a few simple points.

Firstly, parenting is about letting go, not holding on. Secondly, it is about producing children who are unique and not carbon copies. This means recognising that children do not have their parents' experience of life, and especially their Christian experience. Each child has to find their own. This is a hard message for some parents to grasp because they long for their children to have similar encounters with God to their own. We forget that, sometimes, being brought up in a Christian home and church has an effect on how they see life and God. This inevitably means that we, as parents, might be part of the problem. Thirdly, we need to remind ourselves of the story of the prodigal son. Sometimes we have to lose someone before we can gain them back.

So back to the question of how a young adult should behave in their parents' home. There is no simple answer to this. It will depend upon the relationship that the child has with their parents. Is it a dominating home where the child has no say or can't enter into discussion? The probability is that the child will just go off and do their own thing elsewhere. Is it a home where sex and relationships can be discussed openly without judgement or rebuke? Here there is a greater chance of a family being at least aware of what different behaviours mean to each other. Agreeing to disagree yet respecting a parent's position would be a win–win solution. Alas, I have heard too often from young people that the parental attitude is that you must agree with them or get out. This not only destroys a family but also tarnishes the idea of what a Christian parent should be like. Such young people become adults who are angry with their parents and resent the church and therefore Christianity. This is a lose–lose situation. It takes maturity, self-awareness and confidence in one's own identity to disagree with a young adult and yet allow them the space to behave in their own way in what is still their home.

The key for pastoral workers is to help parents to see two things. Firstly, it is important to try and view situations from their child's position, and secondly, to think long term and consider the consequences of their decisions. Sadly, couples often disagree with each other on these matters and this in turn creates additional conflict within the marriage and the home.

It is inevitable that people in a church will handle children's and young people's issues from differing viewpoints. We need the good grace within a Christian community to tolerate differences and yet be supportive as parents have to grapple with major issues in their lives.

We also need to encourage parents to decide on what they consider to be essential rules for the family. It is pointless making lots of arbitrary rules that are really unimportant. It is too easy to have a breakdown in one's relationship with a child because of a rule that, after quiet consideration, is not worth breaking the family for. Also, we need to be careful not to have any rules that we ourselves are not willing to follow. We need to be careful, as Paul warns us, that we do not harass and exasperate our children and in the end push them further away from Christ (Ephesians 6:1-4).

Finally, we need to recognise that this kind of ministry is very exhausting, especially if the pastor has children of their own. It is easy to find that, as we sympathise and support a parent with an issue, we can then drive home reflecting upon our own complex relationships with our children. This can be very discouraging and make us wonder whether we are fit to minister at all. But there are two positives to this. Firstly, our own family experiences bring a deeper understanding to other people's situations, and secondly, I know myself that my parenting skills have improved as I have learned from other parents' joys and sorrows.

Reflections

- Whose responsibility is it in the church to identify childhood problems?
- How can the church work with the whole family with regard to children's issues?
- How do you decide when to refer a problem with a child to a professional agency?
- How can the church support parents?
- If a father figure is lacking in the home, what can the church do to provide a substitute?

- What are the similarities and differences between parenting and pastoring?
- How can the church encourage adolescents to explore and question while providing boundaries?
- Does your church/ministry accommodate the views of adolescent members?

Chapter 42

Care of the elderly

Do not speak harshly to an older man, but speak to him as a father, to younger men as brothers, to older women as mothers, to younger women as sisters – with absolute purity.
(1 Timothy 5:1, 2)

When we lived in a rural parish, my wife and I would open up our home for weekly lunches and cream teas. It proved to be a time for the elderly to not only look forward to a social event, but also to play their full part, whether it was in cooking, washing up or hosting the event. One of the joys of the event was the friendly chatting over the kitchen sink. It didn't matter what age anyone was; there seemed to be a levelling as we all played our part and enjoyed each other's company.

Who are the elderly? It will not be long before there are more elderly people than any other age group in our country. The Church, of course, has always seemed to have a monopoly on the elderly, and usually does well with social groups and lunch clubs, etc. To define what is 'elderly' is a complex business. Someone might work voluntarily for a lunch club serving meals for people younger than themselves. This means that pastoral care in the church is often directed to the elderly but is often also run by the elderly.

Frazer Watts rightly points out that most elderly people are active and in good health in their 60s and 70s, and many in their 80s.[63] We need to be careful not to stereotype people in church according to their age. We might well be missing opportunities to develop all kinds of church programmes which could be managed by those who are retired from paid work but who still have gifts and time to offer. I have talked to a number of ministers who dread retirement as they seem to have no interests other than their church work. We are not a profession that sets a very good example of helping and equipping people for retirement. Too many simply start ministering in someone else's patch, often without permission. Yet retirement is a time not to do what we have always done but to explore new horizons and to be creative in finding new gifts and talents. Ministers

63. F. Watts, R. Nye & S. Savage (2002), *Psychology for Christian Ministry*, Abingdon: Routledge.

should lead the way, showing how we can retire gracefully and practise what we have been preaching for so long.

Erikson talks about eight stages of development where the last two stages represent middle adulthood and old age. The stage of middle adulthood is about the tension between productivity and stagnation.[64] The person has distinct experience to pass on yet also needs to reserve energy for themselves. They are grappling with a change in role of life, of social status and of financial security. They are also wondering what they have to offer the church and community or whether they will be rejected as past their best? Retirement itself is difficult enough to handle, but many find that they are also thrown into grief and loss unexpectedly when they begin to lose friends and perhaps even their partner.

As people pass into old age, there is a tussle between taking stock of one's life and finding meaning in it compared to realising that there is little time left with no point to life. The church can play a healing role if it is willing to engage with people about the issues they are facing. I have never heard a sermon series that looks at life when you are over the hill. If we are not tackling this subject in the pulpit, certainly pastoral carers can engage with it individually. Often the carers themselves are in retirement, so it will require courage to be willing to go on this journey for themselves, let alone for others. But the healing that can be achieved is immense. If we understand the stage of life a person is at, we will be better equipped to minister in a way that the person might need. However, if we are blind to this psychological development, it is unlikely that the subject will come up as both parties will cleverly dance around it.

Loneliness is a great fear of the elderly, yet the church is in a good position to drive out such fears. We can prevent social isolation by offering groups, activities and one-to-one work. In one of my previous churches, through visiting door to door with a questionnaire we discovered that there were a number of lonely people in the parish. We therefore started a lunch club twice a week for which people were picked up by car, given a cooked lunch and then sometimes stayed for entertainment or a church service. Many expressed that it was the highlight of their week. Most of the people who ran the club were in their 60s and 70s. In fact, some were older than those receiving the lunch. Here was Christianity in practice, where pastoral care and evangelism dovetailed.

Visiting seems not to be the flavour of the month for ministers today but it can be a lifeline for those who are housebound. Initiating some kind of regular visiting scheme can maintain a

64. E. H. Erikson, *Identity and the Life Cycle.*

person's link with the church. Visiting the elderly can also provide a sense of meaning and purpose to those who are retired and feel they have little to contribute.

It is always sad when an active member of a church reaches the point when they are unable to attend Sunday worship regularly. It might seem low priority to a growing church, but how we care for these people will reflect what kind of a church we have become. It takes little effort to record or video the weekly service and distribute it to the community. Offering a special midweek service and providing transport can be a blessing. I recently knew of a church that had a minister who moved far away after serving for 17 years in the community. The induction was 300 miles away and seemed out of reach to the young, never mind the old. But an organised pastoral worker hired a minibus and arranged a short holiday for several elderly members to tie in with the induction. This not only made them feel included but the friendships that formed and deepened on the journey gave a sense of revitalisation. This led to some of them deciding to go on a trip to Israel that previously they had thought was out of their reach.

While serving in a rural church, I had the pleasure of being involved in a small 100-pupil primary school. It was a safe community and every autumn each child would be linked with an elderly friend in the community whom they could visit with a parent or teacher. The rewards of such a venture far outweighed the initial aim of just distributing a few harvest gifts. It led to friendships between children, parents and the elderly friends. Some residents would come into school to share their life experiences. A thriving elderly membership in a church can contribute more to the younger members than they might think.

I have hesitated in suggesting that the elderly can become the prayer powerhouse of the church as this removes the responsibility of the whole church to pray. It can seem degrading to suggest that the elderly can pray because they can't do anything else. Encouraging the elderly to pray is fine, but do it with the young alongside. If we fail to get a church to draw together the young and the old, we are in danger of being nothing more than a like-minded social club. This is clearly not the gospel message.

Reflections

- What policy does your church have about middle age and old age?
- How do we address elderly issues in the pulpit? Small groups? Individually?

- What outreach policy do we have to the housebound?
- How can we help people to die well?
- How can we prevent the elderly from drifting away from church?
- How can we respect what has taken place in the past without preventing the church from moving forward?

Chapter 43

Care of those with special needs

The central struggle of parenthood is to let our hopes for our children outweigh our fears.
(Ellen Goodman)[65]

Although as Christians we believe everyone is equal in the sight of God, we also know that minority groups can feel vulnerable and threatened.

Any pastoral care in a church needs to be particularly open to those who are treated differently or feel themselves to be different from the majority. This might be those with mental health issues, physical disabilities or educational problems, those of a different sexual orientation or from a different cultural background.

Jesus particularly found his ministry dealing with people on the edge of the community. The marginalised in his time included:

- Those with physical problems, e.g. lepers
- Those with mental/spiritual problems, e.g. possessed
- Those whose lifestyle was contrary to the norm, e.g. the woman at the well
- Those who didn't fit in, e.g. Zacchaeus, the tax collector
- Those who had issues for a long time, e.g. the paralysed man at the pool
- Those from different backgrounds or beliefs, e.g. the Samaritan woman.

Who might be the marginalised in your church or community?

Regardless of our attitude to these people, we are called to offer unconditional love. Isolating and alienating individuals helps no one, least of all the kingdom of God.

This ministry is not just about caring for people in the church. At the heart of any mission is a pastor's heart of caring for people. Some churches recognise that in their working parish they have special groups of people. One church might specialise in caring for those with mental health issues while another might focus on the homeless and the unemployed. Our pastoral ministry to the edge of

65. E. Goodman (2004), *Paper Trail: Common Sense in Uncommon Times*, Brookvale: James Bennett Ltd.

and to those outside the church will reflect what needs are before us.

The families of children with special needs can face considerable pressure. At times it is difficult to see how churches can cope with so many overwhelming problems in our communities. There needs to be a balance between recognising the limitations of the size of the church and the free time that is available and having a cutting edge that pushes us out of our comfort zone to care.

If a count was taken, we might be surprised at how many people in church are already handling difficult situations within their homes. Sometimes people cling on by their fingertips to manage all their responsibilities. Going to church can be the one time when they have a little space for themselves, to reflect and top up their batteries. The last thing we want to do is to place extra responsibility or pressure on them. For some, just knowing the church knows and prays for them is enough to give them the courage to keep going.

Respite care can be a great provision by a church to those who hardly ever have a break or holiday. A pastor is often the person who detects these needs and has the contacts to link others together to enable healing care to take place. The church is generally good at producing rotas, and they can be used to pull together a group of people to dovetail with a family to share the load. We just need to be aware of expectations and our own limitations. Clear boundaries are essential if we are going to maintain our health and well-being.

Eventually some families have to release their relative to a care home. It can be a terribly upsetting time. Family members can feel guilty or blame others for not playing their full part. A sensitive pastor can at least engage with the family predicament and endeavour to bring some healing to the context.

Reflections

- How welcoming is your church to those who are different from the norm?
- What link does the church have with special-need groups in the local area?
- Is there someone who has specific responsibility to care for those with special needs?
- How aware is the church of the families who have children with demanding responsibilities?
- Could a support group be set up?

Chapter 44

Who cares for the carers?

Too often we underestimate the power of touch, a smile, a kind word, a listening ear, an honest compliment, or the smallest act of caring, all of which has the potential of turning a life around.
(Leo Buscaglia)[66]

Churches are often full of people who spend their time caring for others, be it people in the church, the community or their own family. It is one thing choosing to care for someone; it is a completely different thing to find oneself having to care for a family member on a daily basis. Perhaps it is a partner who has had a stroke, or an elderly parent who lives with you, or a handicapped child who will need care all their lives.

It is understandable that at some point such carers can become depressed. Sadness can hang over them like a cloud. They may experience anger about the situation and lack of support, or perhaps just wonder why this has fallen onto their plate. They will have to adjust to lost hopes and dreams. God may be seen as a great trickster who has rewarded their faith with pain and suffering.

In such situations it can feel difficult to know what to say. We need to beware of the damage we can do if we suggest that they shouldn't be angry with God. The Bible is full of examples of people expressing their anger at God. We now know that anger turned inwards often leads to self-destructive depression. We need to find a way of helping people to recognise their anger without fuelling it and to find a safe way of expressing this powerful feeling. Guilt is often close behind anger, as carers can feel that their calling is a form of judgement. A parent of a disabled child has to find a way of coming to terms with the fact that they may have played a part in their child's problem. Our role is to help the parent to accept that none of us have full control of what happens to us, that their resources are not limitless and that there is only so much care that anyone can be expected to provide.

The problems of a family carer are multiple:

- Finance issues
- Obtaining appropriate support medically and socially

---

66. L. Buscaglia (1996), *Amor*, Barcelona: Emece Editores.

- Learning nursing skills
- Accepting other carers coming into your home
- Not enough hours of the day to do all that is required
- Having time for oneself
- Complex reactions of other family members
- Feeling a prisoner in one's own home
- Knowing when to let go.

It is very easy for carers in the community to lose connection with the church. Caring for one individual can be so all-embracing that it can leave little time to think about one's own needs and social contacts. A pastoral worker can be key in helping such people in specific ways: we can help practically, spiritually and emotionally.

Practically, we can help in giving 'respite' care, even if it is just for a few hours. It might be providing a washing and ironing service or just a regular phone call that says that we have not forgotten about them.

Spiritually, we can find a sitter to allow the carers to go to church and help them to know that they are not forgotten either in God's eyes or the eyes of the church. In an increasingly ageing society, we need to become more sensitive to the needs of people in our churches who care for elderly parents. We must acknowledge that it will become harder for them to get to church and stay in contact unless we make some provision. We can visit regularly and initiate other Christians to visit. This might even involve having a home group in the person's home. We may need to sit down with a person and work out a spiritual care package so that the church is able to meet the needs of the individual. We can supply people with recorded worship or sermons, provide Bible study notes or just keep them informed with all that is going on in the church and community.

Emotionally, we can help people handle the painful feelings that arise from the intense caring for another human being. When we see someone who is tied to us through blood, marriage or friendship suffering in physical pain or handicapped, it can provoke strong feelings. There is acknowledgement of the loss of what could have been for both the carer and the cared-for. Anger can erupt at all the injustices of life. Frustrations arise from feeling imprisoned in an impossible situation. There is hurt when family and friends fail to support. There can be a feeling of powerlessness within carers who see their own plans and hopes slipping away from them.

Finally, there are mixed and confused emotions that come when a carer has to decide to end their caring role or the role is taken away from them. This might be when a severely handicapped child grows up and needs 24-hour professional care or when an elderly relative needs full-time nursing care. The caring role may be taken away suddenly when the person dies. All of this means that the carer finds themselves in a strange place as they suddenly have time on their hands, a different pattern to their days, a great gulf in their lives and waves of fluid emotions. Now the carer has the time they have been craving for yet they can't enjoy it. Release, guilt, vulnerability and tiredness overwhelm many as they adjust to the new situation. Many will not understand this complex reaction, except perhaps a caring, sensitive pastoral carer. We need to remember as a church that it was to the harassed, tired and hurting that Jesus particularly ministered.

If, however, the carer has maintained links with the church, there is a better chance that they will reintegrate into the community and find themselves with new purpose and meaning in life.

An additional role of the pastoral worker, and something that needs championing, is to raise awareness and acceptance in the church of people with disabilities. This is about more than just making wheelchair space available. It is about challenging negative attitudes and ensuring that the church does much more than just tolerating the odd outburst from a person during a service. When a congregation turns and stares, it is enough to make a carer run a mile and never return. This means we need to preach about what true acceptance means within the church, even if it means a little inconvenience to ourselves.

Reflections

- How can we put a policy in place for carers to prevent them burning out?
- How can we prevent ourselves from developing a 'tough skin' towards situations and people while at the same time protecting ourselves?
- How can we develop a support group for carers?

Chapter 45

Funerals

When one man dies, a chapter is not torn out of a book, but translated into another language.
(John Donne)[67]

We intend that no one should blame us about this generous gift that we are administering, for we intend to do what is right not only in the Lord's sight but also in the sight of others.
(2 Corinthians 8:20)

Through the testing of this ministry you glorify God by your obedience to the confession of the gospel of Christ and by the generosity of your sharing with them and with all others.
(2 Corinthians 9:13)

It was a cold, wet day in November as I drove to the large crematorium on the edge of the city. I was about to conduct a funeral of a type I had not done before. As I arrived, the funeral directors were waiting for me, not that I was late; in fact, we were 15 minutes early. 'You're early,' I remarked. One of the men just nodded at the car. 'We want to get this over with as quick as we can.' I knew what he meant. This wasn't my first baby funeral; I had conducted several baby and child funerals in my role as part-time chaplain to a maternity and children's hospital. However, this one felt very different. It was the first time I had done a service where no one was going to be present.

Sometimes when a baby is very premature, families choose not to attach themselves to their dashed hopes. So the hospital takes responsibility and it is left to a funeral director and the chaplain on duty. I robed, prayed and gave the nod to the director attendant. One of the men carried the tiny white coffin up the aisle and placed it on the small table. Now what? I asked the attendants if they wanted to stay but they declined and went out for a smoke. Just me, the white coffin and an unknown name – what until days ago had the potential of life, and hopefully a relationship with God. I decided to do a full service, to the annoyance of a couple of the attendants. It wasn't an experience I would forget in a hurry.

67. J. Donne (1976), *The Complete English Poems*, London: Penguin.

William Gladstone believed that the way a community dealt with their dead reflected the nature and beliefs of that community.[68] Certainly a funeral does provide an opportunity for a family and community to spiritually, psychologically and socially begin to adjust to their loss. At a funeral we seek to acknowledge the reality that someone has died. It is also a time when we can hopefully realise that we are not alone. There has been a big cultural change in the funeral industry over recent years. The number of cremations has increased and the number of burials has decreased; we now have natural burial sites; people have more choice about who conducts the service; there is more focus on thanksgiving rather than mourning and the laity participates far more with eulogies in the service. In addition, we now have full-time priests who have become professional funeral service leaders and are employed by funeral directors. Along with this, people's expectations in our consumer society have changed.

The bereaved want much more of a say in terms of what happens at a funeral, and often a clergyperson can become nothing more than a master of ceremonies. There is also a tendency to dress less formally at a funeral, which, in my opinion, somehow stifles the pain and significance of the loss.

Churches and their leaders have also changed, and there is more of a focus on growth and happiness rather than on the needy and the poor, and there is little space in services for lament. The wider Church seems to be unclear as to whether it really wants to be involved in the funeral business at all. Many Anglican clergy, who in the past would have assisted at all the funerals within their parish, are now being more selective, and some only conduct funerals for church members. This inevitably leads to more secular funerals and the development of funeral firms who employ their own officiates. Whether or not this is a good thing is up to each one of us individually to decide. Clergy have to deal with the tension of whether they are willing to officiate at funerals where they have no church or personal contact. For some this is not an issue, as they see it as their calling to serve all. Others will be more church-orientated and perhaps resent being used almost as a conductor of semi-secular services. How flexible a minister is willing to be with regard to how much Christian content a funeral should contain is a real issue.

Some church leaders are preachers, others are administrators, some are leaders or teachers and others are pastors. Some attempt to fulfil all of these roles. The questions we need to ask are, 'Who will be the bereavement carers in the church?' and 'Who will conduct the

68. R. Jenkins (1995) *Gladstone*, New York: Random House.

funerals and provide the aftercare?' Not all ministers are trained to the highest level. We need to see the importance of the funeral rituals that we provide as doorways to healing through which different types of grievers walk. In Britain, we are in increasing danger of losing our rituals and allowing the community to collude in minimising, avoiding and denying death issues. For those who do officiate at funerals, we need to recognise that we have differing groups of people at funerals, each with their own requirements:

- The chief mourners
- The friends of the deceased
- The friends of the bereaved
- The wider community
- The officials.

It is important to recognise that the needs of these differing groups require a different focus. The chief mourners are probably still in shock and numbness. From my own research I have found that with their higher degree of attachment and the unexpectedness of the loss, the bereaved family tends to recall little of the funeral service. They do appreciate the numbers of people who attend, however. What the minister says tends to go over their heads. They appreciate what we do but will find it hard to forgive us if we make a mistake. They are people who need recognition of their intense pain and grief. The minister needs to stand alongside them in their pain and be their voice as they cry out, 'My God, my God, why?'

I personally find myself doing one thing for the chief mourners at the church, another for the wider community and something different again when I'm just with the key members of the family at the committal. At the church I am identifying with them in the pain, but I use the time at the crematorium as an opportunity not only to say goodbye to the deceased but also to briefly prepare the main mourners for what lies ahead of them on their journey. I endeavour to sow seeds offering further support in the months ahead.

The wider gathering is in a very different place. They are one step removed from the bereaved family. They may be grieving for the person in the coffin or they may be thinking about other losses that this service reminds them of. They may also be thinking about their own mortality. The minister is communicating with these people in a different way. This is the place where the bigger issues of life, death and what might lie ahead can be addressed. This is the group of people who have the capacity in a service to think about 'Who am I?', 'Who are you?,' and 'Where am I heading?'

The friends of the deceased may take this in or they may be very focused on the life of the deceased and want something significant to be said about the person. To achieve this I use a simple technique from Post-Traumatic Stress Debriefing, which allows me to be accurate when speaking to the congregation. I write down the actual words that the bereaved use when describing the deceased. By feeding this back in the service, I know they will accept and agree with what is said, thus providing comfort and acceptance. With regards to the friends of the bereaved, they may or may not have known the deceased. Their focus will be about caring for their grieving friends. They require resources for assisting those who are grieving. We also need to be aware of the need for balance between those who want a reserved, 'common prayer' format, where every funeral is identical, and those who want a more personal and expressive service.

We need to be aware of anyone who feels left out in their grief. Perhaps they were very close to the deceased but no one recognises them. The funeral might be their opportunity to be drawn in to something bigger, to have a moment to express their thoughts and prayers, through hymns, words or prayers, and to say a final goodbye.

So the role of the minister at a funeral is varied and, if done well, achieves communication across the congregation. We also communicate to other officials at the funeral. The engagement therefore needs to be real and congruent, otherwise we are just going through the motions, which can easily be detected. I have found myself in this position at times, and it has left me feeling frustrated and unfulfilled. Who knows how the congregation felt?

The funeral acts as a ritual, as Tony Walter puts it, 'to transport the deceased to the land of the dead, and the bereaved back to the land of the living.'[69] There is a kind of conveyer-belt process going on here. We start out as chief mourners in a daze, then we find ourselves in subsequent months attending other funerals, this time sitting further back from the coffin. Each time we attend a funeral we process different aspects of the event and what death means to us.

So to summarise, as ministers, what are we doing at a funeral?

- We are acknowledging the reality of death.
- We are providing a vehicle to express emotion.
- We are recalling and sharing our memories of the deceased and their significance in our lives.
- We are providing opportunities to reflect upon previous losses.
- We are helping people to acknowledge that we are in a process of change.

---

69. T. Walter (1990), *Funerals and How to Improve Them,* London: Hodder & Stoughton.

- We are opening up possible ways of bringing change.
- We are helping people to recognise that we are not alone but part of a community.
- We are opening ourselves to the unknown, to wonder, awe and mystery.
- We are enabling others to say, 'I am not an island but I need others to successfully journey in life.'
- We are teaching a sound Christian approach to God's creation of forgiveness and hope.
- We are celebrating God's involvement and the work of Christ in our lives.
- We are providing an evangelistic opportunity by being pastorally sensitive.
- We are producing a 'good enough' service that will sow seeds of positive attitudes towards rituals, faith and the church.

Memorial services in church

There has been an increase in the number of memorial services that occur after the body has been taken to the crematorium or cemetery. The main reason for this has been logistics. When I ministered in the countryside, it could take an hour and a half to get to the crematorium and back in time for the wake. By then, most of the congregation had moved on. It is therefore understandable that people might want to do the committal first, just for close family and friends, and then have a thanksgiving service afterwards, perhaps days or weeks later. I can see nothing wrong with this approach, provided it is not because the community is unable to handle the reality of death. With no coffin, we are softening the impact that death has upon us. I have heard it said that 'it is too upsetting to see the coffin in church'. Yet one of the purposes of a funeral is to offer an opportunity to express emotion in a safe way. Without that opportunity of release, we can simply be lingering in denial and storing up emotions for the future.

The role of thanksgiving and memorial services can be therapeutic. In Britain we only have two occasions every year to remember the dead. The first is Remembrance Day in honour of those who have died during wars or armed conflicts. This is very much a national occasion. The second is more of a church event on All Souls' Day. Both of these events occur at a similar time in the year, namely in the autumn (1 or 2 November and 11 November), which leaves a large part of the year with no special occasion of recall. This doesn't leave much opportunity to remember the dead at other times of the year. Hence memorial and thanksgiving services can be a very helpful part of the grieving journey.

In Poland, All Souls' Day is a huge national event and an extremely moving occasion. It is likened to going to a football match with crowds of people blocking the roads, carrying flowers and candles as they walk to the cemeteries. We may not have such an occasion here in Britain, but we can mark time out for special thanksgiving events over the calendar year.

Roadside memorials

Today it is impossible not to notice roadside flowers, usually marking the place of the death of an individual. It is complex as to why this has developed in recent years. It may be partly linked to the mass of flowers that arrived at Kensington Palace after the death of Princess Diana. It may reflect that people feel less in touch with church as a sacred place of remembrance. It may also be due to how the world communicates today, where one event is quickly shared with the world through the media and the internet and is then instantly copied over and over again.

What is special for the bereaved is that this spot is where the deceased was last seen alive. It is now a place of significance. If the Church wishes to engage with the bereaved who identify and mark such places, we need to also recognise them as temporary sacred places. How do we then help these families transfer their grief and remembrance to the Church? We have to engage where they are at when we first meet them. This might mean being willing to go with the family to the location of death to carry out a short, prayerful service of remembrance. By making a link with the bereaved, the deceased and the location, we are in a better place to help the family move forward and make a connection with the church for the months and years to come. For the bereaved to find meaning will involve understanding what took place at the point of death. We need to be willing therefore to engage at that point.

The heart of ministry is always being willing to go where people are at, before we are able to move them forward in their faith towards God. By offering the church and our ministry as a gift to the bereaved and the local community we hope to avoid any criticism that might be levelled at the church for being uncaring, and offering a good example of loving our neighbour.

Reflections

- What role do funerals play within the life of your church?
- Is this responsibility carried only by the minister or do lay workers offer support?
- Does the church see funerals as one-off events or the beginning of a pastoral journey with the members of the community?
- How do the following two verses of Scripture reflect your church's funeral ministry?
  - John 11:35: 'Jesus began to weep.'
  - John 14:6: 'I am the way, and the truth, and the life.'

Chapter 46
Bereavement

Come sit with me on my mourning bench.
(Nicholas Wolterstorff)[70]

How can we help someone who is suffering from loss? In the midst of many grief theories, pastoral workers need to develop their own appropriate approach. Perhaps a simple model to use would be to consider the three phases that we engage in with the bereaved.

Opening phase

In this phase the pastoral worker is seeking to build up trust, rapport and an understanding of the bereaved person's history. This allows us to form an assessment of the extent of the loss and what the bereaved might be seeking from us. It then allows for clarification of expectations from each other. We have to be very careful not to promise something that we can't deliver. Often bereavement work is not a short-term fix but requires someone who is willing to journey with a person over an extended time. If we can't offer that kind of support we need to be clear right from the beginning. It is better to say that we will just be able to call a couple of times and recommend other support agencies than to promise we will keep visiting and then stop after a few weeks.

I often feel when I do a pastoral visit that I am a kind of detective, absorbing information. This needs to happen in a natural and unforced way. But by simply observing the surroundings, asking open questions and developing good listening skills, it is amazing how much information we can glean from what a person casually shares. In this early stage of a relationship we are looking to gather information relating to four specific areas.

The type of death

We need to find out whether the death was sudden or gradual. Was it a shock or did the bereaved have time to adjust? Were they able to be with the person before death and able say goodbye? If the death was sudden and unexpected or untimely, then the bereaved may

70. N. Wolterstorff (1987), *Lament for a Son*, Grand Rapids: Eerdmans.

have additional issues to resolve. This would also be true if it was a horrific death or perhaps mismanaged at some point.

The nature of the relationship

As previously said, the closer a person perceives themselves to have been to the deceased, the greater the impact of the death. Therefore we are looking to see what kind of relationship the person had with the deceased. Were they independent of or ambivalent towards the deceased? Was it someone that they were dependent upon? This might have been for financial support, emotional support or regular contact, or was the person a part of a their regular daily routine? What you will not know initially is whether there was any complexity in the relationship, such as violence or abuse. It takes time for someone to trust you to be willing to share more complex and possibly deeply painful issues. Clearly, such complexities will play a role in how a bereaved person recovers from their loss. If we are unaware of such issues, we may be confused at how the bereaved is behaving.

The character of the survivor

We all react to loss in a way that reflects our personality and past experience. The baggage we carried before the loss is the same baggage that we carry into the loss. Therefore a grief-prone personality or a person who is insecure and suffers from low self-esteem will undoubtedly find loss hard to handle. People who have previously suffered with mental illnesses or who show signs of excessive anger or self-reproach will require particular attention. This will equally apply to people with some kind of disability, which might frustrate or confuse how they are able to express their feelings. One character type who might easily slip under our radar might be someone who finds it hard or impossible to express their anger. We might think they are coping very well as they appear to be calm. It is only as we build up gentle trust with the person that they will gain the confidence to share with us, as well as acknowledge to themselves, how they are really feeling.

The social circumstances

A key factor in how people recover from loss is the kind of social support they have. What kind of family support does the person have? Are there family complexities that this death will make worse, or easier? Have they friends who will travel with them on their journey? Have they employment that will provide a sense of purpose and direction or are they unemployed with lots of time on their hands? What kind of responsibilities do they already have? Have they dependent children? Have they experienced other significant losses in their lives that might make the situation more complex? These social issues can play a big part in how a person adapts to their loss.

Intermediate phase

This is the largest chunk of the work of a pastoral worker as they journey with the bereaved. Part of this is to begin to see where there might be areas of complication or hindrance for the bereaved that prevent them from adapting to their loss. This might include looking at any tasks they are finding difficult and helping them to find ways to overcome these. Everyone has their own adaptive coping strategy. This needs to be recognised, affirmed and supported. Grief is something we 'do' rather than something that just 'happens' to us. This means we can help people make all kinds of decisions, such as:

- Do I view the body?
- Which funeral director shall I use?
- Do we have a cremation or a burial?
- Do we use a church or not?
- What do I do with the ashes?
- What do we put on the gravestone?
- How long shall I take off work?
- Do I need medication or will it hinder my recovery?
- Do I share my grief or keep it private?
- What about my finances?
- How do I fill in these forms?
- Do I move house or stay put?
- How do I remember yet move on?

The questions keep coming. It is important to stress that there is no right or wrong about what a person decides, but they may well need support to come to answers they are comfortable with. Along this journey we are helping people to find new meaning in life and to reconstruct their own personal stories. This might mean going through this reconstruction process many times until it begins to makes some sense.

Another thing we are doing through our presence is gently reminding the bereaved person to include God in their reflections. This involves identifying things to be thankful for, recognising his presence now and finding some hope for the future. It is by incorporating faith in our conclusions that we can come to a healthier position.

- What is God saying about the past?
- What is God saying about the present?
- What is God saying about the future?

During this period we are providing an opportunity for people to talk about the deceased and retell their story. Sometimes our visits are the only opportunities they have to do this, the only times they feel they have permission to talk about the deceased and express emotion with another rather than always by themselves. This is about being willing to use the deceased person's name and encouraging the bereaved to talk about them. It is very hard to reconstruct our identity alone. We need others to help us to reflect. It's like doing a jigsaw puzzle together. The person holding the piece is the only one who can place it, but another person's eyes can help with suggestions of where the pieces might go and in which order.

The jigsaw can never be the same, which is hard for both the bereaved and the pastoral carer to accept. As we struggle to cope with the bereaved person being different since their loss, they themselves have to grapple with how their life will never be the same. There is a parallel process going on here, which is well worth recognising and acknowledging with the person at some point.

Be aware that grief issues can seem far worse during the winter. It is a time of short days and long nights. We find ourselves drawing the curtains so early in the day that it can make us feel more alone and isolated. Those who suffer from SAD syndrome will find that their grief exacerbates the problem. A good pastoral visitor will be aware of this and will particularly keep in contact with people during this period. It may be just a regular telephone call in the evenings over the first winter of the person's loss.

The final phase

This phase can be difficult for both the bereaved and the pastoral worker. It is made easier if clear expectations are clarified at the beginning of the relationship. It is important always to terminate a pastoral relationship in a positive way. This requires preparation in helping the person to be aware that the relationship in its present form will end.

This does not necessarily mean the worker will not see the person at church or in the community at some point, but that the regular specific meetings relating to the loss will end. An important part of the termination is to have time to review the progress the person has made as well as identifying issues they may still need to work on. It is also an appropriate time to point out other types of support that can be called on within the community. It is important that people know that they have other places to turn to and that they never feel trapped. How will we know when a person has reached a satisfactory position? After all, they will never be back to how they were, but coming to terms with the difference is a sign of adaptation. We can look for pointers of recovery. They will initially include going back to work, eating normally and regaining some kind of sleep pattern. Later they might include:

- Regaining an interest in life
- Finding a sense of hope and purpose
- Beginning to be more thankful
- Finding new roles and positions in the community
- Taking new initiatives
- Forming new relationships.

For many, the mourning never ends, but they do regain a lifestyle that provides them with a degree of satisfaction while playing their part within the community. When we see a person who recognises that they are beginning a new chapter in their life, then we can be encouraged that our care has been worthwhile.

Is there a time to talk theology?

From my own research of interviewing bereaved parents, I have found that the early stage of grief is not the time to talk theology. At this stage the family want someone who will be there for them, to identify in their pain and to cry out with them in their despair. It is only later, perhaps three to five months on, that people can engage in a more open discussion about theology. Unfortunately, often the church has lost touch by this stage. There are, of course, stories of conversions in some bereavement situations days after the death. But the reality is that this is not the norm.

We therefore have to think of a better strategy to engage with the bereaved. It may be that a carer has been visiting and over time they recognise that it would be beneficial for the 'theologian' pastor to visit in order to relate to particular faith questions. This type of teamwork works well and makes the most of people's gifts and time. The key is still to be engaged with the bereaved in order to reach this point. I find that faith issues arise naturally out of conversations as the bereaved share their stories with me. I use a range of pointers that enable me to help a person extend their narrative. I then seek to help the bereaved weave their faith within the narrative.

- Use open questions to invite the story, e.g. what does loss mean to you? How would you describe your feelings on a typical day? How has it changed over time?
- Convey interest in the hardest part of the story, e.g. what is the most painful part of your experience? What are the parts of your story that people hear least?
- Consider the impact of this loss on the survivor's worldview, e.g. has the loss changed the way you see things? About life? Yourself? Future?
- Evaluate the impact of the loss on the griever's social life, e.g. how has it affected their relationship with other people? What concerns do others have about you?
- Balance the need to build the working alliance with the person and the need for sufficient information, asking more specific questions as necessary for clarity.
- Do not force questions but encourage a natural flow in the conversation, putting questions into the narrative as appropriate. Remember, people connected with others usually experience better outcomes.

Remember to look for beneficial changes in their narrative and outlook of life. When faith arises, explore how the person views God and their faith. Bereavement listeners have a range of open questions that they can use to help a person open up about their experience. These are helpful in giving us confidence to have a rough idea of what we can explore with a person. Although I don't have a list in front of me during a visit, I do have a series of open questions that incorporate religious and faith issues ready to help the bereaved explore their experience and how they see themselves now within their faith (or lack of it).

- What experience of loss would you like to explore?
- What do you recall about how you responded to the death?
- How did others respond?
- Who were you as a person at the time of death?
- What does this loss mean to you?
- What is the most painful part of the story?
- Has the loss changed the way you view life? Yourself? Your future?
- How has it affected your relationship with others?
- How has it affected your relationship with God? The church? Religious friends?

- What concerns do others have about you?
- Close your eyes and visualise a scene connected with the deceased. Who or what is your focus of attention? What is happening? Where are you? What feelings do you notice now in your body? What was the most emotionally significant part of the experience?
- Do you have trouble accepting the loss?
- To what extent has it been hard for you to trust others?
- Are there any Bible stories that relate to your story?
- How has it affected your prayers?
- Do you pray differently now?
- Do you feel angry about the loss? Towards whom? Yourself? The deceased? God? The Church?
- Do you feel uneasy about moving on with your life? Which areas are difficult for you? New friends? Interests?
- Do you feel emotionally numb or feel disconnected with others since the death?
- To what extent do you feel life is empty or meaningless?
- Do you feel that the future holds no meaning or prospect of fulfilment?
- Do you feel on edge or jumpy?
- Have you thought of writing a letter to the deceased?
- Where is the deceased now for you?
- What beliefs do you have about life beyond?
- What philosophical beliefs contribute to your adjustment?
- How did you make sense of the death when it happened? And now?
- How has your faith changed? Do you view God differently?
- How has it affected your priorities?
- What was your view of yourself before? And now?
- What metaphor or image would symbolise your grief?
- What steps could you take to help your healing?
- How might your faith assist you now?
- What would you have said to someone experiencing loss before this event?
- What can the church do to help you?
- What would you like me to pray for, with you, or later by myself?

These questions are just catalysts in enabling a person to see their situation from a new perspective. I might only use one or two of them as they naturally arise during the conversation. There must be no sense that you are simply working through a list. People's narratives are unique and individual. The bereaved are in the process of finding out just what their narrative means, where it ends, where it begins again and what link there might be between the past and the future. If our sensitive questions can help in this, we will help the person take a step forward with their lives and hopefully with their faith.

Reflections

- Think about a time when you have been in need and someone came and supported you. What was it about their visit that supported you the most?
- Think about a recent pastoral visit that you have done. Can you picture it, smell it and hear it? Go through in your mind what you actually thought, said, did and how you reacted in the situation.
- What do you think you were actually doing in that visit, and what do you think the person was expecting and wanting?

For a fuller discussion of loss issues in churches see *Grief, Loss and Pain in Churches: A handbook for understanding and advising in a Christian context* by Bill Merrington (Kevin Mayhew, 2011).

Chapter 47

Disenfranchised grief

Grief tears a hole in the fabric of life, we spend the rest of our lives trying to mend it.
(Steven Jeffers and Harold Smith)[71]

In one of the churches I worked in, we had a team who would do house-to-house calls on everyone in the parish of 4,000. We had a team of lay people who would send letters first of all saying that the church would be visiting on a particular day. People had the choice to contact the church office and decline the visit. When the team did call, they had a small questionnaire, which ended with the question of whether they would like the vicar to visit. Most declined, but I was asked to visit a stranger. She was a single lady, approximately in her forties. After a cup of tea and a friendly chat I enquired why she had particularly wanted a visit. She slowly and hesitantly shared how she had had an affair with a married man who had three children. He was a work colleague and the affair had gone on for about four years. Unfortunately, the man died suddenly of a heart attack. She felt unable to go to the funeral. No one at work knew of the affair and she hadn't shared it with her parents or friends. It was now 18 months later as she finally shared with me how she was feeling.

Much of what is being said in this chapter is what we recognise as something called 'disenfranchised grief'. Disenfranchised grief is where a person experiences a loss that is not or cannot be openly acknowledged, publicly mourned or socially supported. Some of the signs of this form of grief might be:

- Exclusion of care
- Lack of social support
- Exclusion from funeral rites, etc.

Disenfranchisement can come in many forms. For example,

- When people do not reconstruct the story of their lives
- When someone is surrounded by silence
- The loss of an ex-spouse

71. S. Jeffers & H. Smith (2007), *Finding a Sacred Oasis in Grief*, Abingdon: Radcliffe Publishing.

- When a workplace fails to recognise a loss
- Caregivers who fail to give time to recognise a loss
- When nursing home or hospital staff are dealing with multiple deaths
- When a person can't acknowledge that they are broken-hearted at the death of an animal
- When a person has been adopted and their loss is unclear and vague
- When many children have been fostered, all of whom have moved on
- When ministers engage with a large number of funerals.

We need to remember that grief is complicated when it is delayed, suppressed, interrupted or merged with additional losses. One of the roles of a pastor is to intervene where appropriate; in doing so, we can help to facilitate grief and prevent disenfranchised grief from developing.

People often don't raise the subject of loss in a society that tends to deny its existence. But a pastoral worker can skilfully open the floodgates. If we are able to patiently ask open questions in an environment where the person can see that we are genuinely interested and actively listening, they will gain confidence to truly share their thoughts and feelings about their loss experience. Tears can often be close to the surface when a sensitive pastoral carer visits. As well as listening skills, we can provide a continuity of care through regular visiting. We have the skills and knowledge to see when someone is struggling and, with our networking contacts, we can link the grieved with appropriate support agencies. Unlike other secular community workers, we can also help people in their faith struggles. In this capacity we have an ability to love and to absolve guilt. It has been said that there are regrettable things in life but no regrettable people. Our calling therefore is to work through the negative issues in people's lives so that their self-esteem is restored. It was Proust who said, 'We are healed of suffering only by experiencing it to the full.'[72]

Therefore, good grief means working through our painful experiences and feelings. If we do a Bible study of Jesus' encounters with people, we will see that he met a good number of disenfranchised people. To name but a few:

- There was the woman with the flow of blood. Jesus healed her physically; despite the fact that he was rushing to heal a dying

72. Marcel Proust (1871–1922).

child, he stopped to hear her story. She no doubt needed not only physical healing but also emotional healing via the telling of her story. Would the healing have been complete if Jesus had not heard her? (Luke 8)

- We are told that Mary, the mother of Jesus, right from his birth stored up all that happened to her, right up to seeing her grown-up son suffer death on the cross. At the point of death, Jesus directed her to his friend, John, that he might care for her. Was Jesus providing a channel for his mother to express her long stored-up grief? (John 19)
- Zacchaeus was a tax collector who carried the baggage of being a loner, isolated from the people from whom he collected taxes. It's no wonder he had to climb a tree to see Jesus, as no one would let him in to the crowd to get a good view. Jesus, however, embraced the man by asking to stay at his house, thus making him acceptable and relevant. (Luke 19)
- Jesus engaged with the woman at the well who clearly had a story that others were reluctant to listen to. (John 4)
- There was the man who had been ill for 38 years with no one to put him in the pool when the water was disturbed by the Spirit. (John 5)
- The Apostle Peter after the death of Jesus seemed disenfranchised in his grief and from his fellow disciples, until Jesus redeemed him. (John 21)
- The lepers whom Jesus touched and healed had been previously ostracised by the community. (Luke 17)
- In the parable of the prodigal son, we might identify a number of people who were grappling with loss issues. (Luke 15)
- Finally, the individual who was and is a challenge to us all – was Judas an example of a disenfranchised individual that no one reached out to save before it was too late? (Matthew 26)

Reflections

- Can you identify stories of other disenfranchised people in the Bible?
- Have you ever been disenfranchised?
- Can we provide a care system so that our ministers and those in the church who are in caring professions are supported so that they do not become disenfranchised?
- How can we help people to express their mourning in a church context?

Part five

Health issues

Chapter 48

Anxiety

Every tomorrow has two handles. We can take hold of it with the handle of anxiety or the handle of faith.
(Henry Ward Beecher)[73]

I recall as a 6-year-old running out of the house to a mobile sweet shop. I bought some penny chews. By accident I picked up two chews that were stuck together but I only paid for one. Afterwards I felt anxious and guilty. It must have been a deep emotional reaction, as I can still vividly recall it today.

The next few health topics, with all of their fancy titles and descriptions, will all involve this simple but powerful word: 'anxiety'.

Today, we live in a very anxious world. People try all sorts of things to remove it, deny it or suppress it, but anxiety is part and parcel of life and the sooner we learn to recognise it and handle it the more fulfilling our lives will become.

Anxiety is the body's way of grabbing our attention about something. The first signs might be butterflies in the stomach, sweating, feeling breathless, a headache, shaking, poor sleep or just becoming irritated. All of this is telling your brain that something important is happening and you need to sit up and take note. Anxiety is often triggered when there is a threat or danger that might challenge your beliefs, rules and goals of life. When there is a clash between beliefs and behaviour a tension is created that causes an alarm reaction within.

All of this gets the body to be ready to react to the potential danger. It releases the hormone adrenaline, increases your heart rate, and glucose is released to provide energy for the brain to become more sensitive. It is only after all of these reactions that the brain begins to think about the situation and to speak to itself about what to hope for or what to do. All of these reactions are perfectly normal and affect everyone every day. However, sometimes events of the past become so significant that they trigger an oversensitive reaction in the present. This is like an echo, which causes us to overreact to something because we are really reacting to an event that happened long ago. This can then lead to what are called 'panic attacks'. Here, a cycle develops which can spiral out of control.

---

73. H. W. Beecher (1813–1887).

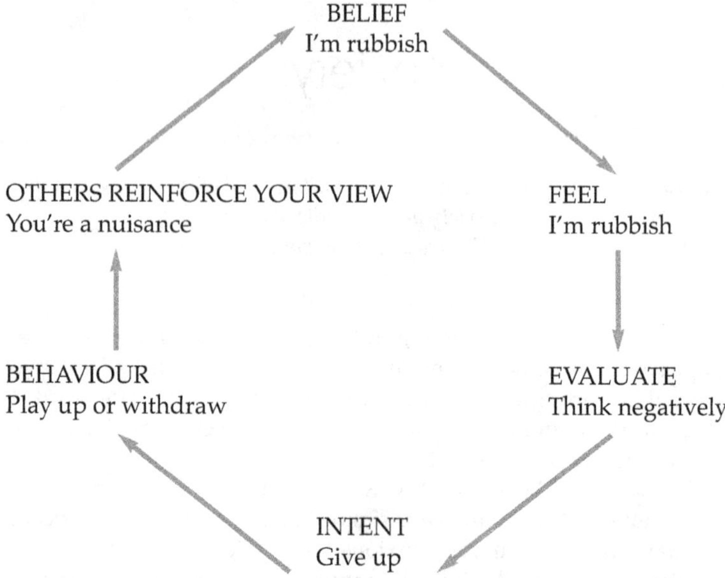

Figure 14: The Behavioural Cycle

Let's think of an example. A child, for whatever reason, has developed a negative view of himself. He tells himself he is rubbish and then he feels it. This affects his thinking. At school he doesn't try because he doesn't believe he can do the work. So he lives out his belief and plays up in class. Others confirm his attitude by rejecting him, which in turn ostracises him even more. His belief about himself is confirmed and deepened.

The key to anxiety, along with all of the symptoms that will follow in this section, is to face the 'foe'. Recognising and acknowledging the anxiety is the beginning of recovery. When the smoke or burglar alarm goes off it is telling us something. But what? We don't actually know whether it is overcooked bacon, burnt toast, a burglar or whether it is windy and the curtain has knocked over an ornament. If we ignore it, the alarm will keep going off. But if we check it out, 99 per cent of the time we can sort it out and get on with life without a worry.

An accumulation of anxiety eventually leads to stress. If we are willing to analyse the way we experience anxiety, we can then begin to compensate for it. We can reflect on how we think in such situations, and whether we have regular thought and behaviour patterns. In this way we can begin to challenge some of our fears. All of this can take time. Anxiety-related behaviour creates ingrained habits which take persistence to change. But with the right support, a greater degree of control and peace can enter a person's life.

When we are dealing with people who are full of fear and feeling hopeless, it is understandable that we will pick up on their anxiety. It can be so strong at times that we can become overwhelmed by it. Our natural response can be to play down someone's anxiety with a desire to cheer them up or talk them out of their worries. Yet this is often not in a person's best interest. We have to recognise that there is a reason why someone is anxious. Our role is not to change people but to help people to understand themselves better so that they might know what they need.

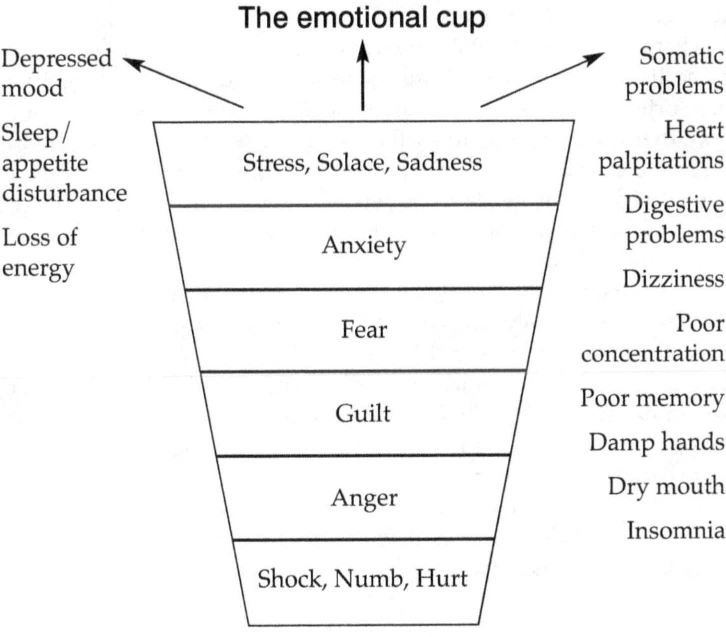

Figure 15: The Emotional Cup

The emotional cup is a simple way of understanding how people become anxious. Imagine someone has dropped a brick on your toe. The first thing you would feel would be pain and hurt. Within a split second, anger would follow. The anger may be expressed verbally or physically or it might be suppressed, but anger would be there. If you imagine these feelings as liquid chemicals filling a plastic cup, it gives an idea of the fluidity of the experience. Guilt of some sort follows anger when we regret our reaction or thoughts. Then the other person pick up a second brick, and fear instantly fills the cup. We have a saying in England: 'once bitten, twice shy'. It is so true. If a dog has bitten you, it will make you very cautious the next time you see a dog. If you keep seeing dogs (or the other person has more bricks in their hand) anxiety will begin to fill your life. If it remains, sadness, stress and solace will eventually follow.

All of these reactions are emotions, but they build up and begin to affect the body physically. Hence people then go to the doctor with real somatic systems such as eating disorders, headaches, digestive problems or lack of energy. If you think of this as a closed can of soft drink that has been shaken, what happens when you bump into it and open the can? If you meet a person who is so full of emotions, you will be unsure as to whether the person is about to get angry with you or burst into tears.

There are clear Christian answers to these emotions. Hurt needs to be listened to ('Blessed are those who mourn, for they will be comforted' – Matthew 5:4). Anger needs to be expressed in a safe way that does not lead to further hurt. We often advise people in marriage guidance not to allow the sun to go down on their anger (Ephesians 4:6). It needs to be released and let go of. The Church encourages forgiveness every Sunday. God brings release from guilt, hopefully others forgive us, but we still need to remember to forgive ourselves. Scripture tells us that 'perfect love casts out fear' (1 John 4:18). Finally, we are told to bring all of our worries and concerns to God in prayer (1 Peter 5:7). If we can take some of these Christian tools and practise them, then we will find that our emotional cup will be less full, thus reducing our anxiety. It also makes room in the cup for the Holy Spirit to embrace us and enable us to bear fruit (Galatians 5:22-6).

People don't change when others try and change them. To bring the presence of God we need to be with a person such that they feel truly loved, accepted and heard.

Solution-focused method

There are other tools that can help us relate to people when they are in an extremely anxious state. Here I will mention one specific technique which can be a very useful resource to those in the pastoral role.

This approach is really quite simple. It begins with forming a relationship in which the client is able to explain their problems with the confidence that they will be listened to. Secondly, there is affirmation that the client has already taken a huge step forward by being willing to make the effort to come and talk to you. Thirdly, there is recognition that the person has already begun to seek answers to their problems. We need to help them to reflect on what has worked, even if it is only in part. We then begin to orientate the client to looking at possible solutions. We can do this with what is called a 'miracle' question:

'Suppose, tonight, you go to bed and fall asleep, and while you are asleep a miracle happens. The miracle is that the problem is solved. But when you wake up you won't know it has happened because you have been asleep. So when you wake up what will be the first things that you will notice that will tell you a miracle has happened?'

We then get the client to think further about what else might be different and begin to explore how this miracle might have already started to happen, even in very small ways:

'When have you already experienced changes? Have there been times when the problem didn't exist?'

We then get the client to think about what number the problem is at now, using a scale of 1 to 10, where 10 is when the miracle has happened and 1 is when the problem is at its worst:

'If your situation is currently at level 4, what might be happening when it is at level 5? What will you be doing?'

In this way, we have identified the problem, looked at exceptions when the problem is less evident, described a day after a miracle and looked at how the problem can be scaled. We have given a client an opportunity to see the situation differently and to recognise ways of how it might improve, even if it is slowly.

This approach can be easily seen from a Christian faith perspective using a person's faith to begin to think about the situation as if God had brought about the change that was desired. There is also emphasis for the person to 'pick up their pallet and walk' into the new visualised situation. Here we are building on a person's desire to hope for change.

Reflections

- How do you differentiate from everyday anxieties and more long-term affecting anxieties?
- Are there people in the church who are prone to excessive anxiety?
- How can the church help anxious people?
- How does an anxious person affect you emotionally?

- Think about the last time you were anxious. What was it about? How did it make you feel? How did it affect you physically? What thoughts kept running through your mind? How did you resolve it?
- What is your worst case scenario at work? In the home? With your health? Would it really be that bad?
- Breathing into a brown paper bag can bring calmness to a situation during a panic attack (it increases the carbon dioxide in the body). Also meditation, contemplation and mindfulness can all reduce anxiety.
- If you could wake up tomorrow and a miracle had happened, how would it be different? What would you feel? How would you think? Give it a try.
- Give the anxiety a number from 1 to 10. How does this compare to other anxieties in your life? At which number does it feel that you are out of control?
- Who can help you think through your anxieties? Often just talking about them reduces them considerably.

Chapter 49
Stress

The fear of flying:
to be sure of being involved in a major air accident, you would have to take a jet every single day of the year for 26,000 years!
(Arnold Barnett)[74]

Although those who feel called to general church ministry, or specifically to pastoral care, express high levels of job satisfaction, it doesn't mean that there are no stresses. In fact, the church can be a place that creates stress. The best way to tackle this subject is to understand it.

Stress arises when individuals perceive that they cannot adequately cope with the demands being made upon them or with threats to their well-being. Stress results from an imbalance between demands and resources. If you imagine a pair of scales, when the pressure put upon you is greater than the support you experience, the scales are tipped and stress results. This is a psychological, physiological and behavioural response.

Stress is not something in the outside world that happens to us; it is rather our own set of feelings and reactions towards what happens in the external world. Too much or too little pressure can result in stress. Contrary to popular belief, stress itself cannot be a good thing: it is always harmful. It can lead to angina, high blood pressure, heart attack, diabetes, mental disorder, ulcers, rheumatoid arthritis and cancer.

External stress factors or life events that are perceived as stressful affect us in three ways: psychologically, physiologically and behaviourally.

- Think back to the last time you felt stressed. Did you have any of these symptoms?
- Everyone reacts differently but most people will have a recognised pattern. What's yours?

74. A. Barnett, the George Eastman Professor of Management Science, MIT Sloan.

Psychological effects	Physiological effects	Behavioural effects
Anxious, angry	Palpitations	Accident proneness
Depressed, nervous	Tight chest, indigestion	Poor work, increased smoking, irritability
Guilty, apprehensive	Nausea, tiredness	Sulking, absence from work
Hurt, jealous	Vague aches and pains	Talking, walking or eating fast
Ashamed, tense	Clenched fists and / or jaw	Change of appetite
Cynical, helpless intake	Asthma	Increased caffeine
Low self-esteem	Migraines	Poor time management

Figure 16: The Effects of Stress

Psychological effects

The psychological effects of stress often come from thinking errors that have developed within the individual. These fall into a few categories:

- **Focusing on the negative** (and ignoring the positive): 'Things are going wrong in my life; nothing good is ever going to happen to me.'
- **Discounting the positive**: 'I only did well in the exam because I was lucky and the examiners were feeling generous.'
- **All or nothing, with no middle ground**: 'A job is not worth doing unless I do it extremely well,' or 'I hate my tutor; there is nothing good about him. My only option is to leave university.'
- **Mind-reading**: 'He must think I am incompetent for forgetting our appointment,' or ' She is pretending not to notice me; we're obviously not friends any more.'
- **Labelling**: 'Failing the exam proves I'm a complete fool,' or 'The lecturer is an idiot; he can't even arrive on time.'
- **Fortune-telling**: 'I know I won't get on with my tutor.'

- **Magnification**: 'If I fail this course, it will be the worst thing that could ever happen to me,' or 'I've overslept and will be late for the lecture; everyone will laugh at me.'
- **Minimising**: 'I was just lucky to pass the exam.'
- **Emotional reasoning**: 'I don't feel like studying now, so I'll do it when the time seems right,' or 'I feel like an idiot therefore I must be one.'
- **Personalisation**: 'My group work mark is low; I only have myself to blame,' or 'My students have not passed all their exams; I only have myself to blame.'
- **Generalisation**: 'What's the point of applying for a job? I applied for three and got nowhere.'
- **Shoulds, musts, have tos, and oughts**: 'I must always perform well whatever the task,' or 'I must always be approved of by significant others,' or 'My children should always get top marks.'

To overcome these effects we need to first recognise how we think. Then we need to befriend ourselves by turning our internal critical voice around and acknowledging the positive voice within us. Trying to find some middle ground in our thinking can help. Asking others for feedback about this can bring some balance to our thinking.

By de-labelling ourselves, we can also attempt to not label other people in a restrictive manner. Instead of filling our minds with strong words of 'ought' or 'must', we can try using words such as 'it's preferable' instead. This is something that needs to be practised daily. Ask yourself, 'Am I really 100 per cent to blame?'

We can use constructive imagery to help. Think of ways to overcome the stressful problem. Visualise yourself in six months' time, two years' time, etc. Will this problem still be so important?

Physiological effects

Physically we can help ourselves in a number of ways. Positive mindful relaxation exercises can help. Stress biodots can be used to measure stress levels. These are simple stickers that are placed on the wrist and which change colour according to body temperature. A stressed person is more likely to have cold hands. If relaxation exercises are practised one can see how the biodot changes colour. In this way, we can train ourselves to be in a relaxed state.

Nutrition can help considerably. Eating fresh food, avoiding processed food and drinking low-calorie beverages can help. Also, taking exercise with brisk walks, using the stairs rather than the lift and simply not eating late at night all help the body to relax. This has an effect on the sleep pattern. Trying to keep to a regular pattern for most of the week will improve health and well-being generally.

Behavioural effects

To lower stress levels we need to become more assertive. We have the right to say no, to consider our own needs as important, to make mistakes, to not understand, to be ourselves, to set our own priorities, to be assertive without feeling guilty.

Time management can make a big difference. Avoid procrastination, do what's important first and don't put off what you can do today. Allow time for the unexpected. Work in short bursts. Remember to play as well as work.

Having a broad social network brings variety and support through the difficult times of life. However, we do need to know which friends encourage us and to avoid those who are negative.

In the end, a Christian should be living a balanced life with more than one dominant thing in their life. In the squares below, identify nine areas of your life that are important. When the topic in one square encounters difficulty, you are still supported by the other eight. Stressed people often only have two or three areas, which they then place too much emphasis upon.

Figure 17: Signs of a Balanced Life

First-aid kit

We all have a rough idea what goes into a green first-aid box. But what do we have in our emotional first-aid box? I've asked many groups this question. At the top of the list is often chocolate and a glass of wine. Other responses include phoning a friend, having a hug, jogging, walking the dog, prayer and sleep.

Bear in mind that if you turn to drink and chocolate as an emotional aid, eventually the prognosis is not good for your physical health. We need to find healthy habits in our emotional first-aid box if we want to stay healthy. We also need to look out for particular signs of unconstructive behaviour:

- Not having regular days off
- Beginning to drink more or needing alcohol to relax each day
- Not booking regular holidays and retreats
- Not allowing oneself to have a couple of hours off work to just relax and do nothing
- Becoming lethargic
- Not having other interests outside the church
- Believing that the church can't cope without you
- Finding it hard to give time to prayer
- Not being able to keep empty space in the diary.

Having recognised that there is a danger of overwork for many ministers and pastors, there is also a subtle stress that comes from feeling unneeded. The phone doesn't always go, there are not constant emergencies to deal with, everyone in the parish is out at work, church members have moved to other churches. If you are a lay worker and the vicar chooses not to use you in the ministry of the church, it can be terribly frustrating. I found that in a rural context, although there was always plenty of work to do, there were also times when life in a rural rectory was relatively quiet. This created its own pressures.

Today, unless we are in a growing, relatively successful church, we can feel like a dinosaur in a secular culture. There is always cultural pressure to tell a member of the church or another pastor just how pressurised you are. But it is not always the case. We need to recognise that unemployed people are under a lot of stress too. Psychologically we can put a lot of pressure upon ourselves to maintain the illusion that all is well and everything is successful. Unfortunately, this is just not the reality. Participating in work-based learning groups in a confidential way has led clergy to begin to be open about how they really feel at times in the ministry. Allowing individuals to be real and to express how it really is in ministry is often the beginning of change.

Reflections

- What increases your stress levels?
- Does the church increase people's stress levels?
- What are the signs of a healthy church?
- How can you address stress within the life of the church?
- How could you teach and model a balanced Christian lifestyle?
- Can you develop a healthy first-aid kit in your life and church?

Chapter 50

Eating disorders

Anxiety does not empty tomorrow of its sorrows,
but only empties today of its strength.
(Charles Spurgeon)[75]

Eating disorders are on the rise, whether they be anorexia or obesity problems.[76] Eating is an essential part of healthy life. For most people it is instinctively natural and has no serious issues for them throughout their lives.

The reasons why some people have problems with food is very complex. Genetics, background, upbringing and personality type all play a part. Some of us simply couldn't become obese; our metabolism just wouldn't allow it. But for some people eating becomes a battleground over which they initially have control but which ultimately begins to control them. Sooner or later the problem affects not just the individual but it begins to affect the wider family and friends. What is clear is that all eating problems have a physical effect on a person as well as an emotional beginning. Over- or under-eating will have an effect upon the well-being of a person's physical health. This cannot be taken lightly.

Anorexia means the loss of appetite. However, that is not actually the case, as it is more about a conscious control of the appetite. It is, in fact, a form of self-starvation.

Extreme cases of eating disorders will usually be picked up by the NHS, but the vast majority go undetected in the community, with family and friends often colluding with the person that there is not a problem. The feelings of shame, guilt, fear and embarrassment mean that many go untreated. This is where a pastor can play an important role. We can often be a catalyst in encouraging and enabling a person to have the strength to do something about the problem.

Whether it is anorexia or obesity, individuals find themselves desperately trying to hold their lives together. This results in a desire to at least be able to control one thing – their eating. They are usually trying to escape an issue in their lives such that they see controlling their food intake as a quick fix, which gives positive feedback in the first instance. This in turn leads to fixed rules that

75. C. Spurgeon (1834–1892).
76. National Centre for Eating Disorders, London, 2012.

they must obey as the only way of making things better. The drive to follow these rules becomes so great that the person ignores the signs from the body warning them that something is wrong. The more the family tries to force the person to eat, the greater the person becomes determined not to eat. Along with this comes a distorted body image where, instead of looking in the mirror and seeing a very thin person, they think that the mirror shows that they are fat. Strict rules are played out, with increased anxiety if the person thinks they have put on any weight. The person begins to feel cold at the extremities of hands and feet. If a person reaches a critically low weight, they will need to be admitted to hospital and given a controlled high-calorie diet.

An individual suffering from anorexia will probably have a very low self-esteem, be consumed with self-hatred, grapple with inner turmoil and have a degree of depression. All of this usually means the person has limited or no social life or outside interests.

This is very drastic behaviour in order to avoid other issues in life. The result is that it leads to low blood pressure, weakening of the heart and general muscles, anaemia (lack of red blood cells), infertility, osteoporosis, digestive problems and the loss of electrolytes.

The causes of eating problems can be multiple, ranging from bullying, abuse, traumatic experiences, anxiety, stress to depression. But why do people turn to food control? There can be several reasons. It seems that this control is offering them something positive to their lives (at least temporarily). Food control gives the person power, which they lack in other areas of their lives. They are giving off a message about their lives, and they feel that this is the only way to communicate this message. It can also be an avoidant reaction, showing others that they need special attention and protection from other stresses in life.

Recovery can be very slow and rather a roller coaster. Eventually the person has to grasp that short-term gains will not reap what they want in the long run. Secondly, they have to begin to be honest about the pain they are feeling through lack of food. Thirdly, they need to begin to accept that change is achievable. Fourthly, they need to set realistic goals of recovery. This is a process and a journey and not something sudden. There will be times where they feel they are taking two steps forwards and one step back. Finally, they need to accept that they can't do this alone but need help and support along the way. Recovery is not necessarily getting back to a normal level of eating. Most recovering sufferers will always have hang-ups of one kind or another with food. What is required is a willingness to eat enough to live a normal functioning life that does not put unhealthy strain on the body.

We need to be aware of the role of purging in those with eating disorders. It comes about because of considerable panic, fear and guilt. Purging is never a safe way of controlling weight and it can become immensely addictive.

The pastoral team can play an important role in supporting people with eating disorders.

- At first, don't talk about how thin the person is or how little they are eating. There will be plenty of others pointing this out to them.
- Build a relationship of trust where you are willing to listen to the person's story.
- Encourage them to think about obtaining professional help. Regular visits to the doctor to be physically checked out can be helpful. This begins the process of helping the person to be informed about the negative effects of the lack of food on the body.
- Rather than merging the problem with the person, attempt to keep the person separate from the problem, but acknowledge that they have a dynamic, changing relationship with the problem. Often the person sees himself or herself as the anorexia rather than as someone separate from it.
- Trace the history of the problem and explore how it has developed.
- Help them to reflect on how the problem influences their relationships and whether this fits into their morals, hopes and desires.
- Help the person to think of alternative ways of being him or herself.
- Recognise that the person will be hearing dual voices in their head in regard to the positive and negative effects of their problem.
- Help the person to reflect upon the tension between what anorexia (the problem) is saying to them compared to the pain that they are experiencing within.
- Help the person to think about what anorexia (the problem) has promised in their lives and whether this has proved to be correct.
- Be prepared for the person to be thinking thoughts about anorexia that they never express to you.
- Help to bring an alternative version of themselves into the light: as a person who is loved, of worth, admired, wanted, respected, talented, capable and worthy of love.
- Help the person to realise that they have choices in this situation.
- Linking with support groups can be a lifeline. This might be via the internet at first. Helping the person to meet others who have made a recovery can also be encouraging and help the person to be motivated to begin to change.
- Help the person to find others who have recovered from anorexia

and to read stories of accounts of those who have conquered their issues.

- Anorexia has the ability to separate a person from their communities. We need to challenge this and encourage the building of safe relationships with others.
- As supporters we need to be very patient. It is easy to try too hard with a desire to see the person recover. However, this just adds pressure to the person and you may begin to lose their trust.
- Practical help can make a big difference, especially if the person lacks energy and strength to get out and about.
- Supporting the wider family and friends is also important. To watch someone appear to starve themselves is extremely stressful. Those closest to the person will need a listening ear and an opportunity to express their feelings of guilt, anger and fear. We can help the family to view the eating disorder as separate from the person themselves.
- Be aware that we cannot become an alternative to anorexia. The person themselves must claim authority.

Reflections

- Remember that recovery is possible.
- You don't have to be thin or fat to have an eating problem.
- Make a pros and cons chart of the effects of your eating. What is the short-term gain? What will be the long-term consequences?
- What does recovery look like for you?
- Remember, small steps over a long period are better than sudden changes.

Chapter 51

Drinking and drug problems

Every habit he's ever had is still there in his body, lying dormant like flowers in the desert. Given the right conditions, all his old addictions would burst into full and luxuriant bloom.
(Margaret Atwood)[77]

Drink and drug addictions are syndromes that affect far more than a person's mind and spirit. They have an effect upon their thoughts and actions as well as their family and friends. We need to understand that physiological dependency is at the centre of a person's addiction. The body needs the chemicals of the substance to feel pleasure and to avoid the pain of withdrawal.

The addict is driven by the need for more of the substance to achieve the desired high, resulting in obsessive thoughts and compulsive actions that drive the addict to get what they need. Addiction has been called a form of chronic adaption to the body's reward system. Once the message is received that 'more of the same will feel good', the drug and the thought drive each other. It is now recognised that many addictions are dependent upon an individual's genetic, developmental and environmental factors. Some people would simply never become addicted while others are highly vulnerable.

We need to recognise that if we get involved in pastoring people with such difficulties, we will need professional help. The absence of a drink or drugs for a day is not a long-term solution. The chemical addiction is a relapsing and progressive disease, meaning that the addict has to stop over and over every day. They therefore need help from someone who understands this process and battle.

One of the commonest accounts that is heard over and over again is when a new pastor with little experience in this field is led to believe that a person is 'clean' and just needs 'some finance' for a train ticket to an interview or to visit a seriously ill relative. We can all be taken in, as the lies can very convincing. However, this is only the tip of the iceberg compared to what the family experiences.

Although we may well refer on in such situations, we can be a key resource for the suffering family. It has to be recognised that stopping something is only half of the battle. If we focus only on the drink problem, we fail to see the whole picture. Even taking away

77. M. Atwood (1939–).

some of the stresses that might have driven someone to drink or drugs might not be enough. An empty life has to be filled with something meaningful. This is exactly where the Christian church can play a key role for recovering addicts of any kind. The Alcoholics Anonymous system recognises this.

The twelve steps of Alcoholics Anonymous[78]

1. Admit we are powerless over alcohol – that our lives have become unmanageable.
2. Come to believe that a Power greater than ourselves could restore us to sanity.
3. Make a decision to turn our will and our lives over to the care of God, as we understand him.
4. Make a searching and fearless moral inventory of ourselves.
5. Admit to God, to ourselves and to another human being the exact nature of our wrongs.
6. Declare we're entirely ready to have God remove all these defects of character.
7. Humbly ask him to remove our shortcomings.
8. Make a list of all persons we have harmed, and become willing to make amends to them all.
9. Make direct amends to such people wherever possible, except when to do so would injure them or others.
10. Continue to take a personal inventory and when we are wrong to promptly admit it.
11. Seek through prayer and meditation to improve our conscious contact with God, as we understand him, praying only for knowledge of his will for us and the power to carry that out.
12. Having a spiritual awakening as the result of these steps, we try to carry this message to alcoholics, and to practise these principles in all our affairs.

Whether a person engages with AA or not, there are some aspects that the pastoral team can focus upon. Firstly, we can engage in the subject of forgiveness. When trust has been destroyed with the church and family members, it can be hard to build fresh relationships. We need to recognise that forgiveness is not a quick fix but can be a long-term struggle. Sometimes wounds need to be healed before others can forgive. Helping the person to understand this can enable them to be realistic. An alcoholic can do such damage that relatives find themselves unable to forgive this side of heaven. God

78. www.alcoholics-anonymous.org.uk (accessed 9 October 2012).

may forgive us but we still have to live with the consequences of our deeds.

Secondly, we need to be careful in case the person becomes dependent upon us. This can prevent them from growing maturely into independence. The carer can feel trapped and guilty if they end their care, yet they may also be afraid of not being wanted and needed. This is where a group can be more supportive, distancing the dependence.

Thirdly, we need to maintain boundaries so that the addicted person does not interfere or dominate the carer's private life. Here the balance between an all-embracing God who calls us to love while protecting our families and ourselves can be complex. (Watch an episode on TV of *Rev* to appreciate this.) We need therefore to work in a team so that a balanced perspective can be maintained.

Reflections

- Does the local church engage with people with alcohol/drug issues?
- What do you think lies behind a person's addiction?
- How do we balance treating the symptoms and the cause?
- How equipped are you to handle a person's lies?
- Is your church willing to get involved with people who have addiction problems?
- How can the church be honest about some of the members' own addictions?
- Should the church be more equipped for people to express their emotions or to suppress them?
- Does the church grade people's sins by the way we treat people?

Chapter 52

Abuse problems

If you can't be thankful for what you have,
be thankful for what you have – escaped.
(John Wayne)[79]

Susan was an attractive 14-year-old whose family had been in the church for many years. She was a part of the youth group, although she was very shy and didn't seem to have many friends. The church had a paid youth worker who had been security checked. He had built up a good team of helpers and everything seemed to be going well with the young people's ministry. However, one day one of the lady youth helpers came to see the vicar. She was very concerned about one of the male youth helpers who seemed very close to Susan. The person in question was a married man in his fifties with two grown-up children and one teenager. The vicar assured the lady that this man was very respectable and suggested that perhaps there was a misunderstanding. He said he would have a quiet word with the man, and nothing more was heard about the situation.

A year later a formal complaint came into the church from a parent of one of Susan's friends. She informed the vicar that a man in the church was sending inappropriate text messages to Susan and that these messages were upsetting her. Susan hadn't told her parents. At first the vicar wanted to keep the police and social services out of the situation, but the mother informed him that she would take action if he didn't. The para-church authorities were finally informed and the police initiated an enquiry. The man in question, although he didn't have a police record and had come through clear on the CRB check, had in fact been grooming a number of young girls in the church. When it came to light that the issue had been raised with the church a year previously, the church's reputation was greatly tarnished in the community. The youth leader left and the youth work declined for a number of years.

Abuse comes in many forms. Sadly we have heard much about sexual abuse recently, particularly in the Catholic Church. However, there are other forms of abuse that take place in God's name that receive far less coverage.

---

79. J. Wayne (1907–1979).

Abuse can be physical, sexual, emotional, verbal, social, economic, intellectual or spiritual, all of which can be found in the church. Each case involves intimidation or manipulation of another person or an intrusion into another's inner being. The ultimate purpose, whether realised or not, is to exercise a degree of control over another person. It is generally a long-term pattern of behaviour that has developed in an individual, although specific short-term interactions can be labelled abusive.

We mustn't think that abuse is to be found only in the church. It can also be found in families, schools, sporting clubs, community organisations and the workplace. However, that is no excuse for its presence in the church that aims to set a higher example to the community. Yet we shouldn't be surprised that it occurs in church. Abuse usually occurs where a weaker person is manipulated by a stronger person. Since churches genuinely seek to care for the weak and vulnerable, it is understandable that an abusive individual might find the church an easy place to exercise their abuse. It might manifest itself as an individual grooming children. I recall an organisation that particularly cared for boys who didn't excel at primary school. It helped boys to gain their confidence through various sporting activities. The leader was a solicitor who had excellent references from school leaders and county youth authorities. The organisation had just begun to rent a church room when they were accused of abusing boys over several years. As the vicar of the building and the local chairman of the school governors, I was warned that my reputation might be tarred on account of my links to the organisation that was being accused. I wondered what might unfold both for my ministry and my faith, and how it might affect the local church and school. A nervous few months followed. The police and the church authorities told me that I mustn't speak to anyone about the situation. I wasn't allowed to speak to the accused or offer support to those damaged by the organisation. All I could do was to grapple with feelings of anger at those who should have known better, guilt for not double- and treble-checking references and carry a blurred pain for those who I didn't know whose lives had been blighted.

Fortunately and correctly, the church and school were not linked with the case. But this is an example where the church was on the edge of an accusation. But how would it have been if it had been a church activity? When abuse takes place it not only destroys individuals physically and emotionally but also attacks the heart of organisations and communities. Ripples go out that shake people's confidence in the church. The community naturally reacts with anger and rejects the church when this takes place. It can take years to rebuild trust and confidence.

But abuse doesn't have to be high profile to do harm. In fact, many people may not even fully realise that the church has abused them. They are simply left with a struggling faith, confused feelings about the church and a lack of direction. In the church, abuse might come from a youth leader or from within the group itself. A youth leader can groom a group of young people not for sexual purposes but to boost their own ego. It is not unusual for young people to feel pressurised into conforming to a belief system that they personally don't seem ready for. Youth groups are famous for being cliques and can be quite cruel to those who don't fit in. What results is a young person who is seeking God but who feels rejected by him because of poor youth work. It is one thing presenting Christ to young people and another to suggest overtly or covertly that to receive Christ you have to be a part of a particular youth group. The loss experience a young person is left with is one of confusion, of not fitting in, of wondering whether God is not for them and yet still longing for something more in their lives. This type of loss can linger for decades, unfocused and unresolved.

Since the characteristic of abuse is one of power misused over others, one might expect church leaders to be susceptible to causing abuse. The influence that a preacher or elder has in a church is considerable. Church gatherings, like any groups, are vulnerable to being led either in a healthy way or in a destructive way. Being a shepherd is a demanding role. Scripture teaches about the high expectations of Christian leaders, but why? Is it because of the deep damage we can do to people's lives, their faith and ultimate fulfilment of their calling in God's kingdom?

Leaders do damage when they:

- Have favourites within the church
- Make people feel guilty for non-biblical reasons
- Perpetually preach sin at the expense of grace
- Continue to treat Christians as not saved
- Prevent Christians from growing into maturity in case they challenge their authority
- Exploit people's financial generosity to build their egos rather than the kingdom of God.

Each of these situations causes an emotional reaction within people that damages both their individual life and the life of the church. Unhealthy leadership leads to Christians who feel undernourished spiritually, who lack self-esteem and who don't reach their full potential within the church. But ultimately the greatest loss is to the church as a whole.

Abuse doesn't just lie with the leaders; a good number of church leaders have been emotionally destroyed by attacks from church members. I can think of one church leader who was told that his children could play in the garden but not in the street, and that the congregation wanted access to the toilet in the manse. As months passed, he was then told that he was a common person and not up to the requirements of the congregation. Every Sunday he was presented with a religious newspaper with the comment, 'There's a job in here for you.' What kind of impact would such a personal attack have upon someone who has given up their career and taken a step of faith to retrain? Some are able to cope with such pressures and see it through, hopefully to a more stable time of ministry. After all, the one we follow was also treated with scorn. But not everyone is suited to such pressures. In such a situation there can be multiple losses. There can be a loss of that sense of calling that took the person into the Church and ministry. It now challenges any future calling as to what is the right way forward. There can be an attack on the person's self-esteem as they reflect on whether it was their own lack of faith that got them into this position. Then there are those who wonder whether God was in the calling in the first place.

We mustn't forget the damage that occurs to a minister's family and the wider congregation when a leader leaves the ministry. I served in one community after a minister left after great divisions. Several years later people were still telling me that they would support my ministry but wouldn't venture into the church and associate with those in the church.

What does all of this teach us? Firstly, that ministry is costly and we shouldn't doubt what some pay for their calling. Ministers who suffer greatly at the hands of other so-called Christians deserve our love, support and help to find a place within the Church where they can find healing and use their gifts for the good of all. When we fail to care for them effectively we simply do further damage to the wider Church.

Secondly, we have to recognise the fallenness of the Church. We not only attract hurt people to the church but also unfortunately at times create further hurt within individuals. If we can at least acknowledge this within our churches we allow the congregations to be honest and truthful. Too often we simply sweep issues under the carpet, which fails to set a godly example to others. We then wonder why people lose interest in what the church is saying.

Thirdly, when any kind of abuse takes place in the church, we need to recognise that, as with deep grief, it will take considerable time to bring healing both within the church and within the wider community. Most churches these days have clear child protection policies that are guided by their church authorities, but perhaps we should also consider some mechanism to handle other forms of abuse in churches, such as bullying and manipulation. Any policy that involves more than just the main leader taking decisions has to be a healthy practice.

Reflections

- Does your church have a clear abuse policy?
- How would you recognise when a person is being abused?
- What would convince you to report a case to the police or social services?
- Has your church completed CRB checks on everyone who works with children and / or vulnerable adults?
- How can the church bring healing in abuse cases?
- Would you speak out if there were covert signs of bullying in the church?
- Why not invite a regional specialist to educate your church leaders?

Chapter 53

Mental health issues

'Because the poor are despoiled, because the needy groan, I will now rise up,' says the Lord; 'I will place them in the safety for which they long.'
(Psalm 12:5)

It is impossible to be involved in caring for people without being involved with people with mental health issues. Indeed, a caring church will attract people who need to find a loving, caring family that will treat them with respect and care.

We know that one in four people will experience some form of anxiety or depression at some point in their lives. At present there are a greater number of women receiving treatment than men, although this might be because women are more likely to come forward for treatment. Approximately 10 per cent of children receive care from the health service while one in five older people will experience depression, two in five if they are in a care home.

The causes of mental health are still up for debate, but views oscillate between nature and nurture. If it is nature then inherited factors such as family history and family traits all play a part. If it is nurture, the environment is seen as the culprit, which could include trauma in the womb, insecurity and poor attachment as an infant, difficult life stages, abuse, abandonment and bereavement.

The good news is that about half the people who experience a mental health issue will find that they are back to normal within 18 months. However, certain people are more prone to problems. Alcohol and drug usage increases the likelihood. Sadly, most people in prisons will have some experience of mental health deterioration.

Church is not always an easy place to be if you have a mental health problem. Pastors are not always trained well enough to understand the issues or know how to react. On top of this, the Church has only a developing understanding of this subject theologically.

In the ancient world there was belief in spiritual powers, which might or might not be attributed to evil. However, by New Testament times, the concept of evil spirits and demons seemed clear: evil spirits could invade the body and personality, which led to illness and unusual behaviour. However, it can be argued that the Gospels also convey the message that demons may not necessarily equate with the cause of an illness (Luke13:32).

As the Church developed, it became clear that not all unusual behaviour was attributed to madness. Some people were identified as holy men and ascetics who manifested strange behaviour because of God's influence. So the cause could be moral, religious, medical or spiritual.

There have been Church leaders in the past who developed a softer side to ministering the mentally ill. Aurelianus (c.420) disapproved of using chains on those who were ill. Others, like Paul of Aegina (625–690), recommended treatment using music for mental derangement. By the thirteenth century, Bacon, a Franciscan, was arguing that these illnesses were from natural causes.

In the midst of the many witch-hunts of the fifteenth and sixteenth centuries, Johann Weyer published that many reasons could be the cause of unusual behaviour and that it was a crime to punish and torture so-called witches.[80] He called for empathy and compassion. From the Enlightenment period, Christian psychiatrists began grappling with these issues. Mania and melancholy began to be seen as not caused by supernatural powers. Freud's negative attitude to religion influenced many psychiatrists to see things from a non-religious perspective and develop their own theories.

Then, eventually, clinical theology developed, with Dr Frank Lake forming the Clinical Theology Association (1962). Others such as R. D. Laing (1969) believed that psychosis was a natural reaction to bad circumstances. By 2001, the Pope spoke out to defend the mentally ill and called on the Church to defend their rights and dignity.

Today, despite all the efforts of charities like MIND, there still exists a stigma to mental health. Some see sufferers as childlike and therefore consider that they need looking after. Others use another's misfortune to feel happier about themselves. Still others think that if a person is not responsible for their illness, this means it could happen to anyone. Therefore people create reassurance for themselves by stigmatising the illness. This can lead to blaming parents and the wider family for their wrongs, thus reducing the guilt in the observer. Some people also have an issue with the disruption that mentally ill people can make to the norms of a community so they distance themselves as a form of protection. The church is not always good at dismissing such stigma. If we see the problem as demonic and fail to bring order to the individual, the only conclusion is to distance ourselves.

We need to develop a healthy church attitude to mental health so that we communicate a God who loves all people equally, including people with mental illnesses. People with mental illnesses are

80. J. Weyer (1563), *On the Illusions of the Demons and on Spells and Poisons.*

entitled to be given the same dignity and respect as other people. They merit special care because they are the poor in terms of status, finance and influence. The love of God shown by people to a person with a mental illness helps that person.

Alongside this, a church needs to develop its own policy of handling mental health illnesses. A support group within a church can be invaluable in recognising needs, understanding, supporting and educating the church as well as keeping boundaries so that people do not become overloaded with issues and personalities. Fostering a link with a mental health practitioner can also be very helpful for advice and guidance as well as a very useful contact in emergencies.

To enable society to get a handle on people's emotional well-being, we have come up with a range of terminologies to categorise people. There is a great danger in labelling people, but it can be helpful for us to know the various ways in which the medical profession views people.

All of these labels can be seen from a biological or psychological viewpoint. One leads to treatment with chemicals (drugs therapy) or by talking therapy (be it cognitive behavioural therapy or psychotherapy, etc.). What we do know is that when people are 'labelled' in any way, they tend to be bullied and treated differently from others. This also leads to family dysfunction, unemployment, poverty and isolation. No wonder the Church needs to get its hands dirty by supporting such people. However, it is costly in terms of manpower, energy and faith. The best support inevitably involves a variety of styles. Biological, psychological, social and spiritual approaches are all needed if we are to get to the root problem and to provide healthy long-term recovery. This means that the local church needs to reflect on where it fits into this structured support.

The world of mental health is full of jargon that can be confusing to those not in the field. Some common terms include:

- COGNITIVE – to do with concentration, memory, understanding, intelligence and judgement.
- NEUROSES – disorders of emotion and behaviour, associated with anxiety and fear.
- PSYCHOSIS – a greater disturbance of mental functioning, including hallucination and delusion.
- HALLUCINATIONS – abnormal sense experiences. This might include seeing visions or hearing sounds or voices that are not regarded as normal.
- DELUSIONS – mistaken beliefs despite evidence to the contrary.

- DELIRIUM – confusion and disturbance of consciousness. This is often linked with alcohol and drugs.
- DEMENTIA – disturbance of higher brain function, memory, thinking, orientation, comprehension, learning and judgement. This affects a person's daily function of eating, cleaning and dressing.
- OBSESSIVE COMPULSIVE DISORDER – a person tries to manage their fears and anxieties by rituals. There can be frequent distressing thoughts or images. The rituals try to prevent these fears and contamination. Common compulsions are repetitive handwashing, repetitive checking or touching. Excessive orderliness and perfectionism may be associated with it.
- ANXIETY PHOBIAS – there are hundreds of phobias that people can become fixated upon. The top few include: spiders (arachnophobia), social where people are afraid of humiliation and criticism (social phobia), flying (aerophobia), leaving familiar places (agoraphobia) and confined spaces (claustrophobia).

Bipolar disorder

This involves marked mood swings between depression and mania. When the person is hypo-manic they will manifest signs of persistent mood elevation with increased energy, feeling very well, increased mental activity, sexual activity and irritability. All of this interferes with a person's normal routine, be it at work or socially. When manic, they will appear to be elevated, have inflated self-esteem and might partake in reckless spending and be aggressive, disruptive and over-optimistic. At first, friends and colleagues might just think they are high and great fun to be with. However, in the manic state, they are in a vulnerable position and could easily harm themselves intentionally or by accident. Excessive aggression, sexual activity, financial generosity and grandiosity can all lead to self-harm. When the manic phase reduces, the person can feel deflated and not themselves, as if they have lost a part of their identity. Sometimes when in such a state, a person will require hospitalisation or even sectioning until their mood descends.

The cause of bipolar disorder is still unknown. We do know that if manic depression runs in the family, you are more likely (5 per cent as compared to 1 per cent) to develop the disorder.[81] The sad fact is that this illness is very likely to recur. Stress can induce an episode.

---

81. M. Seligman et al (2001), *Abnormal Psychology*, New York: W. Norton & Co.

Supporting this illness is complex, but we can help if:

- We help the person to be as free from stress as possible
- Close friends and the pastoral team are informed about the illness
- The pastor has a conversation with the person (when they are well) about the church having a responsibility to call for medical help if they observe a radical change in mood
- There is reassurance that the church will support the person through any episodes
- The pastoral team keeps the person in a calm environment, free from arguments (especially of a spiritual nature)
- The pastoral team protects other church members from getting drawn into situations that might encourage manic behaviour
- The church recognises that the bipolar person's family will also need ongoing support.

Schizophrenia

This is a word that is often misunderstood. The term means a 'split mind'. Jekyll and Hyde comes to mind where a person can change identity and can become suddenly dangerous. The reality is far from this, however.

The word represents a group of mental illnesses, which lead to the disorganisation of a personality. Here the symptoms interfere with thinking, emotions and cognitive thinking. It can lead to the need for long-term psychiatric care. Hallucinations by hearing voices, delusions of false beliefs and distortion of thought processes are common. All of this accumulates into a sense of aimlessness, poor social connection, lack of motivation and limited speech.

Schizophrenia can affect people of all ages and affects one in every 100 people.[82] Unfortunately, repeated episodes can lead to being ostracised and isolated, which doesn't help effective medical treatment. Symptoms include hallucinations, seeing things that are not actually there, hearing voices and developing false beliefs that become fixed and hard to change. This delusion often brings with it a high degree of fear. Alongside this is a reduced ability to feel or express emotion and a lack of motivation. Personal hygiene can therefore be greatly reduced. Add to this a belief that the person's thoughts are being controlled leads to confusion, disorientation, agitation and distress. It is as though all of the person's senses have

82. M. Carson (2008), *The Pastoral Care of People with Mental Health Problems*, London: SPCK.

been magnified and they are receiving messages from everything around them. This can lead to thoughts of grandeur, belief that they are hearing voices from God or believing they are God. For others it leads the opposite way into deep fear and depression.

Sufferers don't have an ability to filter out stimuli – why are there all these red cars? Why are these people looking at me? The person is bombarded with input, which they struggle to sieve. One sufferer put it this way: 'Everything is so meaningful, impregnated with meaning. Everything around you is a sign to influence or mock you, so you are knocked about like a pinball machine.' Everything becoming significant is a sign that a person's dopamine level has risen.

Yet despite all of these symptoms, the person themselves may not realise that they are ill. This can make it very difficult for family and friends to handle.

The cause of schizophrenia is still under debate. Some believe the problem is biological while others believe that it is environmental. There does seem to be a greater likelihood of occurrence in cities and built-up areas than in smaller villages and the countryside.

Treatment usually involves either neuroleptics or anti-psychotics. The aim of these drugs is to reduce the auditory and visual hallucinations and, in turn, the anxiety. Unfortunately, many patients default with their medication, partly because of unhelpful side effects. Talking therapies and cognitive behavioural therapy may be helpful for some.

Pastorally, caring for a schizophrenic can be very challenging. Church and Christianity is all about thinking about who you are, where you have come from and how you relate to Christ in your life. If, however, you lose any sense of relatedness, either to yourself or to others, there seems to be no handle of support. We need to hold on to the fact that although a person may have lost a degree of their own identity, they are not lost to God and therefore not to the Church either. However, we need to recognise that our normal model of supporting people in need may be problematic. Usually we would build a relationship based on acceptance and empathy. In this safe relationship a person can begin to look at themselves and others afresh so that they gain a new perspective of life (hopefully a Christian one). But this approach can be very threatening to a schizophrenic since they struggle to build relationships and tend to withdraw, for their own protection. It is also hard for a carer to empathise when we really do not understand what is going on in the person's mind.

It is common for a schizophrenic to have delusions related to a topic they are particularly interested in. Religious delusions are very common and can be confusing and upsetting for a Christian carer. The Christian faith is very open to visions, dreams and inner senses of a calling. So at first, a carer might find themselves going along with the delusion and may in fact be excited by what they are hearing. Only time reveals the evidence for such visions and ideas, but if it all turns out to be delusionary, the carer can feel rather foolish and perhaps disappointed with themselves and God.

Yet our role can be very helpful to mental health professionals who try to make sense of what the person is saying and may need guidance as to what is a 'normal' Christian perspective. Christian maturity is needed in order to be able to analyse the content of what is said as well as the insight behind it. We believe in a God of order and control who produces grace, forgiveness, love and patience. 'Normal' divine insight will incorporate these elements. There will still be a normal lifestyle routine attached to the person's life, along with a willingness to test out their experience with other mature Christians. It will be a vision that dovetails with the tradition of Scripture and the history of the Church's beliefs. Finally there will be fruitfulness to the conclusion of the situation. The receiver and those around them will be blessed by the message. However, with a schizophrenic, there is often a state of chaos, disorder and lack of peace.

We need to develop a different approach:

- We need to think in terms of long-term practical care.
- We need to read accounts of schizophrenics to begin to grasp their situation.
- We need to recognise the person's fears and take them seriously.
- We need to listen in a non-judgemental way.
- We need to listen and accept the delusionary accounts. There are different opinions about relating to the voices the person hears. In the past, carers would ignore talking about the voices. But it is increasingly believed that the schizophrenic can build a balanced relationship with the voices such that they can control them. For a church carer, we need to focus on the positive aspects of what the voices may be saying and keep away from the negative. Ideally, we want the person to gain some control over the voices so that they can dismiss the negative, more harmful suggestions.[83]
- Reliability and being consistent with the person can be very helpful and reassuring to the person.
- Consistent practical help can be invaluable.

83. M. Romme & S. Escher (2000), *Making Sense of Voices: A Guide for Mental Health Professionals Working with Voices Hearers*, London: Mind.

- The person may need protection from others who want to exploit them.
- There may be a time when we will have to call in more professional medical help. This may damage your relationship with the person but nevertheless it may be necessary for the safety of the individual.
- The family around the schizophrenic will need additional support. They will have to cope with a range of behaviours from extreme laziness, excessive anger, constant smoking and disturbed sleep patterns to leaving the home vulnerable to fire, flood and burglary. Anything the church can do to support the family in creating a calm, stress-free home environment will reap benefits.
- The carer can help the family and friends work through their own feelings of guilt, disappointment and fear.

Personality disorders

These are persistent, lifelong, deeply ingrained maladaptive patterns of inner experience and behaviour. They are the expression of an individual's lifestyle and deviate markedly from the expectations of their culture. There are four types of behaviour according to DSM IV (Diagnostic and Statistical Analysis Manual).[84]

Narcissistic personality disorder

This consists of grandiose self-importance with an inferiority complex of feelings of inadequacy. Such people seek admiration but may keep others at a distance. Criticism is seen as someone else's problem and not theirs. They may treat people as objects and can be abusive.

Antisocial personality disorder

This often occurs in young males who have had complex childhoods. They tend to fail academically, have a low tolerance of boredom and poor work performance; they can feel victimised and have a low level of intimacy. Alcohol and drug abuse is common. There is a disregard for society's laws and they often end up in prison.

Paranoid personality disorder

These people show extreme mistrust of the world. They may have few friends, be anxious in a social context, can often under-achieve and may be eccentric with grandiose ideas.

---

84. DSM IV (1994), *Diagnostic and Statistical Manual of Mental Disorders*, American Psychiatric Press.

Borderline personality disorder

This might involve outrageous behaviour, erratic social behaviour or uncontrollable emotional outbursts. Most churches will have experience of parishioners who might be classified in this way. Such behaviour might have its roots in childhood experiences or post-traumatic stress disorder, sexual abuse, childhood losses or even inadequate pathways in the brain. 'Splitting' is common, where the person sees people as all good or all bad. They may idolise people when they first meet, only to have their opinion shattered when the person doesn't do what they want. There is a constant need of reassurance and acceptance for fear of rejection. Yet they may also rebuff people before they have time to be rejected themselves. Anyone who supports such people can experience a roller coaster of emotions and find themselves easily exhausted and quickly worn out.

To understand these traits we need to think about what forms a stable personality. Dimensions of agreeableness, emotional stability, openness to experience and conscientiousness are identified as being a part of a person's identity and are detectable by how a person relates to others. We all have observable traits, dispositions and characteristics. However, certain traits can be troublesome and some people seem unaware of how damaging these traits are in terms of their interaction with others. If these traits persist, they can become a personality disorder. However, we have to be careful with such labels, as they are extremely culturally determined. Should we be so judgemental when in fact this is not an illness as such? There are often other factors involved such as drug abuse or physical illness. It may be helpful to see such situations as bio-psychosocial. In other words, we recognise that the person's life is being affected biologically, psychologically and socially.

Such behaviours, because they are complex, can be very hard to treat. However, there are several things a church can do.

- Respond in a low-key and gentle way in order not to overwhelm the person.
- Listen and ask for clarification if confused.
- Offer encouragement with regard to self-esteem.
- Be prepared not to believe everything you hear. It can take time to fully see a person's true behaviour.
- Respect information provided by previous churches that the person has been involved with. They may have a much better picture of the situation than you first observe.
- Be aware of manipulation and persuasion techniques.
- 'Harm reduction' within the pastoral team and the wider church can be monitored and controlled.

- Do not assume all spiritual talk is genuine. It can often be very shallow, despite enthusiasm.
- Recognise that they may have a sad story to tell about their past, but observe whether they are able to recognise their own failures and responsibilities.
- Be as consistent as possible with our support. This means we may need to offer less not more in the first instance.
- The overall aim is to help foster a stable sense of identity with consistent values and beliefs.
- Clarify boundaries and maintain them. We have to protect the general congregation, the innocent and ourselves. Once the ground rules are agreed, do not allow them to be twisted or manipulated.
- Do not excuse behaviour that is unacceptable.
- Watch out for manipulation which might range from giving you a cake, emotional blackmail ('You are the only one who understands') to threatening violence, self-harm or suicide.
- Allowing a person to simply come to church services with no other support is very valid and may be a healthy strategy for the good of all involved.
- Always relate to the person in a location where others are nearby and where you will not be cornered.
- Not hesitating in phoning the doctor or the police. There are times when we need clear intervention for the safety of all involved. Even if professionals might struggle themselves in knowing what to do, they need to be informed. We all have different levels of what we can tolerate but it is important to be aware of one's own reaction. If you are feeling overwhelmed, unsafe or threatened or deeply alarmed, try and excuse yourself and dial 999.
- At the end of the day, we might have to let the person go for the good of our own health and that of the church. God still loves them even if you find it impossible (Romans 8:38, 39).

Self-harm

Self-harm is when a person deliberately harms himself or herself physically without the intention of suicide. This might involve cutting skin, burning, headbanging or taking harmful drugs. The person does this as a way of finding some release from emotional pain or as a cry for help. A chemical change takes place as endorphins are released after cutting, for example, that brings a temporary 'high' feeling. Some believe self-harm is a result of childhood abuse and/or a way of expressing anger internally.[85] I have heard it argued that Jesus allowed himself to be crucified and his followers wearing crucifixes around their necks condones self-harm. This is a rather twisted theological perspective. However, we have to be aware that when someone is not thinking clearly, they can manipulate Scripture to justify their behaviour.

A pastoral approach should include making sure the person's physical wounds are treated. They may need someone to support them when being attended by medical professionals. We need to keep affirming that we don't reject the person because of their actions. They also need to know that we will support them whether they continue to self-harm or not. This can mean we have to be prepared for the long haul, as there is no quick fix with this ministry.

It is helpful for us to have 'harm-minimising' techniques up our sleeve. This might include elastic bands on the wrist, which they can pull, or holding an ice cube.

Beware that ultimatums to stop self-harming seldom work. The problem is not that simple. This is where self-help groups can be informative and supportive.

It can be a difficult ride for families with young people who self-harm. They may need additional support to allow them to express their bewilderment and anger.

In all of this we need to look out for 'rescuers' or 'over-zealous' Christians. People with personality disorders are very good at sniffing out such people in church. Christians with these tendencies can feel that the church is rather uncaring towards people in need. However, they can quickly burn out and then need pastoral support themselves. The key is to try to identify personality disorders as early as possible and then to identify a small, controlled support group who can, with clear ground rules, share the load. We then need to be clear and firm with the over-sensitive carer to stay well away for their own good. There are always plenty of others for the rescuer to care for.

In the end, all of these conditions can be exhausting, both for the carer and their family. Right from the beginning we need to put into place limitations concerning what we can provide, clear protection for ourselves and our families, and access to a supervisor who will look out for us. We need to be aware that the relationship might end with the person annoyed with us. All of this challenges our own understanding of who we are, our limitations (living with things we can't understand), our sinfulness and selfishness, reminding us that we live in a world where God's kingdom is far from complete.

85. F. Gardner (2001), *Self-Harm: A Psychotherapeutic Approach*, Hove: Brunner-Routledge.

Reflections

- How equipped is the church to support people with mental health issues?
- How can you support people without overloading?
- Have you a mechanism to prevent over-zealous Christians from taking on too much?
- Does the church have a contact within the mental health services?
- How can you look after your own mental health well-being?
- Have a look at www.time-to-change.org.uk.

Chapter 54

Depression

Sadness is to depression what normal growth is to cancer.
(Lewis Wolpert)[86]

Today, almost everyone seems to claim that they have been depressed at some time or another. I'm not sure whether this is misusing the term. Real depression is not just having a mood swing or feeling under the weather for a few days.

Depression is when your life feels as though it is dangling by a thread. You feel as though you are on the edge of an abyss, surrounded by darkness with nowhere to turn. This may be because of a chemical imbalance or result from an accumulation of feelings of worthlessness, hopelessness, failure, despair and even self-disgust. For some, their faith only seems to make it worse. This is therefore not a time for platitudes. But we do have at the heart of Christianity a God who knew something about the agony of the cross. This, at least, for the depressed can offer some comfort. We need to recognise the signs of depression because the sooner a person receives medical help, the sooner the pain can be eased.

Physical

- Sleep problems
- Exhaustion
- Restlessness
- Change in eating patterns
- Bursting into tears

Feelings

- Overwhelming sadness
- Worthlessness, guilt or shame
- Loss of interest in life
- Feeling alone

Thoughts

- Poor concentration
- Seeing everything as hopeless

86. L. Wolpert (1999), *Malignant Sadness: The Anatomy of Depression*, London: Faber & Faber.

- Loss of confidence
- Hating oneself and believing others hate you
- Suicidal thoughts

Depression shows itself with a familiar pattern. (Dorothy Rowe identifies six characteristics of a depressive, see Appendix 7.[87]) This includes disappointment, sadness and self-pity. There are various degrees of depression, from mild through severe to psychotic. Symptoms include depressed mood particularly when waking, loss of interest, inability to make decisions, loss of energy, change in eating habits, tiredness, poor sleep patterns, low self-esteem, crying outbursts, high guilt, feelings of unworthiness, hypochondria, depersonalisation and suicidal ideation. When it becomes psychotic it might include delusions of poverty, sin, imminent disaster or physical illness, hallucinations and hearing voices.

Depression may be caused by external circumstances such as prolonged strain and stress or by a distressing life event. However, it is generally recognised that depression always involves a chemical imbalance in the brain. The neurotransmitter serotonin becomes depleted. This transmitter particular controls sleep, appetite and sexual function. The new anti-depressant drugs such as Selective Serotonin Re-uptake Inhibitors (SSRI) aim to kick-start the serotonin level back to a normal level.

Depressed Christians can feel extremely guilty for lacking the faith to recover. This can lead them to withdraw and be isolated from the church. They need someone to listen to them, to persevere when they do not recover as quickly as expected, to be patient when they have heard the story before, to restrain from trying to cheer them up (as this falls on deaf ears) and have consistent and regular but balanced visiting. Short passages of Scripture can assist, particularly those focusing on love, forgiveness, God's perseverance and hope. It is generally better to stay away from Old Testament passages, bar the Psalms, as if a degree of psychosis is present, it can lead to confusion and fear. The carer needs to hold on to hope even when the depressed person can't see any way forward. Eventually, with medication and talking therapy, hope will return along with thanksgiving and praise.

We may think that drugs are not really dealing with the problem. This might be the case, but we do know that when people, especially young people, experience an imbalance of hormones, for whatever reason, they can become suicidal. With medication, the risk can be reduced considerably, which then allows for counselling and other forms of therapy to work with the underlying issues.

---

87. D. Rowe (2003), *Depression: The Way out of Your Prison*, Hove: Routledge.

What the church requires is not to ostracise people who are depressed, but to be willing to stick with someone in a controlled, healthy way. Sustaining our contact can be so important when someone is feeling very down. A regular routine of care can make such a difference. I have known people go in and out of depression almost all of their lives. But they have been fortunate to have a friend who has stuck by them faithfully. This is not glamorous work, but it is kingdom work.

Just listening to someone can give them great consolation. A depressed person doesn't want us to try and persuade them out of their reality. If we think we can, then we miss the depth of the problem. Even psychopharmacology only achieves a 30 per cent recovery rate. Another 30 per cent might require several attempts to find the right medication to help. The remainder find themselves trapped in long-term depression. That's a large number when you consider that five million people are experiencing depression at any one time in the United Kingdom. For many, the long-time solution is not a cure but a remission that allows normal functioning and well-being.

In the past, we would simply say that someone had had a nervous breakdown, which does capture how a person feels. This total collapse involves a breakdown of thoughts, beliefs, emotions, sleep and appetite. It's as if they have fallen flat on their face physically and in every other psychological way. They can't just pull themselves together, any more than a blind person can make themselves see.

As Christians we can have a tendency to view things simplistically. Yet most professionals would agree that depression is often made up of various factors that can cause or trigger a depressive episode. There is a diagnostic questionnaire called the Beck Depression Inventory that attempts to measure degrees of depression.

The problem for the depressed is that they no longer feel themselves. They have lost their identity and now don't know how to find themselves again. How can you live as yourself if you do not know who you are?

How can we help? What a depressed person doesn't want is someone who tiptoes around them and ignores the reality of the problem. We do, in fact, know more about depression than we realise. We all know something about loneliness, confusion and being misunderstood. We need to make sure we don't just abandon them to their pain. Our experience might be a tiny fraction of what they are feeling, but it is a connection that we can build upon. However, it requires us to be vulnerable just as they are. This makes a connection that breaks their loneliness.

If a person doesn't feel confident with you when you ask how they are, they will give you the standard British reply: 'I'm fine.' 'Fine' means Flawed, Insecure, Neurotic and Emotional.

We can fall into the trap of thinking that 'positive thinking' will make all the difference. Professional therapy can help, but the individual has to choose to put it into action. The beginning of recovery is accepting what has happened to them. They can't change their parents but they can accept them; they can't change their past but they can learn from it. Therapy brings knowledge, just as the Christian faith does, but the individual still has to do something with it.

The depressed are in fact already working hard.

Every time you feel sad, you are abandoning yourself.
When someone hurts you and you say you are fine, you are abandoning yourself.
Every time you don't eat, you are abandoning yourself.
When you are tired and refuse to sleep, you are abandoning yourself.
When you deny your own needs, you are abandoning yourself.
When you fail to ask for help, you are abandoning yourself.

It is here that Christian theology of taking up your cross and denying yourself creates a problem. It can lead to an inability to care for oneself. Jesus' teaching was never meant for this kind of situation; he spent too much time bringing healing to people to encourage unhealthy self-persecution.

For many depressives, there is an underlying default position that says, 'If there is a problem, hide.' This leads to them distancing themselves from friends, not answering the phone, hiding in the house and staying in bed. When they are out in the world they can manage to put on a mask that says, 'All is well,' even though they are feeling a living hell inside. We all have times when we say one thing and feel another, but this becomes exaggerated, and when people react according to what they see (unaware of what the person is really feeling), the person can feel more isolated and confused. The habit of wearing a mask and not asking for help can go deep and can take a lot to break down. For the carer this is wearisome, to be constantly offering help, aware there are needs but the person does not respond. We can only stick around and persist in offering a hand of care.

When the offer is accepted, what can we do? Firstly, we need to be careful of quick-fix answers. Although there are many theories about depression, there tends to be a combination of factors contributing to the problem. Childhood disruption and confusion with poor attachments may be a foundation, although many become depressed after what appear to be perfectly normal childhoods.

Secondly, feelings of deep insecurity and being disconnected can arise for various reasons.

Thirdly, some people simply have a chemical make-up that is prone to depression and need to correct the balance with pharmaceutical drugs.

Fourthly, in an increasing drug culture, some young people, particularly during their teenage years when their brain pathways are developing, can be severely affected by illicit drugs. This might not manifest for a few years but when it does it can lead to a degree of psychosis and depression.

Finally, life events and problems can accumulate to such a point that something small can push an individual over the edge.

So trying to make sense of the cause of the depression can be a muddle. We need to see ourselves in two roles. Firstly, as a resource to encourage a person to receive professional help, and secondly, to be part of a team approach to support the individual. That might include the family, friends, other church members, the local GP, a counsellor and perhaps a mental health worker. It can take this team approach to make a significant difference in a person's life.

We can make one of two errors here, however. We can think the church and our own effort isn't significant, or we can think that the Christian approach is the only way to help the person. The reality is that the God of creation is actively using every resource to bring healing to his child. We need to see ourselves as part of his activity that might involve both a talking cure and drug cure.

What does the Christian pastor particularly bring that is unique to the situation? Firstly, we can bring a community of acceptance. This is vitally important for those who are down and depressed. Knowing that they are always welcome in the church without judgement is so important. Getting a church community not to judge is the hard part. So send cards, ring regularly and surprise them with small gifts like flowers. Don't worry if they hardly respond; this doesn't mean that they are not grateful or that it is not having an impact upon them. This is what is called 'unconditional positive regard'. Here we are formulating a connection with a person that can be a lifeline back into life.

Secondly, there is the ability to identify 'triggers' within the person that cause them to stumble and fall. Helping someone identify these trigger-thoughts can enable a person to defuse them. We can become sensitive in observing these signs when someone seems to be regressing. We might notice that they are not coming to church as regularly, losing weight, or seem to have an inability to concentrate.

Thirdly, we can offer prayer ministry as we seek healing from God for the situations and events that the triggers take the person back into. We can pray into these, seeking a deeper healing for the individual. If a person's pattern of behaviour and their negative thought patterns are linked to childhood, praying into these memories and experiences can help. On top of this we can practise Christian Cognitive Behavioural Therapy (CBT). This is based on the idea that emotions are simply thoughts in action. If a thought produces an emotion, we can learn how to think differently. The use of Scripture can be a great help here, and can help us to change negative automatic thoughts.

Supporting those who live with someone who is depressed

It is very natural for relatives and friends to feel that they are to blame when someone close to them tumbles into depression. We want to take responsibility for what has happened and attempt to tidy up the mess. Unfortunately, the person will only recover when they take responsibility for themselves. It is understandable that parents will consciously or subconsciously believe it is entirely their fault. The role of a parent is learned on the job, so no one ever gets it right. Secondly, there are many people and events that influence a child through into adulthood. Of course, parents can be the cause of depression and, unless the parents are willing to face their own demons and enter into a healthy open relationship, it becomes difficult for the child to move on. In my university chaplaincy role, I often engage with depressed students who have had very complex relationships with their parents. The students feel a huge responsibility to perform according to their parents' expectations. They feel guilty if they are failing and are frightened of the consequences. This can come to a head when they are about to graduate and have to face the reality of adulthood and finally trying to break free.

A supporter can make a tremendous difference. Firstly, by just being there. A depressed person is living in an isolated hell. If we can come and sit on their 'mourning bench', we can at least keep them company. This is draining and exhausting so the supporters need to ensure that they look after themselves.

Secondly, we have to come to terms with the fact that the person is depressed. This means accepting them as they are, warts and all. A depressed person has very low self-worth and we must do all we can to help them regain their self-esteem. This means we have to show our love for them even when they are depressed. They are of equal worth whether they are well or depressed. Depressed people are extremely selfish; it is the only way they can survive. It is only when we realise and accept this that we can begin to support them. A depressed person might struggle to get up in the morning because of enormous fears of facing the day. We have to acknowledge this.

When a person is down, they can easily slip into a role of saying 'yes' to all of our ideas and suggestions. But we very quickly discover that this is a game. In the depressed head, there are many reasons for not doing as we suggest, all rooted in the common symptoms as mentioned before. If we find ourselves in this game, it is best not to force our suggestions. What we can do is to listen when they want to talk. We can also encourage them to express what they are feeling. Expressing confused thoughts and feelings into a story or narrative can be extremely helpful. This can lead to a discussion of other possible interpretations. The thought that there might be different answers is the beginning for the depressed person to choose to head in a different direction.

The road to recovery involves very small steps as the person begins to change their thinking which in turn changes their feelings. A part of this might mean practical help to enable them to reach this. It might be taking the person for a walk, going swimming or helping them do some cooking.

Finally, we have to allow the person to begin to change. Sometimes we want the situation to remain as stable as possible, but a depressed person has to change in order to recover. That requires a degree of experimentation and a willingness by the supporters to back off and give space. Fear in the supporter can in fact strangle the depressed person into submission and remaining depressed.

In the end, there has to be a dovetailing of what the depressed person and the supporters want. There has to be an end to the 'yes' game and a willingness to recognise this. When the person is willing to be kind to themselves, there is a chance that they might begin to feel positive feelings. This involves saying thank you and not having to reciprocate the kindness (i.e. being able to receive just for the sake of it). Also, beginning to recognise and acknowledge what a person is good at is a sign of breaking the false humility that depressed people hold on to.

This is not the time to discuss medication and antidepressants, but if a person is recovering they need to be very careful in coming off their drug routine. It needs to be done with the knowledge of their doctor. Alongside this is the need for a healthy diet with plenty of fruit, vegetables and healthy fluids. The role of drugs will be debated, depending on people's opinions. Psychiatrists will be more positive as they generally see problems from a chemical perspective. Counsellors and pastors will have their own approach. There is no easy answer here as human beings are complex and consist of biological and chemical reactions as well as having some cognitive free will to choose how to live and change. What we mustn't do is see prescriptions as a weaker option. If the problem is chemical, then an appropriate chemical will bring the required healing. The brain is one part of the body we have much to learn about. We are not yet in a position to make narrow judgements. In the end, the depressed person has to make the decision (unless they are a danger to themselves).

Whichever approach is taken, relaxation exercises are often part of the scaffold of recovery. This is something that can be done with a friend or family member. It may be a Christian meditation exercise or a secular approach. The key is that it has to be something that the depressed person is comfortable with. Whatever the practice, it needs to be worked at both when the person is struggling and when they are well. The more it becomes a part of a person's routine, the more the person will be able to access it when things are tough.

Next, the person has to begin to take some risks in trusting themselves and their friends – i.e. the risk of being 'good enough'. Here we often think about trusting God. This is fine, but we need to be clear about what sort of God we are trusting. When terrible things happen to ordinary people, we have to develop a view of God that is not of a genie who only helps the good and punishes the bad. This will only put the depressed person into a state of fear. If it is trust in a God who loves regardless of the person's behaviour or feelings, there will be some benefit in this trust. This is part of people accepting themselves as God accepts them. We need to acknowledge that there are some very healthy and very unhealthy projections of God within the Church and outside it. If we get trapped with the wrong image, we can do more harm than good.

A loyal, consistent friend who journeys with a depressed person without judgement can be not only a lifeline but also a very godly example of the God I at least believe in.

Ways of handling depression

- Practise grabbing positive thoughts when they come along and try to hold on to them.
- Do something that makes you laugh. Practise smiling.
- Playing like a child can help the mood.

- Choose not to deny the losses in your life, but rather to reflect on them, 'cry them out' and begin to release them.
- Remember that alcohol lowers the mood and will not help.
- Practise saying that 'I am OK; I am good enough.'
- Put things into perspective. Will this worry be important in years to come?
- Connect with nature every day by walking, swimming, gardening, and so on.
- Deal with big issues at the beginning of the day; save the pleasurable things for later.
- Keep away from listening to the news on the TV or radio and reduce your time on the computer.
- Practise breathing in and out, becoming more aware of your senses. Do meditation, contemplation, and mindfulness exercises.

Reflections

- Do you know people in church who have suffered with depression?
- How might they help others who are struggling?
- Would you recognise a depressed person? What would be the signs?
- In what ways can Christian faith and/or the Church help the depressed?
- When is anger constructive and when is it destructive?
- How can you help someone who is consumed with anger?
- How can you balance the desire to support and yet not become dragged down with depression yourself?

Chapter 55

Suicide issues

Kill yourself, what's the point, it achieves nothing, precisely,
it achieves nothing.
Nothingness is what I want.
(Udo Grashoff)[88]

Notice that this is a different topic to mental health. Not everyone who attempts suicide is mentally ill, although this is hard for society to accept. Can one actually be clear in one's own mind yet choose to end their life?

Suicidal people have an inability to differentiate between dying and living. They want to escape the problems that overwhelm them but may not have thought about not living. This is less about death and more about becoming defeated by the long, hard struggle to stay alive. There is an inability to see that things may be hopeless yet it is possible to be determined to make things better.

Having to handle a suicidal situation can seem rather overwhelming to anyone. The thought that anyone might want to take their life and be in their right mind can be rather disturbing. We might rationalise some understanding if a person is chronically ill and goes off to Switzerland to have a controlled death. But when someone who is physically well, has gifts and abilities along with supportive friends, talks of suicide, it can disturb our own equilibrium.

Every six seconds someone contacts the Samaritans. Every 60 seconds the contact expresses suicidal feelings. Over five million people contact the Samaritans every year. Thankfully, most of them live to tell the tale. However, every day men under the age of 35 die from suicide. According to the Office of National Statistics, in England and Wales in 2008 17.7 men per 100,000 committed suicide compared to 5.4 women per 100,000. Suicide rates have increased steadily since the 1960s but have slightly decreased over recent years apart from men between the age of 15–34. In this age range, suicide accounts for 25 per cent of deaths. There are more suicides on Mondays than any other day of the week.

---

88. U. Grashoff (2006), *Let Me Finish: An Anthology of Suicide Letters*, London: Headline Publishing.

Unfortunately, today there is a new development called internet suicide. There are people on the internet who will talk to a suicidal person and actively encourage them to succeed. They will offer advice on how to do it and what to do with their last hour (this is called 'catching the bus'). Some people, called Trolls, are not interested in suicide for themselves, but they just get a 'high' by inciting and encouraging others.

It is fairly common to hear of a train or tube journey being delayed because someone has taken their own life on the track. However, many choose to commit suicide quietly without fuss or attention.

There seem to be various reasons for suicide, such as unemployment, drugs, alcohol, money and relationship problems. Although one or two of these issues alone would not tip someone over the edge, when they come together, it can take just a small thing to lead someone to attempt suicide. This does not include those with ongoing mental health issues.

A caring church will inevitably attract people with emotional needs of many different kinds. I can recall one town church where we had attracted many people with counselling and mental health issues that I was spending considerable time going to the mental health hospital. I began to wonder whether the church was actually causing some of these problems but was reassured by a psychiatrist who was a member of the church. He expressed appreciation of the pastoral care that the church was providing, recognising that this freed up the NHS to handle the more serious cases.

There is still a stigma for some in acknowledging that they have a mental health problem. Some might think it is for the weak-minded and those who can't be bothered to sort out their lives. The church should be a safe haven for such people. People with mental health problems can feel extremely lonely and isolated in the community. If we are to have a ministry for the mentally ill or those bereaved from a suicide, we will need to understand the depth of the complexity of the subject.

To engage with suicidal individuals we need to first remove any preconditions that we have previously formulated. There are several misconceptions in the community about suicide:

People who talk about suicide won't do it

This is simply not true. Sometimes someone attempts suicide several times and then, when no one is expecting it, they succeed. There may be lots of reasons why someone does not succeed, but it doesn't mean it wasn't serious. We should always take suicide attempts seriously.

If a person is determined to commit suicide, there is nothing we can do about it

The reality is that most suicidal people do not want to die; they simply want their pain, whatever it may be, to be taken away. Even severely depressed people have very mixed views about ending their lives. There can be a wavering in their decision right up till the last few seconds.

Suicidal people fail to seek help

Alas, most people who commit suicide have had some medical help at some point over the previous months before death.

Suicidal people are mad

Most suicidal people are not necessarily psychotic or insane. They may be in deep depression, grief or overwhelming distress.

I'm worried about putting the idea of suicide into someone's head

The reality is that the opposite is true. By bringing up the subject you are defusing a situation. Allowing a person to talk about their thoughts on the subject allows them to feel both normal and accepted. It also allows them an opportunity to not feel trapped in their thoughts on the subject; they now have someone else to talk about it with, and help to be able to begin to see things from a different perspective.

I don't know how to bring the subject up

We can simply ask, 'Do you sometimes feel so bad that you think of suicide?' If the answer is yes, there are a few other questions we can ask, such as:

- Have you thought of how?
- Have you been thinking when you would do it?
- Have you talked about this to anyone before?
- Have you tried suicide before?

If the person has a clear plan and means of achieving it and has decided when, then the risk of suicide is extremely high. If you add either a suicide in the family history or drug or alcohol abuse, the risk increases.

How to respond in the crisis

When someone lets us know they are thinking about suicide, we need to be clear about what is expected of us.

Our role first and foremost is to keep someone safe. If we think someone is in immediate danger, the suicidal person should not be left alone and medical help should be summoned immediately. If the person is telephoning, encourage them to phone the Samaritans while you call the emergency services. Before you hang up, get the person to promise that they will not hurt themselves in the meantime.

Secondly, we can help by drawing the unmanageable, fearful or negative thoughts into the open where they become less fearful and more manageable. Our natural tendency is to focus on reasons to live, but we must first deal with the person's dominant thoughts that are negative. Helping the person to express the pain that has led them to this position will build an alliance between you and the person as well as ease their pain. It also begins the realisation that the person is not alone and has support. Only when they have fully expressed their reasons for dying do we need to begin to raise the case for living. The fact that they are talking to you reveals that there is a glimmer of hope. You could express it in one of the following ways:

- 'You have shared with me your deep pain but I seem to hear that there are things holding you back from taking your life. Can you share what they are?'
- 'There seem to be lots of reasons to take your life that are dominating your thoughts, but can we just for a few minutes let the side of you that wants to live speak?'
- 'I hear your deep pain right now, but you haven't taken your life and you are talking to me, so what does that tell us?'
- 'If the pain that you are experiencing could be dealt with, would that mean you wouldn't need to take your life?'

Being confident with a few well thought through sentences can ease the discussion.

Thirdly, getting the person to reflect upon the impact their death will have on others is often a major reason why a person resists. This includes the effect it would have upon you.

Fourthly, getting the person to talk about what the suicide would achieve can give a clearer picture of how the person might bring about relief from their pain without dying. The technique of 'magical thinking' can help (see Chapter 18, Counselling skills).

Finally, helping a person go about the normal routine things can enable them to get through the day. Very small steps can lead a person away from a cliff edge.

If we believe the person is about to commit suicide we have a duty of care to inform them that we can't stop them but we must phone the emergency services. This sometimes makes a person pause and reflect further. It may result in the end with the person not trusting us in the future, but we don't have any other choice. It is then our responsibility not to leave them alone until extra support is at hand. Remember, the person might be hallucinating or under the influence of drugs; our action might save them from doing something they never really wanted to do.

The Samaritans launched a campaign called 'We're in your corner' in September 2012 which gives advice for men on suicide issues.[89] Appendix 8 is a helpful reminder of what to do in an emergency situation.

The impact on others after suicide

When suicide occurs, the shock is overwhelming. Although family and friends may have been very fearful for a relative, when the event takes place it still brings a reaction of alarm. There are three areas that affect the bereaved:

- The events that led up to the suicide
- The event itself and the immediate circumstances
- The long-term effects of the grief.

The pre-suicide events

People bereaved from suicide tell complicated stories. Some have had to grapple with the stress of handling a relative or friend who has had a turbulent life. They may have tried many times to talk the person out of their depression and despair. It can feel like the sword of Damocles hanging over their head, waiting for the inevitable death. There may have been a long history of the person going in and out of hospital or endless arguments about taking medication. The family may have reached the point of becoming deaf to the person's ongoing plight. If previous suicide attempts have taken place, relatives and friends feel as though they are walking on eggshells in fear that the person might do it again. This in itself adds pressure and prevents the individual from feeling normal.

Shame is a thin strand that runs throughout this subject. The individual who is having suicidal thoughts grapples with their shame for thinking this way. Those who survive attempts can feel

---

89. See http://www.samaritans.org/media-centre/our-campaigns/were-your-corner (accessed 11 October 2012).

ashamed for trying, failing and now living with their past. There is then the shame of the bereaved relatives and friends who have to live with the feeling that they perhaps could have prevented this scenario.

For others, the person can be functioning normally, washing the dishes and emptying the bins on the very day they succeed with their suicide. Here the shock is much greater and can complicate the grief journey. As pastors we need to be aware of the baggage a family brings into their grief and be prepared to hear the full story.

The suicidal event

Often there is a 'final straw that breaks the camel's back' which causes suicide. It can sometimes be difficult to work out why a person did it at that particular moment, but we have to see the whole story to understand why they got to that point and were tipped over into a suicidal crisis. It may be that unemployment alone is not the issue, nor relationships, debt or drugs, but when they occur steadily together and are increasing, this creates a tipping point.

Often the bereaved are treated differently from other bereaved people. They have to deal with the police, an inquest and possibly the media. Unfortunately, a suicidal person's pain is tied to others after they take their lives. At first, people feel disturbed by the news. It is only later that they experience the fullness of the loss and begin to miss the person.

The events of the day of the suicide are often impregnated into the minds of the bereaved. They will be able to tell you where they were and what they were doing at the time. Some experience the trauma of actually finding the deceased. The impact of this is hard to come to terms with; the image lingers for a long time. The bereaved also have to cope with the knowledge that the deceased probably knew who would find them first; they have been especially chosen, for good or ill, to cope with the event.

In addition, there is the complexity of what the bereaved might have said to the person only minutes or hours before they took their life. This can give ground for considerable guilt and regret about the way they reacted at the time.

Another complexity is the suicide note. Not everyone leaves a note when they take their own life. Even if they do, it may create more issues than it resolves. Some contain profound utterances; others are vague, abstract and incomplete. Some appear to be totally false and incorrect to the surviving relatives. 'I spent ages wondering what to write or whether I should write a note. And that's because the more you think about it, the more difficult it is to maintain any hope of ever being understood.'

Some letters are left to create guilt; others offer advice about caring for specific people, while others express love and thanks.

Long-term effects

There is one thing that lingers for the bereaved for as long as they live: the unanswerable question 'Why?' that torments so many families. On top of this there is the taboo that we don't talk about suicide, which isolates the bereaved.

There are many 'bad' parents whose children don't commit suicide and many 'good' parents whose children do. But suicide can tear families apart. Siblings can often retreat into themselves; their isolation only causes further pain and fear for the parents. Friends are at a loss to know what to say or do.

The bereaved wonder what other people might be thinking about them: 'What kind of mother, father or family did this person have?' The reality is that the issue of suicide is not usually about the survivors; they are not the focus of a suicidal person's mind. This is hard for the bereaved to accept. This is especially the case if there had been arguments before the death. Often there are arguments before a suicide, when people say things that they didn't mean and now greatly regret.

> I told him to get out of my house and never come back. That was the last words I ever spoke to him.[90]

Anger is an overwhelming emotion for many bereaved. 'Why did they do that?' is the thought that echoes in people's minds. However, sometimes the bereaved also have a sense a relief both for themselves and the deceased: release from the ongoing torture of living with a suicidal person and release that the deceased is not going to be disappointed or unhappy any more.

> You don't really get over this kind of loss; you just have to incorporate it into your life. It is always there, it always will be, because nothing can change it, it has happened, it is real.[91]

There is another thought that naturally occupies the minds of the bereaved: 'If my relative has committed suicide, does that mean that I might?' Some are able to clearly draw a line between the action of

90. U. Grashoff, *Let Me Finish.*
91. U. Grashoff, *Let Me Finish.*

their relative and themselves, but others can't, and that is a difficult thought to forget.

The way a church engages with those who have suicidal thoughts and the bereaved from suicide will depend on what the church thinks about the subject. Freud thought suicide was an aggressive conflict within.[92] More recently, scientific thinking sees it as a pathological thought process, a moment of 'crisis problem development'. Today we call it a pre-suicidal syndrome. One thing is clear: suicide is a universal phenomenon. It expresses the reality that human beings have free will. Today, society may have less fear about it but the impact is just as great. David Hume, the Scottish philosopher, said, 'a man who retreats from life does not harm society'.[93] But the truth is far from this, as it's like a terrorist attack that causes ripples to echo through the community, and that includes the church.

If the parish has a diverse population, poor housing, high unemployment and a high incidence of drug abuse, we are going to experience families with suicidal narratives. A willingness to address the subject in teaching and creating a community that doesn't increase shame will help to draw out the vulnerable as well as the bereaved. Funerals that deny that suicide has taken place just collude with the shame and denial within the community. The church has a chance to be a light in raising the subject and offering appropriate care. Whether we choose to engage in this ministry or not, suicidal thoughts and experiences will be present in any church.

Reflections

- What do you think is your church's attitude to suicide?
- What kind of conditions in your life would cause you to think about suicide?
- How can the church support the bereaved after a suicide?
- Read the account of Judas' life and suicide in the New Testament. Can we learn anything from Judas?
- How do you think Jesus coped knowing that he chose Judas who would betray him?
- How can we support people who live with relatives who are often suicidal?
- How can we help people to be absolved of guilt and shame?

---

92. S. Freud (2001), *The Complete Psychological Works of Sigmund Freud*, London: Vintage Classics.
93. D. Hume (2005), *On Suicide*, London: Penguin Classics.

Chapter 56
Dementia

I hate to sound this way, but why me? Why me with dementia?
(Pat Summitt, basketball coach)[94]

With people generally living longer these days, the Church is going to find itself with an increasingly older membership. Alongside this come mental health problems for the elderly. Old age brings with it a slowing down of movement, a preference for a regular routine, a tendency to avoid risks and to become more introverted, a weakened short-term memory yet a strong long-term memory. Depression is common, but with good support and medication it can be controlled.

Perhaps the biggest fear in old age is of developing dementia. This is a collection of symptoms that are produced due to changes in the brain. There are various forms of dementia, all with differing effects. The two most recognised are Alzheimer's disease (SDAT) and multi-infarct dementia (MID).

Dementia is more than just having a weakened memory. A person might find themselves forgetting the names of their children or getting lost in their local village and not remembering where they live. Dressing, washing and general household chores can become very difficult to manage. There can be catastrophic reactions with emotional outbursts and uncontrollable rages. Some find that they are unable to recognise familiar objects or recall what they are used for. So they might put food in the wardrobe instead of the fridge, or they might wear their clothes inappropriately. Alongside this comes a restlessness that results in pacing up and down and wandering with no clear purpose. There will be flashbacks of lucidity but gradually the person will lose all insight into their condition.

How can we help? If we can imagine what it is like to be bewildered, terrified and totally abandoned, we will get a glimmer of what it is like. (Read a Christian's account of his experience: *My Journey into Alzheimer's Disease* by Robert Davis.[95])

The church can be a place for familiarity, routine, optimism and encouragement. Services with consistent liturgy can be helpful –

---

94. P. Summitt (2011), TV interview, Tennessee.
95. R. Davis (1989), *My Journey into Alzheimer's Disease*. Available as a free pdf download from http://disorders.free-books.biz/My-Journey-into-Alzheimers-Disease-PDF-837.html (accessed 21 September 2012).

familiar scripture verses, hymns, creeds, and the Lord's Prayer. Also having the words available in large print can make a difference.

We need to recognise the person's personality and individuality and seek to consistently affirm it. Regular visiting with Holy Communion, praise and prayer can be beneficial. Even if the person reaches the stage of not participating, we are providing a message that this person is still loved by God, made in his image and not forgotten. God still speaks even when we're in a strange land (Psalm 137:4). I have known patients in residential homes who appeared to be totally unaware of the communion served, but then responded and wanted to receive the bread and wine. We also have to be prepared for those who will look at the bread and not know what to do with it.

Talking to sufferers' families and supporting them can be so important in helping them to come to terms with what is happening. Denial is often an early reaction by the sufferer themselves as well as the family. There may also come a point when the family may need encouragement to recognise that it is becoming impossible to continue to care for the person in their home. Here issues of failure, guilt and anxiety need to be discussed. We might find ourselves being the only one willing to raise such issues with the carer. But if we can provide consistent practical help both to the sufferer and the family carer it can help to reduce the build-up of stress.

Reassurance to the sufferer that the church will be there for them and their loved ones can bring a degree of peace. Affirming that the church will perform the funeral when the time comes can also bring comfort to the sufferer, although we have to acknowledge that we might not be the one to do the service, as we can't guarantee where we will be at the time.

When the time comes for the sufferer to enter a residential home, the church may well have good advice to offer, particularly where there is an element of Christian involvement in the care. We may also need to sound the alarm if we feel that a person is not being treated appropriately in the nursing home.

Finally, we need to be open to what can only be called 'epiphany' moments, when the person has glimpses of their old self again. When they respond to our spiritual presence, it can be a very humbling experience.

Reflections

- How aware is the church of who in the congregation is grappling with dementia, either in themselves or in relatives?
- Could you shadow a carer for a few hours to begin to understand what it must be like living with a person with dementia?
- Could the church offer realistic practical help?
- How would you know when to raise the subject of burnout or signs that the carer is not coping?
- What fears arise within you when you see dementia?

Chapter 57

Long-term problems

Endurance is not just the ability to bear a hard thing,
but to turn it into glory.
(William Barclay)[96]

We know that some people have been very poorly treated in life. Perhaps they have been pushed by a critical, cold parent and this has led to them spiralling downstairs into a depressed, isolated, fearful and angry position. To get someone to walk up this staircase into an environment of care and love takes a combination of strategies. For many, it is too easy to fall back down the staircase.

We may respond to such a person in love, but because of their previous experience they may not have love-shaped receptors so our care and love is rejected. It takes time for a person to develop a love-shaped space within them and allow people to fill this empty space.

This is why counselling is not enough. Pastoral care is not enough. What we need is a church community that is willing to be a caring 'womb' over a long period of time. Only then can people learn to develop new ways of coping when problems come at them. The Church is the redeemed, new family, so we need to behave like it. If we can't cope with those on the edge, those who are different to ourselves or those who continue to struggle in life, we fail to be 'good enough' parents and will see people fall down the staircase again to pain and despair. They may one day experience heaven and a new beginning, but the Church is called to bring the heavenly kingdom on earth now.

By creating an environment of acceptance we will create a safe place for people to blossom and mature in a Christlike way. To do this we need to integrate our policies with regard to preaching, welcoming, home groups, one-to-one care and mission in order to create a corporate safe environment. Some secular organisations have clear green, DDE or fair-trade policies; perhaps we need to learn from these kite marks, go back to the beginning and remind ourselves what the church is meant to be.

Long-term care involves a deep commitment to both individuals and a community. It is here that the wider community begins to see

96. W. Barclay (2010), *The Letters to the Corinthians*, Norwich: St Andrew's Press.

what it is to be a Christian as they observe the fruit of the Spirit in action. A church that becomes known for its care is an evangelistic tool in itself. Of course, we have to be realistic as we balance wanting to live in the kingdom whilst still having our feet in this world. This means that a church has to be honest about what it can achieve in the community, about how it can help individuals with deep problems. For a small church with very few helpers, developing a caring ministry could capsize the boat.

This is also true for larger churches that gain a healthy reputation in this area. Needy people are very good at smelling out a place of love and care. Ensuring that we have the right number of helpers for those in need can be a real problem for church leaders. Once again we come back to reflecting upon what is happening, developing ground rules to protect the carers and being willing to accept that we can't do everything, otherwise one needy individual can wear out keen members of the church to breaking point. If we are to have a long-term care policy in the church we also need strong leaders to protect the carers. Sometimes carers themselves do not appreciate a strong hand from a pastor who is trying to prevent burnout and overload. However, we have to remind ourselves that ministry is not about being liked but seeking the best for the whole church and not just one individual. Living with failure and the inability to do all the things we want to do is all part of being a Christian in an incomplete world. We need to constantly reflect this in our preaching and prayers.

Reflections

- How can people use Christianity as a way of keeping themselves stuck in their unhealthy thinking?
- How can the church tackle a person's long-term problems?
- How can you safely confront someone about their unhealthy religious thinking?
- How can you protect others in the church from being manipulated?
- How does the church decide what not to do?

Part six

Understanding ourselves

Chapter 58
Storytelling

You can discover more about a person after an hour of play, than a year of conversation.
(Plato)

If you break down the components of pastoral care, you will end up with the fact that we are practising love in word and deed. This is the action of helping people search for the meaning in their lives. This marks us out from social workers, doctors and counsellors. Since religion has been pushed to the margins of people's lives, we find ourselves engaged in helping people make sense of their everyday lives. One way to do this is through storytelling. When we remember a story from our lives we are digging deep into our memory banks and, in a sense, reliving the experience. This takes us away from dogma or laws.

We tend to categorise our accounts. Where there are powerful accounts of falling in love or grieving a friend, for example, these memories are often attached to emotion. There are memories of significant events that have redirected the course of our lives. This might be bumping into someone who then affected us, or hearing a sermon which caused us to head in a new career direction. Then there are events that puzzle us and leave us with a sense of mystery. We take all our memories with us, and they all play their part in how we see the present and the future. So when we engage with the present, it is not that we are standing on a mountain top and deciding where to go next; it is rather that this is part of a continuous thread that makes up our lives. The present moment is as significant as any other moment in life. As we progress, we constantly see life from a different perspective. What was felt to be a difficult period of life at the time may later be reflected upon as an important time of self-development.

The journey of self-awareness does not end until we die. This means that our understanding and interpretation of life is always fluid and open to change. We might not think this when we meet people who have fixed views of life, yet we are often encountering people at a crossroads in their lives, at the very time when they are beginning to see things differently. We see this take place in the Book of Job. Here, Job tells his story, laments, complains, asks questions and then, after reflection and God's guidance, he reflects afresh upon his story. This recollecting is both painful and cathartic. It allowed Job to find a deeper healing and transformation rather than just a temporary sticking plaster repair. Job found a new theology that fitted his experience more comfortably.

Job's story is just one account of many in the Bible where people speak out about their joys, sorrows, doubts and hopes. The stories do not give us definitive answers but they do help us to find a path for our own story to develop.

Cognitive science has shown that we organise our life events into stories with a plot structure with a beginning, a middle and an ending. This self-narrative is the way we think, feel and act and is like a garment that we wear. The micro-narratives of our lives (and the reason why so many people enjoy watching soap operas) lead to a macro-narrative of who we are. This gives rise to many types of stories. There are:

- Healthy narratives
- Disorganised narratives, such as trauma
- Disassociated narratives, which often include silent stories such as incest or suicide
- Dominant narratives that constrict – e.g. depression, where the self is problem saturated, like the loss of a child where the parent finds their grief all-encompassing
- Frozen narratives (such as Miss Haversham in Charles Dickens' *Great Expectations*).

Some people have such rigid, oppressive and destructive narratives that they find it hard to change. They get trapped in a meaningless cycle. Consider Ecclesiastes 1:2-9:

> Vanity of Vanities, says the Teacher, vanity of vanities! All is vanity.
> What do people gain from all the toil at which they toil under the sun?
> A generation goes, and a generation comes, but the earth remains forever.
> The sun rises and the sun goes down, and hurries to the place where it rises.
> The wind blows to the south, and goes round to the north; round and round goes the wind, and on its circuits the wind returns.
> All streams run to the sea, but the sea is not full; to the place the streams flow, there they continue to flow.

> All things are wearisome, more than one can express; the eye is not satisfied with seeing, or the ear filled with hearing.
> What has been is what will be, what has been done is what will be done; there is nothing new under the sun.

Stories come in many forms: personal, social history, myths, tales, novels and everyday stories, which all make up most of our lives. We build our stories from the many assumptions we make in life, and there are three major assumptions that we make. Firstly, that the world and its people are benevolent. Secondly, that there is meaning, justice and control in the world, which is not random. Thirdly, that we have our self-worth and our own goodness; we are under control and have our own luck in life. This helps us to:

- Organise past events – we recognise what's familiar
- Direct our choices for the present – we cognitively master our environment
- Anticipate intelligibly for the future – we predict what will happen.

So we develop self-awareness through trust, based on a number of things:

1. Faith in our ability to perceive dangers – I know where I stand
2. Faith in our ability to handle dangers that arise – I can cope
3. Faith in my whole body image – I am intact, a whole person.

And we develop trust in others:

1. Others will be available to protect me – I can rely on other people
2. I can evoke the care of others and reward them – people like me
3. I can coerce and influence others to help me – people do what I tell them.

and develop trust in the world:

1. Faith in the lasting absence of danger – the world is a safe place
2. Faith in protective powers – God, police, law, rules of life.

We skate on a sheet of ice of certainty, over a lake of faith.[97]

97. S. Jeffers & H. Smith, *Finding a Sacred Oasis in Grief.*

We constantly live in this assumptive world. We make thousands of assumptions every minute of every day that enable us to function with minimum worry and anxiety. This became real to me one day when the ceiling in my lounge collapsed, only just missing me. Ceilings are things we rarely look at or think about; we just assume they are safe. But my assumption that ceilings are safe had been shattered. For months later I would find myself looking up in rooms and checking that the ceiling looked safe. It is the same when a person has been burgled. The trust that their home is safe has been removed. As they return home every time they have been out, there is an element that is wondering whether it has happened again.

In pastoral ministry we are dealing with people whose lives have been thrown into confusion and where their assumptions have been challenged. It is like a jigsaw being thrown up into the air: some of the pieces stick together, others are upside down and some get lost. We go from being organised, with everything in its place, to a state of chaos in thoughts, values and beliefs. We then spend a considerable amount of time trying to make sense of it all.

So here we are in a complex web that is made up of various relationships with people alongside ideologies, assumptions, beliefs and hopes. This web makes up who and what we are. But when things happen to us that challenge this web, we have to reorganise our story to find fresh meaning in life so that it makes sense to us and allows us to continue in daily life.

When the narrative of our lives is disrupted, it can lead to a loss of meaning. Viktor Frankl, from his experience as a prisoner during the Holocaust, found that those who had some meaning or purpose in life tended to survive the prison more than others. He developed something called Logotherapy – that the primary motivation of humanity is to find meaning in life.

> Why do we not commit suicide?
> Because we have found a reason to live.[98]

A pastor's role is full of stories. We are storytellers, we listen to stories and we help people make sense of stories. And the Bible is a story-making machine.

Giving life 'meaning' is the way we make deep sense of things. It is how we articulate our purposes and goals in life, the significance we give to things and the values we cherish. This includes theological meaning to bring purpose, order and direction to people's lives. And it is through stories that we create, learn, value

---

98. V. Frankl (2004), *Man's Search for Meaning*, London: Rider.

and reflect meaning. Families have their own language for this. What sayings characterise your family? Are any of these familiar?

- Work hard
- Be honest
- Just do your best
- Cleanliness is next to godliness
- Let it all hang loose
- Family comes first.

When this life narrative falls apart, a person has to reconstruct a life worth living by giving it fresh meaning. They might need to add more 'plot' to the story or come up with a new interpretation.

A Chinese farmer lost a horse. 'Bad luck,' everyone said. 'Maybe,' he replied. The next day the horse came back with seven wild horses. 'You're lucky,' everyone said. 'Maybe,' said the farmer. The next day the farmer's son rode one of the horses and broke his leg. 'That's bad,' everyone said. 'Maybe,' said the farmer. The following day the army came and conscripted all the young men except his son (because of his broken leg). 'Great,' everyone said. 'Maybe,' said the farmer.

Constructing narratives has to be done in relationship with others. The church can play a key part. God can shape stories. Bringing in a different Christian perspective can lead to different stories, meanings and interpretations. Part of this is the acceptance of mystery. Here, there is even meaning in mystery.

- There is suffering and God is love
- There is pain and God is love
- There is loss and God is love
- There is mystery and God is love (Romans 8:39).

We had the experience but missed the meaning.[99]

Statistics show that people with some religious connection at some point in their lives are more likely to turn to religion at times of crisis.[100] We know that children from stable religious homes are more likely to grow up as Christians, just as those in stable atheistic homes are more likely to become atheists. Those from unstable homes are more likely to have a conversion experience one way or another. Here, we begin to grasp that religion consists of many things and does not just come from our own narrow personal perspective.

99. T. S. Eliot (2001), *Four Quartets*, London: Faber & Faber.
100. M. M. Kelley (2010), *Grief: Contemporary Theory & the Practice of Ministry*, Minneapolis: Fortress Press.

People relate to religion through many channels, such as:

- Prayer
- Meditation
- Sacred writings
- The Bible
- Rituals
- Communal worship
- Tradition
- Reasoning
- Art
- Intimate relationships
- TV's *Songs of Praise*
- Social compassion.

We need therefore to have a broad canvas of how we relate to and support people pastorally and spiritually. People can engage with religion through different doors, be it through religious beliefs, religious practices or religious community. The pastor needs to find the most appropriate way of relating to each person. We do this by hearing the person's story.

Pathways through a story

Firstly we need to listen to and hear the story about ourselves, others and God in a way that honours and cherishes. By listening to a person's account, we can help to expand the narrative and bring new shape and meaning. We and others can provide consistent support. We are in the business, as Revelation 21:5 puts it, of 'making all things new'. This is initiated by asking open questions to invite the story. Here are some examples:

- What does this account mean to you?
- How would you describe your feelings on a typical day?
- How has it changed over time?

We need to convey interest in the hardest part of the story:

- What is the most painful part of your experience?
- What are parts of your story that people least hear?'

By doing this, we are engaging the person to self-reflect at a deeper level. We are also considering the impact of their experience on their worldview:

- Has the loss changed the way you see things about your life, yourself, your future?

We also need to include and evaluate the impact of the story on the person's social life:

- How has it affected your relationship with other people?
- What concerns do others have about you?

It is important to balance the need to build a working alliance with the client with the need for sufficient information and to ask more specific questions as necessary for diagnostic clarity. These are not forced questions but come from a natural flow in conversation. What we are doing is putting sensitive, carefully chosen questions into the narrative (see Appendix 9).

Reflections

- Is your story chronological or does it have a different structure?
- How did you decide when a chapter ended or began?
- When did your story begin?
- Is there a need for a foreword?
- Is your story evolutionary, gradual or sudden?
- Do your early childhood attachments reflect upon your first attachment to God?
- How would you describe your attachment to others? To God?
- How does this influence how you minister to others?
- If it were a novel, would it be a comedy, adventure, romance?
- What are the major trends and themes in your story?
- Where is the story anchored?
- Who is the primary author? Is there a co-author, or any others who deserve credit/blame?
- Who is the relevant audience for your narrative? Who would enjoy it? Who would want to edit it?
- How different would it be if you wrote it as a child, teenager or in the future?
- How different would the story be if others wrote it?
- What is the title of your self-narrative?
- Think about your experience of loss and grief. How has your grief been shaped by your attachments to others? To God?
- How might the attachment theory throw light on those you minister to with struggles and how you care for them?
- How can a church bring security of attachment?
- What from this list of questions should you take to prayer? A spiritual director? A friend?

Chapter 59

Know thyself

My entire job is output, so I need some input.
(Chris Doulton, pastoral worker)[101]

I recall one day seeing my spiritual director and sharing the pressure I felt I was under. She quickly suggested that I had what was called 'the Jesus Syndrome'. I was about to take it as a compliment until she explained, 'You think you are Jesus with all that you are doing.' At this point I began to cry as the stress poured out. I went back to the parish and signed up for a 'how to delegate' course.

The kingdom of God will always lead us to a new view of ourselves, along with a new view of others around us. This requires us to be increasingly self-aware. There is a Latin proverb that says, 'nemo sat quod non habet,' which means, 'you can't give what you don't have'. It is as we encounter other people's stories that we inevitably meet some of our own taboos. Here we discover that we see the gospel through our own tinted view of life. Our beliefs, our attitudes, our wants and our assumptions have been shaped by our upbringing, our culture and our experience. All of this shapes how we see God and his world. We cannot just ignore these but need to bring them into the light of God's perspective. This can come about through the help of supervision as well as ongoing knowledge-based learning and reflection.

If we are willing to be open to the concept of engaging in people's stories, it is inevitable that we will find ourselves reflecting upon our own stories. Part of this is the need to be aware of our own strengths and weaknesses. Tools that help to define personality types can be very helpful here. A range of options is available, for example:

- Myers-Briggs is a common personality indicator. Working on one's shadow-side can be enlightening and help to develop a balanced personality.
- Belbin is helpful with regard to how you fit in a team.
- Margerson-McCann provides a team-management wheel.
- Enneagram is a more spiritual personality-type indicator.

101. C. Doulton (2012), at an ACC conference.

These exercises all help us to think about how we function using our right and left brain activity and whether we have a particular preference. Try looking at the world through only one eye for five minutes and you will soon understand what it is like to see life from a biased viewpoint.

A church can appear to be full of indispensible individuals who are convinced that the church will fall apart without their busy involvement. It is common for a new minister to take charge of a church and take on the mantle of full responsibility without pausing to reflect upon the history or the character of the church. From day one, they choose to be in charge, to make all the decisions and hardly pause to reflect upon the differences between their previous style of ministry and what is now required. Thus they carry the full pressure of the church alone. Pastoral carers need to be warned not to fall into the same trap. A pastoral worker can easily slip into the role of handing out verbal tranquillisers, along with the slight suggestion that they know best. Here, all decision-making is kept safely in their hands, which makes people entirely dependent upon them.

We need to recognise our own tendencies in ministry and come to terms with them. Part of this might be that we have a tendency to treat people as children rather than as mature adults. If we are always caring for people we think of as children, we will always be needed as a foster parent. But if we can begin to treat people as adults, we will be far more willing to let go when our work is complete.

I can hear someone reply, 'Yes, but this person is so lonely. They need me.' There are many situations that create a gulf in a person's life that we cannot fill. The best we can do is to help the person to recognise and accept their situation and see it as part of what it means to be human. We ourselves cannot be the answer to every person's loneliness or heartache. We need to constantly have our antennae up to make ourselves aware of situations where we might be becoming part of the problem:

- When we continue to see a person as a child or immature
- When we don't like it when a person makes decisions without first informing us
- When we get upset when a person chooses to seek advice from others
- When we are making arrangements to meet with someone and not the other way around
- When we are unable to allow a person to try and walk in case they fall down
- When we are not willing to learn from someone we have been helping.

Part of helping individuals to become mature is never to stop growing into maturity ourselves. After all, we are to be a model of maturity.

So when we react to a situation, be it in words, feelings or deeds, we need to reflect upon the purpose that lay underneath the reaction. The conclusions can reveal a great deal about ourselves. As we react in conversation and action, we reveal our own identity. This is why we need to be in an ongoing process of self-awareness, self-reflection and self-understanding. Since we are always changing, this journey needs to be a constant one. Unless we are willing to be aware of how ministry affects us, we can very easily lose sight of where we will end up spiritually. Too many ministers become consumed with never-ending Christian work and discover years later that they are spiritually dry and lost.

Pastoral work, like all Christian ministries, can never be done in a vacuum. God is always present, and in any case we are always working within the context of others. This is where self-awareness is developed. It is as we relate to others that we are given the opportunity to reflect at a deeper level about who we are, where we are going and what we want from life. It is up to us whether or not we choose to take this opportunity. Caring and ministering to others is no substitute for caring for our own needs. It is here that a spiritual director, supervisor, coach and / or a mentor can be so valuable.

A spiritual director can be our compass to remaining truly God-focused. A supervisor will help us maintain our boundaries and keep us ministering safely. A coach can work alongside us on a particular aspect of ministry that we want to develop. A mentor can be a sounding board to help keep our vision open and wide.

All of these roles allow us to hear ourselves speak and to reflect on what we are saying and why this is important to us. How can this sharing change how we see our ministry, God and others? When should we stop doing what we are busy with and move on to a new chapter? A worker who is isolated from openly sharing with another will in the end develop a 'blind spot' about themselves and their ministry.

It is inevitable that ministry will change our perspective on life, on others, on ourselves and on our faith. There has been much historical debate about whether Jesus himself experienced a growing self-awareness. After all, he began his ministry when he was about 30 years of age. What took place before then as he reached his mature position? What impact did the loss of his father early in life, with perhaps a 'clingy mother', have upon him? Donald Capp suggests that Jesus had a melancholic, depressive and diffused identity, which drove him to resolve the issue.[102] Hebrews 5:8 tells us that he learned obedience through his suffering. How Jesus balanced his divinity and humanity is complex, but what is clear is that we ourselves are definitely on a self-discovering journey.

This journey can, if we are not careful, create a crisis in our identity. If we enter ministry believing that our faith will not be affected by our work with others, then we will create a fracture between a 'frozen perspective' of ourselves and the reality of life in the present. This can lead to considerable emotional turmoil. If it is not dealt with, it can be like a boil that needs lancing. It will suddenly erupt, with serious consequences. This is where we suddenly hear of a minister leaving his wife, or a pastor resigning his or her orders, or a lay pastor giving up the church altogether. At first, it seems that there is no known reason for the change until eventually the truth comes to the surface that the individual had been living with tension for a considerable time. Such crises can be avoided if we are more self-aware and choose to care for ourselves with the same degree of importance as we give to others.

A friend at work asked a man if he was interested in swimming. 'No,' replied the man, 'I'm not from that kind of family.' However, he was persuaded to join an introductory evening and enjoyed it so much he joined the Alpha swimming club. He learned all about the breaststroke and how to be safe in the water and enjoyed good fellowship and hospitality. Before he knew it, he was a signed-up member of the club and became a great salesman for their activities.

One day, another work colleague suggested he should go to his club where they learned the crawl swimming technique. He took advice from his other friends who tried to dissuade him, saying he wasn't ready yet for a new technique and he should build on the swimming he had already learned. He listened to his friends, but months later he became a little dissatisfied with doing just the breaststroke. So he quietly went to the other club and really enjoyed learning the crawl with a group of people who stimulated his interest.

Having achieved all the qualifications he could in the two clubs, the man began to wonder if there was more to life than this. He was bored and frustrated at the clubs and thought about giving up swimming altogether. It just didn't seem to scratch where he was itching. Whenever he talked to the first club leaders about developing other muscles or learning new techniques, they seemed to become very worried and kept emphasising how he had not yet

---

102. D. Capp (1998), *Living Stories: Pastoral Counselling in Congregational Context*, Minneapolis: Fortress Press.

mastered the breaststroke. So he secretly went off and found out about a most interesting but challenging concept called 'the butterfly'.

The man never mastered this technique but he loved dabbling in it; it stimulated him and he enjoyed talking to people who were willing to look at things from a different perspective.

One day someone asked him why he never swam in the sea? 'The sea,' he thought. Surely it was beyond his reach or thinking; a place with no walls or barriers, erratic, uncontrollable. It both frightened and excited him. He decided to try it, but wisely he didn't tell his old club mates.

The man reflected upon his experience of swimming. He had had an interesting journey. At first, he had been very anti-swimming, but he had come to love it and feel safe in the club. He still loved to attend and had many loyal and good friends there. But there were times when it did not satisfy all of his needs, questions and concerns. He found that although he could never be a master at swimming and have all the answers, by being stimulated by others, trying to grasp the butterfly technique and encountering the waves in the sea, he was a more fulfilled swimmer. He never told his friends that he swam in the sea; they just didn't seem to understand or seem to have the same need. He knew he wasn't better at swimming than they were; he was just someone who had learned to adjust and adapt while maintaining his love of swimming.

This story expresses the concept of 'developmental faith,' which recognises that Christians often go through faith shifts to accommodate their experiences. The creeds were written after people experienced God, not before. Theology is formed in the crucible of life as we relate to others and make sense of it all with a godly perspective. Some people's faith seems to remain fairly static and solid, a faith that is reliable and sees them through life. But others can find that through ministry, new questions arise that challenge the old answers that they were previously content with. We find ourselves on a journey in which some people get lost and leave the church altogether whilst others find new answers and maintain membership in the church. The key is to recognise that we are on a journey, and like any relationship, that journey will mould and shape us. If we can engage in this developmental shift, we can grow in our faith, and maintain our relationship with God whilst accommodating parts of our lives where gaps and mystery linger.

Paula and Sally Nash talk about engaging in a trialogue, which involves us listening to the voice of God through our Christian heritage, our own beliefs and values, and our experience.[103] We then

103. P. Nash & S. Nash (2009), *Tools for Reflective Ministry*, London: SPCK.

have to sift and weigh up the merits of each voice to come to a conclusion.

Carers encounter situations that can affect us in at least four ways:

- The situation affirms our beliefs – e.g. a son dies of an overdose, which reaffirms our belief that bad actions lead to devastating consequences.
- Our faith is found wanting in the situation and we struggle to find a suitable answer – e.g. a parent once said to me, 'I have come to terms with the death of my son but not the loss of all that I believed.'
- The situation leads us to adjusting our spirituality – e.g. you change the way you pray.
- The situation deepens our faith in God whilst acknowledging that we understand less than we did before.

Nicholas Wolterstorff, an American theologian, lost his son in a climbing accident. It challenged his perspective on life. He says,

> Suffering may do us good, may be a blessing, something to be thankful for . . . in the valley of suffering, despair and bitterness is brewed. But there also character is made. The valley of suffering is also the valley of soul-making. How do I receive my suffering as a blessing while repulsing the obscene thought that God jiggled the mountain to make me better?[104]

We cannot expect others to be challenged by life and not appreciate that we too will be affected by their stories. Unless we make provision to reflect and be supported ourselves and to allow shifts in our theology, we may be challenged more in our faith than we can accommodate. We need to give ourselves permission to do several things. We need to ask questions, even if others are not interested, until we find some acceptable answers. We need to give ourselves and others time and space to express doubts and acknowledge that we don't have all the answers. All too often a 'doubt' is assumed to be in a theological form. However, we need to reflect upon whether in fact our doubts relate as much to psychological theories that don't seem to fit our experience. Or it may be socially, recognising the failure of the community and club culture to meet people's needs. We can find ourselves disillusioned by a church community that says one thing but does another. This is not necessarily a religious

104. N. Wolterstorff (1987), *Lament for a Son*, Grand Rapids: Eerdmans.

problem but might say much more about how that particular church functions socially. Or it may be the cultural behaviour of the community. Here, for example, the local culture may have rejected a healthy way of acknowledging death and grief. If we don't spend time reflecting upon our doubts, they can all too easily focus only on our faith. Finally, we need to allow ourselves to adjust our faith and spirituality without feeling that we are failing or falling away from our faith and church.

Church ministry is a privileged role that allows us to minister right at the heart of the community's soul. However, there is also a cost. Often without a clear job description and, as previously outlined, sometimes without adequate professional supervision, we can find ourselves working very long hours. When a job becomes a way of life it brings with it great satisfaction, but with the added sting that there seems to be no end of what is required of us.

Over the years I have asked clergy to fill in various questionnaires so that I could carry out stress analyses. The conclusion I have come to is that most clergy are 'A' types in terms of behaviour, where they are prone to be workaholics – the type we find in coronary care units. Ministry clearly has an impact upon us and may affect particular character types more negatively. It is interesting to note that one Anglican diocese recently found that the greatest job satisfaction came from non-stipendiary ministers rather than those in stipendiary posts. Perhaps this lay in the fact that these people were carrying out their roles almost as a 'hobby' (I say this in a positive and creative way) compared to their main financial career that had very different pressures. In contrast, stipendiary ministers hold the responsibility for the overall ministry. 'Carrying the can' inevitably leads to greater pressures. On top of a demanding role comes the psychological pressure of always having to relate a ministry to one's own personal belief system. This endless self-analysis can be wearisome. When we then add into this a whole range of emotionally draining grief and loss issues within the parish, it is easy to see where the stress comes from. So when it comes particularly to dealing with bereavement issues, we really need to 'know ourselves' if we are to not only survive in the ministry but thrive and last the course set before us.

One of the first requirements in ministry is to know what our gifts are and to make sure we use them well and without distractions. In my understanding, everything else comes second. It is here that we find our fulfilment in ministry. Everything else in ministry then has to be managed effectively.

So what happens if funerals, counselling and all of this grief work is just not for us? We need to remember that not all church leaders want to be involved in funerals or bereavement work. This is perfectly fine provided the church appoints others to carry out the role in a professional way. This is not just about abdicating responsibility to whoever seems interested but about seriously appointing a trained individual, or someone who is willing to be trained, who will be a credit to the church and wider community. The professional example we offer at funerals is a huge marketing opportunity that is not just to be passed to any retired priest or lay reader who might not have a heart for and commitment to the task. We therefore need to allocate a budget to this ministry which includes ongoing training costs. If this is effectively managed, the minister can learn to let go and allow the overseer to fulfil the role; they do not need to be responsible for every situation.

Whether or not a minister is involved in loss issues in the parish, they need to be responsible for themselves. As we have said before, this includes respecting the needs of their own family and setting a godly example to the congregation. If we simply copy the laity and become workaholics, what example are we setting? Most Anglican churches have the tradition of placing a plaque with the names of all the vicars going back to the church's birth. In some instances, the names go back a thousand years or more. It is sobering to realise that the church was there before we were, and will still be there long after we have moved on. We therefore need a better frame of mind that recognises the importance of looking after oneself. We need to set an example to the congregation about the importance of days off and holidays for ourselves and our families.

We very quickly becomes aware in church ministry of when we are feeling stressed, exhausted and ready for a break. After a year or two it should be clear how the pattern of ministry affects our health. We are then in a position to plan ahead and book breaks well before a crisis point. This not only applies to our long-term ministry but also on a daily basis. I have known ministers who cope fine with several funerals each week and others who find that just one drains them physically and emotionally.

We need to recognise our own psychological make-up and, if necessary, book time after events to restore ourselves spiritually. Otherwise we may find that 'disenfranchised grief' soon builds up within us. We may not recognise why we are feeling the way we do or what these feeling are connected with. Who else can look after us but ourselves? To love our neighbour requires us to first love ourselves and to formulate a healthy self-esteem for the good of our families, the congregation and ourselves. In this way we will have a long and fruitful ministry.

> You were taught to put away your former way of life, your old self, corrupt and deluded by its lusts, and to be renewed in the spirit of your minds.
>
> *Ephesians 4:22, 23*

Reflections

- Do you/your church recognise your minister's gifts, abilities, strengths and weaknesses?
- Does your church delegate or abdicate responsibilities?
- What care is in place to support lay people who take responsibilities within the church?
- When was the last time you or your minister took a spiritual break?
- When was the last time you said 'No'?!
- What history do we bring that clouds our present ministry?
- Have we identified and accepted our uniqueness in ministry?
- Can we naturally talk about our weaknesses?
- Have we a rule and rhythm of life?
- Is there peace between my inner and outer self?
- Try keeping a journal of your outer ministry and the inner feelings that it produces.
- What energises you? What pulls you down?
- What colour would you use to describe your role?
- What keeps you going?
- What disappoints you?
- What are you grappling with at the moment?
- Who can I reflect these answers with?

Chapter 60
Humour

A sense of humor is a major defense against minor troubles.
(Mignon Mclaughlin)[105]

Humour can be a lifesaver for a pastor. This can both be in our ministry with others as well as our in own reflections upon ourselves. Laughter is often seen as a release from pent-up nervous energy. Freud thought that humour was an energy that is a hangover from our thinking such that it needed to be discharged.[106] Others think laughter reflects the difference between what we expect to happen and what actually takes place.

There are certainly plenty of situations where humour arises in pastoral care with individuals. It is believed that the average adult will laugh at least 17 times a day, and children more often.[107]

Humour can be beneficial in pastoral situations in that it can be a way of opening a door through which the truth can be seen more fully. We can use humour both to release tension and to help someone see a situation in a new way.

Humour, of course, can be used completely inappropriately and can be offensive in the wrong situation. Some people use it as a way of mocking, putting down and deriding others. The Pharisees tried this approach with Jesus when they were attempting to turn the crowd against him (Luke 16:14; Matthew 27:41-3).

Humour is a tricky subject to understand. Some people are naturally humorous and seem to have a gentle touch with it. We have all met people who use humour as a sledgehammer at totally inappropriate times or who constantly repeat the same old joke that is well past its sell-by date. The worry is that humour can also be used to mask our own insecurities and fears in a situation. It can be a kind of get-out clause which eases our tension (although it may increase the tension of those around us).

It is therefore wise to steer clear of humour in pastoral situations unless we are very congruent with ourselves and with those with whom we are relating. Being humorous for our own sake is not a

105. M. McLaughlin (1963), *The Neurotic Notebook*, Indianapolis: Bobbs-Merill.
106. S. Freud, *The Complete Psychological Works of Sigmund Freud.*
107. R. Martin & N. Kulper (1999), 'Daily Occurrence of Laughter, Relationships with Age, Gender and Type A Personality' in *Humor: International journal of Humor Research.* 12:4, pp. 355-84.

good enough reason to introduce it in the presence of others. If in doubt, humour and laughter should be kept for our own release with ourselves, or for when we are back in the safety of our own home with those who understand us.

Yet humour can be very important to both sufferer and carer. It is an ability to be amused and enthused about life.

Laughing at ourselves can be a great way of releasing stress. Many times I have laughed aloud in the car after a pastoral encounter. It may look strange to other car drivers but it has certainly helped me not to carry emotion into my next task. It would be worrying if I were always laughing at others in my thoughts but most of the time I'm laughing at my own reactions, thoughts and concerns. It also reminds me of my own small significance in the great scheme of things and hopefully encourages humility.

God himself seems to remind us of this when we get carried away with our grand schemes and reminds us of our true position (Psalm 2:1-4).

In Genesis 21:6 Sarah laughs at the impossible situation of bearing a son at her age. She attributes this laughter to God himself.

The story of Ruth presents a different view of life compared to Nehemiah and Ezra, which are more serious accounts of establishing the kingdom. Both books emphasise the purity of the Jewish nation and how they should not integrate with other tribes. Yet Ruth, a Moabitess, is revealed as a descendent of David. If you grasp the extreme backgrounds of the characters, you can't help but see that God clearly has a sense of humour. The story of Jonah also conveys a humorous bent of someone being called to reach out to people he couldn't stand.

Despite the enormous tragedies that Job encounters, there is a darker humour present. He lost everything except his wife, yet his wife nags and turns on him. Standing back and seeing Job's so-called friends scolding, arguing, insulting and threatening has to draw a smile. It does seem set for a sick comedy scene. The Jewish nation has developed a very dry humour to see them through the many tragedies of its nation's life. One joke goes, 'Lord, isn't it time you chose some other nation to be special?' A simple Jewish-Christian song expresses it well:

Ten blessings from God,
nine for Jerusalem, one for the rest,
ten sorrows from God,
nine for Jerusalem, one for the rest.[108]

108. Traditional Jewish song from Israel.

This ability to see the lighter side of life has served the Jewish nation well. Job's story ends with his life restored as well as a family and friends and he is able to look back with a smile on his face.

Jesus himself was relaxed enough to use humour in his ministry. The best and most obvious example is when he talked about trying to take a speck out of a brother's eye when all the time we have a plank in our own eye (Matthew 7:3-5). To picture this, we can't help but see the funny side of the story. There are many other examples in the Gospels (see Reflections at the end of the chapter), and so often in the Gospels we find mystery and comical paradox. If Jesus could express real-life situations with a light touch, surely we can. Perhaps it begins when we take ourselves a little less seriously.

So the issues we need to consider are:

- Should I use humour in this situation?
- Am I using humour for myself or for others?
- Will humour build up or tear down the relationship?

How we should use humour is perhaps the key. The problem for us all is that it often occurs spontaneously, without pre-thought – or at least that's what we generally think. We need to use our intuition as to the appropriateness of introducing humour. This doesn't necessarily mean having to know a person extremely well. In some instances there can be a rapport with an individual after only a few minutes which enables us to assess what constitutes appropriate behaviour in that encounter. However, the motto has to be, if in any doubt or you feel at all uncomfortable being humorous, refrain at all costs. The damage that might be done could mean that your ministry with the person comes to a premature end.

Often it is the person we are caring for who spontaneously comes out with a humorous comment. We need to understand and appreciate the deeper need of the person to express their pent-up emotions in a way that is appropriate for them. We need to be able to embrace the humorous remark while at the same time being an empathic listener. There is a risk that we can be so relieved at the comment that we respond with our own humour and then can easily take the conversation into an inappropriate place that is difficult to manoeuvre out of.

Healthy humour in the end allows us to take a step back from a situation and recognise the limits of our mortality. Ultimately, in all pastoral situations, the final word belongs to God whose message is life over death. This leads us from sorrow to joy, from weeping to laughter. We are repeatedly encouraged to rejoice and to experience a deeper sense of joy and hope. Here, healthy humour has the potential to produce a richer experience of the dignity of life and, if it is handled correctly, it can bring a blessing to the listener and the pastor.

Reflections

- How would you define 'humour'?
- Can you recall humorous situations that helped you to cope?
- How can you use humour to bring healing to yourself, others, the church?
- Reread the accounts in the Gospels and see if you can see the humorous side to some of the stories. Imagine it was your story. Examples might include:
  - The birth of John the Baptist
  - Jesus' baptism surrounded by women with Pharisees looking on
  - Jesus talking about how people are never satisfied (Luke 7:31-5)
  - Miracles on a Sabbath (Luke 13:13-16)
  - The Sermon on the Mount
  - The parable of the sower, where God wastes the seed yet reaps bounteously (Matthew 13:1-23)
  - The feeding of the 5000 (Matthew 14:13-21)
  - The link between the kingdom and children (Luke 18:15-17)
  - Prayer and giving (Luke 11:11-13)
  - The story of the prodigal son (Luke 15)
  - The way of the donkey (Luke 19:35, 36)
  - The Emmaus Road (Luke 24)
  - Can you find others?

Chapter 61

Walking with a limp

On the highest throne in the world, we still sit only on our own bottom.
(Michel de Montaigne)[109]

One of the occupational hazards of pastoral ministry is becoming discouraged, be it with individuals, with God or with ourselves. Sometimes it's all three at once. It is impossible to embark on this kind of ministry and avoid a journey through the wilderness during which we struggle to hold on to the God we claim to believe in. It is a strange feeling to find that all our thoughts were good yesterday, but today they seem faded and sour. Sometimes it arises in our shared lives with bereavement, an accident or family problems; at other times it is more within ourselves with discouragement, depression, loneliness or anger. Sometimes the smell of very tragic situations such as the Holocaust, Hiroshima or the birth of a severely handicapped baby drifts our way and we catch a flavour of the suffering and despair.

'I hold and I am held' is a good, traditional prayer to cling to at such times. In the midst of all of Job's sufferings, what comforted him most wasn't what God said to him. It was rather discovering that he wasn't alone, that God was with him. There are times in ministry when we see no light, hear no voice, sense no presence, can't determine the way forward and only fear what is ahead, but we endeavour to acknowledge that God is still in our midst. At other times he is right in front of us but we just can't recognise him.

Although we believe in a crucified Christ, we tend to think more of Christ as the healer, teacher, comforter and guide. We know so well the stories of Peter's mother-in-law, the leper or the woman with the flow of blood, and we formulate a clear picture of Christ the carer. Here he can seem to be the one who is always positive, creative and who has the answers. If we are following Christ, how can we fall into discouragement and resentment? But we do, and we can easily punish ourselves for our lack of faith. Perhaps we need to hold on to a parable Jesus told of himself being sick and ill. It is not the kind of image we have in our minds. We can imagine Jesus struggling in the garden or being beaten and whipped and then

109. M. de Montaigne (1993), *The Complete Essays*. London: Penguin.

suffering on the cross, but we might never have pictured him lying sick with a fever. Yet Jesus' parable does just that.

> For I was hungry and you gave me food, I was thirsty and you gave me something to drink, I was a stranger and you welcomed me, I was naked and you gave me clothing, I was sick and you took care of me, I was in prison and you visited me.
>
> *Matthew 25:35, 36*

We represent humanity with all its weaknesses. There will be mistakes, failures and disappointments. The truth is, we are not transformed fully on this earth. We work towards it but constantly fall short. Realism therefore is required if we are to survive as pastoral workers. Our ministry is not one that is greater than any other but rather it is an ability to see ordinary daily life at a deeper level. It is seeking to see the kingdom in all situations.

> For we do not have a high priest who is unable to sympathise with our weaknesses, but we have one who in every respect has been tested as we are, yet without sin.
>
> *Hebrews 4:15, 16*

We have all heard the analogy about whether our glass is half full or half empty. The reality is, of course, that both are true. The life of a pastor embraces both joy and despair. We need to recognise our own tendencies to veer towards optimism or pessimism. We need to practise not seeing negatives where they do not exist. Yet it is equally dangerous to be a Christian who sees everything through rosy glasses. Otherwise we put ourselves in impossible positions when we encounter very challenging situations. We need to develop a resilience that enables us to handle what life throws at us while maintaining faith and confidence in ourselves.

Our feelings play a big part in this resilience. Feelings can either lift us up and move us forward or make us uncomfortable and put the brakes on. We know that those who are more in touch with their feelings have a better prognosis when they encounter counselling. Perhaps this speaks to us of our own ministries. The more we are aware of our feelings, the more we can work them through so that we can carry less baggage.

> Thank you for the seven marvelous roses. They opened up into countless petals . . . they lived long enough to bring a ray of light. It doesn't matter that they didn't last long. The important thing is that they had the courage not to stay closed up in their

buds, that they were wise enough to come out of themselves and rise toward the sun in delicate red petals. They left the mark of your presence here.[110]

Reflections

- Are you aware of your strengths and weaknesses?
- How will you know when to stop your pastoral role in the church?
- What helps to keep your feet on the ground?
- Is your glass half full or half empty in your pastoral role?
- What aspects of your life would you like still to blossom in?

110. C. Christo (1978), *Letters from a Prisoner of Conscience* (Orbis), p. 65.

Chapter 62

Knowing when to stop

When you lose touch with inner stillness, you lose touch with yourself.
When you lose touch with yourself, you lose yourself in the world.
(Eckhart Tolle)[111]

When a person is constantly 'giving themselves away' to others, it is inevitable that burnout can result. What often occurs before burnout is a feeling that the work is becoming less meaningful, producing cynicism and dissatisfaction with the work. A person goes through the motions and often finds unhelpful ways of coping, such as alcohol, stress-related illnesses or extreme sexual habits. Others collapse with exhaustion. These problems don't arrive at a person's door all at once; they creep up. The main culprit is usually simply doing more and more of the same every day. Any good pastoral worker will inevitably find that their workload gradually increases. Some workers have an internal system that requires them to 'give themselves' to others in order to fill some inner void. At first the void is filled and the worker feels appreciated. But eventually the void returns and the worker has to work harder to keep filling the space within. They become automatic givers, causing self-abuse and resulting in burnout.

It is possible to keep working in Christian ministry long after burnout has taken place. A worker can go through the motions whilst harbouring frustration, resentment and cynicism. Burnout has two components to it.

Firstly, there is a stress disorder which has emotional, physiological and behavioural symptoms (see Chapter 49, Stress). Dealing with people's problems over years can accrue a sense of traumatisation. The endless bereavement situations, painful stories, violent accounts and listening to people's bouts of depression take their toll. A pastoral worker is expected to have an inbuilt resilience to these issues, but we are not supermen and women; we all have our limits. If we fail to refresh ourselves with a healthy input of the positive aspects of God's creation, we will end up with a twisted perspective.

There is also stress that results from the cultural changes that are taking place around the role of religion in our society. At times we may find ourselves working in growing churches that are exciting

111. E. Tolle (2003), *Stillness Speaks*, Novato: New World Library.

and dynamic. This is energising and we can be carried along with colleagues' enthusiasm. Working long hours can seem a pleasure and no burden. But we might equally find ourselves in communities that are full of infighting, where the church is not respected in the community and is struggling to survive. If the church is declining and experiencing financial difficulties, even to pay our wage, we can feel as if it's entirely our fault and that we are just not good enough.

Churches are not very skilled at reducing what they do when they lack manpower. There seems to be an assumption that all we need to do is to work harder, pray more and the problem will be resolved. Sooner or later someone will snap in such a situation.

Stress can result from too much change, where the church is always attempting new things and responding to all of the latest Christian ideologies. In this situation there never seems to be enough time to consolidate the work that is put in. There is also stress that comes from being in an organisation that is resistant to change, where we feel as if we are always pushing new ideas and constantly being told why they won't work. If we feel that every new idea will face criticism and resistance, there develops a weariness about the work and it becomes a heavy burden to bear.

Secondly, there is a spiritual aspect to burnout. This can come in various forms. It may be that a theology is developed that suggests that all the world's problems are your responsibility. Here the task spiritually simply becomes impossible. The light finally dawns that whatever we do, there will always be more needs at the door. Others can become weary of hearing exaggerated Christian hype, be it from preachers who preach one thing but practise another, or church members who expect something from you that they themselves are not living out. There can also be a point in the Christian journey where our faith changes. The answers we once were comfortable with no longer fit. We can find ourselves surrounded by other Christians who do not seem to be asking the same questions or are just not willing to have dialogue on issues without a black and white viewpoint. This is a lonely place to be, especially if we are on the staff and expected to maintain a particular church/religious stance.

What do we do when we honestly acknowledge to ourselves that things are not right within us? There are several things, if we are honest with ourselves and willing to allow others to support us.

Firstly, we should follow the advice that parents give to children: 'If you are lost, stand still.' We began this book with the Genesis passage where God calls to Adam and Eve, 'Where are you?' This is a good starting question for us all when we are weary and worn out from ministry.

Secondly, we need to find someone we can trust, someone who has experience in counselling or spiritual direction. Here we can unload our deepest feelings in a safe and confidential way that allows us still to hold our heads up high.

We then need to decide on a reasonable number of hours to work, with the agreement of our supervisor and the church leaders.

Then we need to create regular time out with our family and friends to bring back a degree of pleasure and fun into our lives. This should include a good holiday period as well as booking in a few shorter breaks over the year. Ministry has its own pattern of business. With experience we will learn to identify when the pressure points arise and therefore we can pre-plan holiday breaks.

We must have a daily routine that is healthy and balanced and which incorporates a quiet time, work, rest, play and relationships.

It is important that we choose to become more aware of our body and the messages it is giving us. We must learn how to care for the gift of life that God has given us. This might involve going to the gym, cycling or going for a walk with a friend. When we are getting stressed, our body gives us clear messages, if we are only willing to listen.

It is a good idea to find two or three people outside the parish with whom to form a prayer triplet. Meeting on a four- or six-weekly basis provides a regular chance to share honestly and pray for one another. Finding others of a similar background can help the group to share things in common.

As mentioned earlier, I was taught by my pastoral tutor at college to choose a new spiritual topic to study each year. This has always given me a sense of movement in my faith, challenged my preaching and theological thinking and prevented me from being static. It has also helped me to form the habit of reading around new topics.

Developing a hobby is a good idea, which we can explore during our day off. I took up woodwork twenty years ago. I wanted to make a rocking horse for my young children. I started doing a little work on my day off when my wife happened to be working. It led me to making a few horses on commission, which provided a refreshing challenge away from my spiritual work. Over the years I moved on to head portraiture. This was just a few hours a week which not only uplifted me but provided a space to allow me to come back to my regular spiritual work energised and refreshed.

Finally, preach into the subject of a church family that supports one another in our work environments. Encourage the church family to care for one another, including you! This means being human in the pulpit and sharing some of the difficulties of ministry. This requires vulnerability, but it also can reap the rewards of a community that takes an interest in your ministry and empowers the laity to share their concerns about you.

If you are single, it is even more important that you provide for yourself a clear support structure that will enable your ministry to thrive over many years.

Remind yourself that ministry is seasonal. God created the seasons for a purpose; we therefore need to attune to them: a time to work hard, a time for new initiatives, a time for fun and pleasure, a time to withdraw and feed off the food from the summer. We need to learn to flow with God's creative timing. Part of this is to make sure we have a Sabbath rest each week and adjust our work according to the seasons.

In the end, we need a ministry that allows us to grow in grace and love over all the years of our work. It is our responsibility to prevent ourselves from becoming bitter and cynical in the Lord's work.

Reflections

- What theological topic would you like to study?
- How far ahead do you plan your holidays? Retreats?
- Can you make time for the development of a personal hobby or social interaction outside the church?
- How will you know when you are spiritually burnt out?
- Who is on 'lookout' to watch over you?

Conclusion

The pastor's task is to help a person out of their sin and to enable them to raise up to their full potential.

Change is all around us; it is something we just can't prevent. Sometimes it might feel good; at other times it leaves us anxious and troubled. Other changes challenge us to think about life in a totally new way. And there are times when we yearn for change to take place but we feel stuck and unable to do anything about it. It is into this situation, living on the edge of change in a time of change, that the pastor is called to minister.

We live in a time of experts, whether it is theologians, scientists, philosophers or politicians. It is also a time of incredible change with cyberspace changing the whole concept of what a community looks like.

Yet all of this can lead to increased fragmentation in our communities and heightened loneliness. We as a society seem to know more about all of the parts of life rather than the whole. We are also learning that health is not just the opposite of illness. It involves becoming aware of our strengths and limitations. We can experience health even in the midst of illness and death. It is this wholeness that the pastor seeks to bring about, or to put it into biblical language, to bring about the new kingdom of God. We are seeking to put new wine into new wineskins.

We do this by believing ten key simple facts:

1. People are body, mind and spirit.
2. We are on a journey of wholeness.
3. We need one another in family, community and society. We can't ignore the fact that we are all connected in one way or another.
4. Human beings are constantly changing.
5. There are positive and negative aspects of life that make up the whole story of our lives (including death).
6. We seek to move away from dominant, oppressive, hierarchical relationships and aim to embrace more equal relationships.
7. We are willing to use all the skills and knowledge available to us to bring about wholeness.
8. We learn to live with things not yet completed.

9. We recognise the uniqueness of each person even though they are a part of the collective community.
10. Pastors are not exempt from any of the above.

We need to hold on to the tension of being professional, learning as much as possible from the growth of knowledge that relates to people's health and well-being while remaining truly Christian and spiritual. This means we need to develop a ministry that is wide in its learning. Being eclectic in our learning is challenging and liberating. However, we need to move to a more mature form of ministry, which is more integrated. This is not where we simply pick and mix our skills and techniques according to the situation; rather we should merge our knowledge into an integrated belief system. This means our approach becomes more mature and holistic and is consistent across our care.

For the average pastoral worker, their task might seem to be rather unrewarding. There is no opportunity to preach and receive a great response. People seldom leave a church and say, 'Thank you for all you have done this past week.' The reality is that people do not know what you have done. This is pastoral care's strength, and its weakness. The caring role is successful because it works away quietly like the yeast in a bread mix. People value it individually because of the confidentiality of the work. But this does leave a pastoral worker feeling rather like the Cinderella of the organisation. Our work can seem rather ordinary and grey from the outside. People think that visiting and listening 'can't be difficult', and 'what a nice job it is.' They hardly realise what goes into being a skilled care worker.

We need to remember that, as we care for another, we are reaching out and touching the hem of the Lord's garment. We don't always recognise the Lord above us, but nevertheless he is there working through our loving actions. This is reward indeed.

Pastoral ministry is rather like the development of a rose in a garden. It needs good roots and feeding if it is to produce a flowering bud. With the right support, prayer and fellowship it can blossom and open its petals to produce a sweet fragrance that blesses those around us and, in turn, blesses us. If you can work on just a few of the aspects mentioned in this book, whatever your context, you will be in a process of blossoming and maturing.

Appendix 1

A picture of a mature Christian human being

Someone who:

- Has been born again
- Can accept themselves without guilt or defensiveness
- Is natural and not artificial
- Will break away from convention if necessary
- Doesn't have to have the last word
- Can find direction in life that motivates them
- Is able to focus outside of themselves and have genuine interest in others
- Is happy with their own company
- Can be independent of other people's opinions and attention yet be able to engage with people as necessary
- Has a sense of humour that is not cynical or bitter
- Is able to relate to people irrespective of race, class, education or religion
- Appreciates the ordinary things of life
- Knows how to say no, and cautiously considers all aspects before saying yes
- Does all things with prayer with an awareness of God's presence in all situations
- Produces the fruit of the Holy Spirit that leads to Christian maturity
- Can relax and enjoy themselves, whether it be in art, music, sport or sexual experiences with their husband or wife
- Lives with their faith and acknowledges their doubts
- Integrates their faith in every aspect of their lives
- Is able to articulate what they believe and stand accountable
- Is able to let go and trust God.

Appendix 2

Example of a pastor's/counsellor's log

Date	Time	Person's name/course			Type of contact			Reason for Contact					Risk			Content/ Themes	Action
		Church member	Parish member	Other	Phone	Email	Face	Enquiry	Chat	Gen Sup	Crisis	Counsel	H	M	L		

Appendix 3

Example of a pastor's/ counsellor's one-to-one session form

PASTOR'S/COUNSELLOR'S FORM

Name	*Date*	*Duration*
	Client/Parishioner	*Self*
Description What took place?		
Feelings Client / self?		
Interventions/ Exploration Incidents / aspects / stories		
Conclusions/ Further actions/ Concerns Learning / development		
Future meeting?		

Appendix 4
A chaplain's protocol in a university setting

The chaplaincy provides a service across the whole university for the staff, students and their families.

We offer:

- Confidentiality
- A sanctuary: we have a quiet room available for anyone to use
- A space to escape, reflect and relax
- A willingness to journey with individuals irrespective of religious beliefs
- A place to learn about belief and no belief; a place to experience new styles of worship, reflection and contemplation. We provide worship for welcoming, memorial, carol and weekly services
- An information service linking individuals with multi-faith chaplains and faith communities. We have a general prayer/quiet room and two Islamic prayer rooms
- Pastoral care which works closely with the university counselling service and medical team. If we engage in counselling, we are independently supervised
- We represent the university to the religious communities locally and nationally
- We provide a priestly/prophetic role and are able to speak into situations with a sense of objectivity and independence
- We seek to remind individuals and the institution of the importance of self-worth, of being affirmed by oneself (and by others), of celebrating achievements and of the importance of enjoyment and fun
- An interface creating discussion between religion and academic subjects
- We run a global café and various courses on topics such as self-awareness, stress, meditation, listening skills, counselling skills, loss issues and faith issues. We also lecture in schools on appropriate topics
- Various events during freshers' week for new students

- A place to share hospitality with free refreshments
- A meeting room for groups
- A safe place for international students and close work with the international department
- A desire to maintain a historical tradition where students have an opportunity not only to learn academically and develop skills for employment but also to grow in personal/spiritual formation
- A safety net for individuals to learn of the dangers of cults and groups that manipulate
- A call-out service as part of the wider crisis management team for issues relating to:
  - Physical illness
  - Mental health issues
  - Bereavement or loss
  - Missing students
  - Victims or perpetrators of crime
  - Redundancy or retirement
- Referrals from support or academic staff
- Support of staff development programmes and induction events.

Appendix 5

Pastoral care ethics and framework for good practice[112]

(For the sake of brevity the word 'client' is used to indicate the person being cared for.)

1. Ethical basis for pastoral care

1.1 Care must be taken not to exploit clients. Because of the vulnerable nature of clients, special care is required and the client should be kept fully informed and given opportunity for discussion at every stage of the process.

1.2 The integrity and confidentiality of the client must be maintained.

1.3 The safety of the client must be guarded and all reasonable steps taken to seek appropriate medical or legal assistance, should the need arise.

1.4 All Christian pastoral care members should be integrated in the body of the local church community and receive appropriate consultative support for their work.

2. Framework for good practice (pastoral care member/client relationship)

2.1 Pastoral care members should take all reasonable steps to ensure that the client suffers neither physical nor psychological harm during caring encounters.

2.2 Pastoral care members are responsible for working in ways which promote the client's control over his/her own life and respect the client's ability to make decisions and change in the light of his/her own beliefs and values.

2.3 Pastoral care members do not normally act on behalf of their clients. If they do, it will be only at the express request of the client.

2.4 Pastoral care members must not exploit their clients financially, sexually, emotionally or in any other way.

2.5 Pastoral care members have a responsibility to establish with clients what other therapeutic or helping relationships are current. Pastoral care members should obtain the client's permission before conferring with other professional workers.

---

112. From the Association of Christian Counsellors and Pastoral Carers (ACC).

2.6 Exceptional circumstances may arise which give the pastoral care member good grounds for believing that the client will cause serious physical harm to others or to him/herself. In such circumstances the client's consent to break confidentiality should be sought whenever possible unless there are also good grounds for believing the client is no longer able to take responsibility for his/her own actions. Whenever possible, the decision to break the confidentiality should be made only after consultation with the person overseeing the caring.

2.7 Pastoral care members need to be particularly aware that the client's right to confidentiality must not be waived in the context of prayer.

2.8 Pastoral care members should monitor actively the limitations of their own competence and involvement and work within their own known limits.

2.9 Pastoral care members should not work when their functioning is impaired due to personal or emotional difficulties, illness, disability, alcohol, drugs or for any other reason.

2.10 It is an indication of the competence of the pastoral care member when they recognise their inability to help particular persons and make appropriate referrals.

2.11 Pastoral care members have a responsibility to themselves and their clients to maintain their own effectiveness, resilience and ability to help clients by seeking help and advice from the person who provides their pastoral care cover.

2.12 Pastoral care members should have received adequate basic training before commencing work and be willing to maintain ongoing training.

2.13 Pastoral care members should take all reasonable steps to ensure their own physical safety.

2.14 Pastoral care members should not conduct themselves in their caring activities in ways which undermine public confidence either in their role as a pastoral care member or in the work of other pastoral care members.

2.15 If a pastoral care member suspects misconduct by another pastoral care member which cannot be resolved or remedied after discussion with the person concerned, they should implement the complaints procedure, doing so without breaches of confidentiality other than what is necessary for investigating the complaint.

Complaints procedure

2.16 The only complaints that can be dealt with by the ACC are those concerning failure to comply with the 'Pastoral Care Ethics and Framework for Good Practice'.

2.17 All complaints should be taken up with the ACC pastoral care member in the first instance, both verbally and in writing.

2.18 If there is no satisfactory conclusion, the complaint should be taken up in writing with the Chair of the Association.

Appendix 6

Examples of issues that ought to be addressed in a pastor's contract

- Agreement concerning the number of hours to be worked per week
- Whether the post is paid or voluntary
- Clarification about what expenses will be paid – e.g. telephone
- What will be expected in terms of work duties on Sundays
- Clear line management with set times to meet
- Review date of contract – at least annually
- Whether the pastor will be a part of the leadership team
- Provision of an external supervisor and spiritual director
- Clarification on where individuals will be seen
- Provision of panic buttons?
- Church provision of insurance cover
- Agreement about policy for working alone
- Contact number for emergencies
- Agreement that the pastor will not be undermined or bypassed by other leaders in the church
- Two named persons to whom the pastor can turn if grievances arise.

Appendix 7

Rowe's characteristics of a depressed person

Dorothy Rowe talks about depression as being a prison that a person puts themselves into in order to feel safe from the dangers outside. She identifies six common thought processes in depressed people.[113]

1. 'No matter how good and acceptable I appear to be, I am really bad, evil, valueless, unacceptable to myself and others.' This comes from the belief that the person thinks that they have to be always good. When they fail to achieve this (like us all), their conclusion is that they are bad. This seems an irrefutable truth rather than just an opinion.
2. 'Other people are such that I must fear, hate and envy them.'
3. 'Life is terrible and death is worse.'
4. 'Only bad things happened to me in the past and only bad things will happen to me in the future.' Dorothy describes life like a house. For most people, the past is represented by a small cosy room with lots of things in it, with a veranda leading to a light-filled future. But for a depressed person this room is large, dark and menacing, and the future is represented by a long dark tunnel. Here the depressed person has collected a series of negative life events that they hold on to. These range from rebuffs, losses, unsettling changes, betrayals, deceits, disloyalties, treacheries, cruelties, criticisms, reproaches, indignities, belittling and rejections. For most of us who experience some of these, we talk them over with someone and they become resolved or dissipate. Not so for the depressed. Guilt then comes along and suffocates us with the past.
5. 'It is wrong to get angry.' It is often said that depression can be anger turned inwards. Once the anger is projected at ourselves it is a small step to blaming ourselves; a recipe for disaster. Along with this is a belief that we should never offend anyone such that we don't understand assertiveness. Trying to please everyone is, of course, impossible.
6. 'I must never forgive anyone, least of all myself.'

---

113. D. Rowe, *Depression: The Way out of Your Prison*.

Although there may well be common traits in depressed people, we need to remember that no two people ever have the same experience of life or ever see things in the same way. What we do know is that our behaviour is determined by the way we interpret what happens to us.

Appendix 8

What to do if someone is in danger of suicide

- Take the person seriously.
- Stay calm.
- Obtain their permission to contact their doctor or therapist.
- Express genuine concern. Give clear reasons why you are concerned.
- Listen attentively.
- Ask direct questions. Ask the person if they have a specific plan for suicide. What method are they thinking about?
- Acknowledge the person's feelings. Do not be judgemental.
- Do not relieve the person of their responsibility for their own actions.
- Reassure. Stress that suicide is a permanent solution for temporary problems.
- Stay with talking about things that make you feel uncomfortable – i.e. the person's pain, rather than talking about positive things that you feel more comfortable to talk about.
- Help the person to reflect upon what the impact will be on others if they do commit suicide.
- Provide hope. Remind the person that that help is available and things can get better.
- Enable the person to think through who else can support them at difficult times. Provide telephone numbers for the Samaritans, etc.
- Do not promise confidentiality as you may need to speak to another medical professional. Do not make promises that would endanger the person's life.
- Encourage the person to agree that they will not attempt suicide without first informing you or seeking additional help.
- Draw up a plan of support for the person, including telephone numbers of support groups.
- Write down what has been said and decided as a reminder to the person.
- If possible, do not leave the person alone until you are sure that they are safe and have adequate support.

- If the person wants to leave, allow them to but inform them that you will seek help.
- Involve others. If necessary call 999.
- Afterwards, keep a clear record and inform your supervisor/line manager as soon as possible.
- Take the issue to your therapeutic supervisor/pastor for your own support.

Appendix 9

The pastor's appropriate questions

As pastors we need to have a range of appropriate questions up our sleeves when we engage with individuals. These questions should flow naturally in the conversation.

Look for benefiting changes:

- What experience of life would you like to explore?
- What do you recall of how you have responded to key events in your life?
- How did others respond?
- What does this story / account mean to you?
- What is the most painful part of the story?
- Has this story changed the way you view life? Yourself? Your future?
- How has it affected your relationship with others?
- What concerns do others have about you?
- Close your eyes and visualise a scene connected with your story. Who or what is your focus of attention? What is happening? Where are you? What feelings do you notice now in your body? What was the most emotionally significant part of the experience?
- Do you have trouble accepting the past?
- To what extent has it been hard for you to trust others?
- Do you feel angry about your story?
- Do you feel uneasy about moving on with your life? What areas are difficult for you? New friends? Interests?
- Do you feel emotionally numb or feel disconnected with others since the event?
- To what extent do you feel your life is empty or meaningless?
- Do you feel that the future holds any meaning or prospect for fulfilment?
- Do you feel on edge or jumpy?
- If you wrote a letter to yourself, what would you say?
- What philosophical beliefs contribute to your adjustment?
- How did you make sense of the event when it happened? And now?
- How has the event disrupted your life story?
- How has it affected your priorities?

- What was your view of yourself before? Now?
- What metaphor or image would symbolise your experience?
- What steps could you take to help your healing?

All of this might seem like a checklist, although that is certainly not the intention. But many pastoral workers wonder what to do when they visit people. It is listening and caring, but it can be so much more. By having these questions in our toolbox of thoughts, we can use them naturally to bring change to a situation. Jesus always seemed to have the right question ready in his encounters with individuals. This came from his in-depth knowledge of human beings. We, too, need to meet and engage with people with a working insight. Hopefully the questions become ingrained in the pastor such that they flow out naturally as appropriate to aid a person's self-revelation.

Bibliography

Books

ADAMS, J. (1979), *A Theology of Christian Counselling: More Than Redemption*, Michigan: Zondervan

ADAMS, J. E. (1979), *Prayers for Troubled Times*, Grand Rapids: Baker Books

ATKINSON, S. (2010), *First Steps out of Depression*, Oxford Lion Hudson

BAGBY, D. (1999), *Seeing Through Our Tears: Why We Cry, How We Heal*, Minneapolis: Augsburg Fortress

BALLARD, P. & PRITCHARD, J. (1996), *Practical Theology in Action*, London: SPCK

BARCLAY, W. (2010), *The Letters to the Corinthians*, Norwich: St Andrew's Press

BAUM, F. (1982), *The Wizard of Oz*, London: Puffin

BILLINGHAM, W. (2010), *Growing a Caring Church: Practical Guidelines for Pastoral Care*, Abingdon: Bible Reading Fellowship

BONHOEFFER, D. (1953), *Letters and Papers from Prison*, New York, Touchstone

BROMLEY, G. (1979), *Introduction to the Theology of Karl Barth*, Eerdmans

BROWN, C. R. (2012), *The Gospel of Good Health (Classic Reprint)*, Hong Kong: Forgotten Books

BUJOLD, L. M. (1999), *A Civil Campaign*, New York: Baen Books

BUSCAGLIA, L. (1996), *Amor*, Barcelona: Emece Editores

CAMARA, H. (2009), *Essential Writings*, Maryknoll: Orbis Books

CAPP, D. (1998), *Living Stories: Pastoral Counselling in Congregational Context*, Minneapolis: Fortress Press

CARSON, M. (2008), *The Pastoral Care of People with Mental Health Problems*, London: SPCK

CHALMERS, A. K. (2009), *Quote Me*, Uplifting Publications

CHAPIN, E. H. (2012), *Lessons on Faith and Life (Classic Reprint)*, Hong Kong: Forgotten Books

CHELMSFORD, J. (2000), *Time to Heal*, London: Church of England Report

CHRISTO, C. (1978), *Letters from a Prisoner of Conscience*, Orbis

COLE, E. L. (1995), *Winners Are Not Those Who Never Fail but Those Who Never Quit*, London: Honor Books

DAVIS, R. (1989), *My Journey into Alzheimer's Disease*, Amersham: Scripture Press. Also available as a free pdf download from http://disorders.free-books.biz/My-Journey-into-Alzheimers-Disease-PDF-837.html (accessed 21 September 2012).

DEEDS, D. (1987), *Pastoral Theology: An Inquiry*, London: Epworth Press

DONNE, J. (1976), *The Complete English Poems*, London: Penguin

ELIOT, T. S. (2001), *Four Quartets*, London; Faber & Faber

ERIKSON, E. (1994), *Identity and the Life Cycle*, London: Norton

FRANKL, V. (2004), *Man's Search for Meaning*, London: Rider

FREUD, S. (2001), *The Complete Psychological Works of Sigmund Freud*, London: Vintage Classics

GANDHI, M. K. (1927), *An Autobiography: The Story of My Experiments with Truth*, London: Penguin

GARDNER, F. (2001), *Self-Harm: A Psychotherapeutic Approach*, Hove: Brunner-Routledge

GILBERT, J. H. (1895), *Dictionary of Burning Words of Brilliant Writers: A Cyclopaedia of Quotations, from The Literature of All Ages*.

GOODMAN, E. (2004), *Paper Trail: Common Sense in Uncommon Times*, Brookvale: James Bennett Ltd

GRASHOFF, U. (2006), *Let Me Finish: An Anthology of Suicide Letters*, London: Headline Publishing

GRASSI, J. (1986), *God Makes Me Laugh: A New Approach to Luke*, Eugene: Wipf & Stock

HERON, J. (1989), *The Facilitators' Handbook*, London: Kogan Page

HICKS, J. W. (2005), *50 Signs of Mental Illness*, London: Yale University Press

HUME, D. (2005), *On Suicide*, London: Penguin Classics

HUNNEYSETT, E. (2009), *Pastoral Care Mental Health*, Brentwood: Chipmunka Publishing

HURDING, R. (1980), *Restoring the Image: An Introduction to Christian Caring and Counselling*, Exeter: Paternoster Press

ISON, D. (2005), *The Vicar's Guide*, London: Church Publishing House

JEFFERS, S. & SMITH, H. (2007), *Finding a Sacred Oasis in Grief*, Abingdon: Radcliffe Publishing

JENKINS, R. (1995), *Gladstone*, New York: Random House

JOYBELL, C. (2010), *The Sun is Snowing: Poetry and Prose*, London: Author House

JUNG, C. (1933), *Modern Man in Search of a Soul*, London: Paul Trench Trubner

KELLEY, M. M. (2010), *Grief: Contemporary Theory & the Practice of Ministry*, Minneapolis: Fortress Press

KEROUAC, J. (2000), *Atop an Underwood: Early Stories and Other Writings*, London: Penguin

KLINE, N. (1999), *Time to Think: Listening to Ignite the Human Mind*, London: Cassell Ltd

KORNFELD, M. (1998), *Cultivating Wholeness*, New York: Continuum

KUSHNER, H. (1990), *When Bad Things Happen to Good People*, Outlet

LAMBOURNE, R. (1975), in *Contact*, No.35

LEACH, J. & PETERSON, M. (2010), *Pastoral Supervision: A Handbook*, London: SCM

LEE, H. B. (1973), *Strengthening the Home*, Latter Day Saints pamphlet

LEWIS, C. S. (2012 Reissue), *The Problem of Pain*, Collins.

LITCHFIELD, K. (2006), *Tend My Flock, Sustaining Good Pastoral Care*, London: Canterbury Press

LOVE, J. K. (Ed) (1933), *Helen Keller in Scotland: A Personal Record Written by Herself*, Methuen.

MADDOCKS, M. (1981), *The Christian Healing Ministry*, SPCK

MAISEL, R., EPSTON, D. & BORDEN, A. (2004), *Biting the Hand That Starves You: Inspiring Resistance to Anorexia/Bulimia*, New York: Norton

MASLOW, A. (1968), *Towards a Psychology of Being*, New York: John Wiley

McCLOSKEY, R. (1920), *Make Way for Ducklings*, New York: Viking Press

McLAUGHLIN, M. (1963), *The Neurotic Notebook*, Indianapolis: Bobbs-Merill

MEAD, M. (1973), *Coming of Age in Samoa*, New York: First Quill

MERRINGTON, B. (2011), *Grief, Loss and Pain in Churches*, Buxhall: Kevin Mayhew

MIDDLETON, K. (2010), *First Steps out of Anxiety*, Oxford: Lion Hudson

MIDDLETON, K. & SMITH, J. (2010), *First Steps out of Eating Disorders*, Oxford: Lion Hudson

MONTAIGNE, M de (1993), *The Complete Essays*, London: Penguin

MURAKAMI, H. (2001), *Norwegian Wood*, London: Vantage

NASH, S. & NASH, P. (2009), *Tools for Reflective Ministry*, London: SPCK

PATTISON, S. (2000), *Shame*, Cambridge: Cambridge University Press

PATTISON, S. A. (2003), *A Critique of Pastoral Care*, Norwich: SCM

PATTON, J. (2005), *Pastoral Care: An Essential Guide*, Nashville: Abingdon Press

PRATT, A. (2010), *Practical Skills for Ministry*, London: SCM

RICHARDS, J. (1974), *But Deliver Us From Evil*, London: Darton, Longman & Todd

ROGERS, C. (1967), *On Becoming a Person*, London: Constable & Robinson

ROMME, M. & ESCHER, S. (2000), *Making Sense of Voices: A Guide for Mental Health Professionals Working with Voices Hearers*, London: Mind Publications

ROSS, A. (2003), *Counselling Skills for Church and Faith Community Workers*, Maidenhead: Open University Press

ROWE, D. (2003), *Depression: The Way out of Your Prison*, Hove: Routledge

SAUNDERS, C. (1990), *Beyond the Horizon: A Search for Meaning in Suffering*, London: Darton, Longman & Todd

SCHULTZ, K. (1993), *The Art of Vocation of Caring for People in Pain*, New York: Paulist Press

SEALEY, K. (1997), *Restoring Hope*, Boston, MA: Beacon Press

SELIGMAN, M., WALKER, E. F. & ROSENHAN, D. L. (2001), *Abnormal Psychology*, New York: Norton

SMEDES, L. B. (1997), *The Art of Forgiving*, New York: Ballantine

SMITH, R. L. (1960), *Towards an Understanding of the Carpenter's Son*, Nashville: Tidings

SPEARING, E. (trans) (1998), *Revelations of Divine Love*, London: Penguin Classics

STEWARD, I. & JOINES, V. (1987), *TA Today: A New Introduction to Transactional Analysis*, Melton Mowbray: Lifespacing Publishing

THOMPSON, N. (2009), *People Skills* (3rd ed.), Basingstoke: Palgrave Macmillan

THRELFALL-HOLMES, M. & NEWITT, M. (2011), *Being a Chaplain*, London: SPCK

TOLLE, E. (2003), *Stillness Speaks*, Novato: New World Library

VANIER, J. (2008), *Essential Writings*, New York: Orbis Books

VANSTONE, W. H. (1982), *The Stature of Waiting*, DLT

WALTER, T. (1990), *Funerals and How to Improve Them*, London: Hodder & Stoughton

WATTS, F., NYE, R. & SAVAGE, S. (2002), *Psychology for Christian Ministry*, Abingdon: Routledge

WEYER, J. (1563), *On the Illusions of the Demons and on Spells and Poisons*

WILSON, M. (1988), *A Coat of Many Colours: Pastoral Studies of the Christian Way of Life*, London: Epworth Press

WOLPERT, L. (1999), *Malignant Sadness: The Anatomy of Depression*, London: Faber & Faber

WOLTERSTORFF, N. (1987), *Lament for a Son*, Grand Rapids: Eerdmans

WRIGHT, B., DAVE, S. & DOGRA, N. (2010), *100 Cases in Psychiatry*, London: Hodder Arnold

WRIGHT, F. (1996), *Pastoral Care Revisited*, London: SCM

YOUNG, F. Y. (1982), *Can These Dry Bones Live?* SCM Press, pp.60-61

YOUNG, W. P. (2008), *The Shack*, London: Hodder

Websites

www.alcoholics-anonymous.org.uk

http://disorders.free-books.biz

www.samaritans.org

Printed in the USA
CPSIA information can be obtained
at www.ICGtesting.com
LVHW090815080124
768391LV00022B/325